HUNTING HEADS

HUNTING HEADS

HOW TO FIND AND KEEP THE BEST PEOPLE

JOHN H. McCONNELL

KIPLINGER BOOKS
Washington, DC

Published by
The Kiplinger Washington Editors, Inc.
1729 H Street, N.W.
Washington, DC 20006

Library of Congress Cataloging-in-Publication Data

McConnell, John H.
    Hunting heads: how to find and keep the best people / John H. McConnell.
        p. cm.
    Includes index.
    ISBN 0-938721-76-3
     1. Employees--Recruiting. 2. Employee retention. I. Title.

HF5549.5.R44 M299 2000
658.3'111--dc21   00-032717

This publication is intended to provide guidance in regard to the subject matter
covered. It is sold with the understanding that the author and publisher are not
herein engaged in rendering legal, accounting, tax or other professional services.
If such services are required, professional assistance should be sought.

First edition. Printed in the United States of America.
9 8 7 6 5 4 3 2 1

Kiplinger publishes books and videos on a wide variety of personal-finance and business-
management subjects. Check our Web site (www.kiplinger.com) for a complete
list of titles, additional information and excerpts. Or write:
        Cindy Greene
        Kiplinger Books & Tapes
        1729 H Street, N.W.
        Washington, DC 20006
        email: cgreene@kiplinger.com
To order, call 800-280-7165; for information about volume discounts, call 202-887-6431.

Dedication

To one individual I owe a particular debt of gratitude. It was he who first introduced me to a professional method of selecting employees, and he is probably the best interviewer I have ever met.

Ralph J. Brown
Interviewer Extraordinaire

Acknowledgments

N O BOOK CAN BE WRITTEN WITHOUT CONSIDERABLE assistance and support, and this was certainly true in this instance. Many of my clients—particularly those who own and operate small businesses—shared their needs, concerns and stories. Rob Kaplan, my agent and friend, provided directions and advice, and Ruth Long suggested many excellent changes.

There were also many people with whom I have worked over the years to find and keep good people. Each taught me something, and the information contained in this book is a product of the combined input of literally hundreds of people.

Several people at Kiplinger Books helped to bring *Hunting Heads* to fruition: First and foremost, my thanks to Patricia Mertz Esswein, who worked wonders with my manuscript; David Harrison, Director of Kiplinger Books; Priscilla Taylor, copyeditor; Cindy Greene, editorial assistant; and Heather Waugh, graphic designer.

To all of these people who directly and indirectly assisted, thank you!

Table of Contents

Introduction

T HE U.S. ECONOMY CHARGES INTO THE 21ST CEN-
tury with the tightest labor market in our nation's
history. The national unemployment rate is barely 4%, and in some metro areas and some business sectors, it is virtually zero. Workers have
unprecedented opportunities to change jobs for higher pay,
better benefits, and more responsibility, and they are doing so
with greater frequency than ever before. Indeed, many firms
find that just staffing their offices and plants poses the biggest
challenge for continued growth.

Hiring and retaining good employees have always been the
key to success in every enterprise, whether for profit or non-
profit. But this fact hasn't always been so evident to managers
as it is today. In previous eras, when asked the essentials of a
prosperous organization, many executives would have first
answered "a unique product," "brilliant managerial vision,"
"modern equipment," or "plenty of capital." When labor was
abundant, businesses assumed that they could always find
enough competent employees to staff their departments. If a
few left, no problem; there would be plenty of good replace-
ments. In too many businesses, employees were there simply to
follow orders. In the "top-down" management style of the past,
the men and women on the front lines—making the products,
dealing with customers—were seldom asked for their ideas on
how to improve the company's products and services.

Well, those days are long gone at most successful companies. Asked today to name their most important ingredient for
prosperity, most executives will answer "our people." And

they're right. Today the most important capital is the kind that resides in the brains, training, and experience of the workforce. Companies that recognize this—and honor the creativity, diligence, and loyalty of their employees—tend to do better than those that don't. Why? Because they attract and retain the best workers, by empowering them to succeed.

Our Experience at Kiplinger

We learned this lesson early at The Kiplinger Washington Editors, Inc., because, from the day we started in 1920, our sole product has been a highly intangible service: judgment on the business outlook, government policy, and personal money management. Our products—periodicals, books, and Web-based information—have no patents, no proprietary processes, and nothing that other publishers can't try to copy. Our success was and is entirely dependent on the intelligence and experience of our editorial staff, backed up by equally talented people in circulation sales, subscriber service, accounting, design and production, personnel, and other support functions. Our physical assets, especially in the early days, have been few and relatively unimportant. It has always been truly said of this business, in 1920 and today, "Our company's assets walk out the door every night at 5 P.M." (or, these days, more typically at 6 or 7 P.M.). That's why nurturing these valuable assets has always been a top priority of the Kiplinger organization.

Sales executives know that it is a lot less expensive to satisfy current customers than to replace ones whose needs are not met. Human resources managers know that the same is true of a company's employees, but until recently they've often had a hard time convincing senior management of this. Now, with staff turnover at record levels, every business is grappling with the high cost of replacing employees—the costs of production forgone, help-wanted ads, interviewing time, and, most of all, training the new hires. As with customers, satisfying good workers is vastly more economical than replacing them.

Building Employee Loyalty

Many managers complain that the concept of employee loyalty is now ancient history. But they fail to recognize the role that they (or their predecessors) played in making this happen. In times of massive corporate restructuring and downsizing, employers came to regard employees as expendable resources and interchangeable parts, and they displayed no loyalty to them. Employees responded in kind when the labor market shifted in their favor. This situation explains in part the high turnover many firms experience today, even when their pay and benefits seem to be competitive.

Here at the Kiplinger organization, we, too, are seeing more staff turnover than we did 20 or 30 years ago, but it's still well below that of most other companies. We attribute this positive situation to a combination of factors, including smart hiring and competitive pay and benefits. But the biggest factors are probably the working environment and broad employee participation in the financial success of our enterprise. As a closely held, family-led business, we can't give our colleagues stock options on publicly traded shares, so popular at today's start-up firms. But profit-sharing and employee stock ownership have been traditions at Kiplinger for decades, supplementing our employer-paid pension plan (a generous "defined benefit" pension that is increasingly rare today). Through an employee stock trust, our colleagues collectively own about 25% of our business, benefiting from annual dividends and gradual appreciation in the share price. This plan rewards long service to our company and helps keep turnover fairly low.

About This Book

This fine new book by John H. McConnell is all about how to find and motivate today's most valuable resource—talented and committed workers. It is much more than just a guide to effective hiring. It is a broad manual of today's best practices in human resources management. While even experienced HR professionals will learn new things from it, it has even more value to senior executives in other fields, giving them an overview of the key issues in finding and retaining talented people. Many executives, after digesting this very readable guide, will want to huddle with their personnel managers to check on whether their own organization is following these recommended procedures. Many leaders of new companies, who've been preoccupied with the challenges of developing and getting product or service to market, will want to use the book to ensure that they set up an equally effective personnel system and avoid the perils of a poorly defined or nonexistent one.

Hunting Heads doesn't just leap into the mechanics of how to hire. It first explores the important matter of how an enterprise decides whether and when it needs more staff, and if so, how this need might be addressed with alternatives to a new, full-time position.

One of the most important lessons of this book is that an organization's treatment of job seekers—especially unsuccessful applicants—is a public relations opportunity that must not be squandered. Companies that treat all applicants with the utmost courtesy, regardless of their qualifications, generate a lot of goodwill, and the converse is equally true.

John McConnell has had years of experience in the real world of employee relations, working as an HR professional at Wolverine Tune, Garan, Inc., M&M Mars, and National Liberty Insurance, and consulting with such organizations as Colonial Penn, Philip Morris, Ford Motor, and the U.S. Navy. *Hunting Heads* puts his savvy and insights at your disposal. I learned a lot from this book myself, and I think you will, too.

From all of us at the Kiplinger publications, our best wishes to you and your colleagues for success in the exciting and challenging years ahead.

Knight Kiplinger

KNIGHT A. KIPLINGER
Editor, *The Kiplinger Letters*
Editor in Chief, *Kiplinger's Personal Finance* magazine
Washington, D.C.
May 2000

HUNTING
HEADS

Finders, Keepers

"The best executive is the one who has sense enough to pick good men to do what he wants done, and self-restraint enough to keep from meddling with them while they do it."

—THEODORE ROOSEVELT

N THE 1950s, LARRY APPLEY, THEN PRESIDENT OF THE American Management Association, put it this way with his simple definition of management: *Getting things done through other people.*

Despite all the technological and cultural changes that have occurred during the half-century since then, that definition still applies, and it applies to all sizes and kinds of businesses. Small-business owners, as well as managers of major corporations, need both to *get things done* and to *get them done through other people.* For many owners and managers, the *through other people* is the most difficult challenge, but only through other people can any business grow and succeed.

Finding, and keeping, good people is a never-ending task for any business. When you start a company, you soon discover that you can't do it all yourself, and as the company grows, you require even more people. People eventually leave and need to be replaced. Changes in your business or in technology create new sets of needed skills. But whenever these situations face small businesses, owners or managers should see them as opportunities. Consider:

■ **When a large organization** of 5,000 employees decides to add 5 new employees, that decision represents only a 0.1% increase in employment and related costs, including the cost of finding and hiring those people, and paying their wages or salary, benefits, and any overhead.

■ **But when a small business**—say, of 10 employees—decides to add just one new employee, that represents a 10% increase in employment and related costs. That decision represents equally significant opportunities. With a 10% increase in your workforce you should be able to produce more products or offer expanded services; as a result, your income should increase and, along with it, your profits.

Whether you're hiring an additional employee or replacing a departing one, your company can benefit, provided it selects the right employee.

On the other hand, if you select the wrong person—one who, say, performs poorly, stays for only a short time, does not contribute to the purpose of the company, or is habitually absent or late—you have not realized the possible benefits from the opportunity. Instead, you may have actually decreased your company's performance. We'll talk more about this later, but at this point it is important to recognize the advantages of finding the right employee and the disadvantages of choosing the wrong one.

A five-person company that builds Web sites was awarded a contract that required an additional employee to fulfill it. Rather than taking the time to identify exactly the competencies required, the company hired someone who appeared to have performed similar assignments with another firm, but because of the hasty selection, the company didn't verify the person's degree of experience.

The company soon discovered that the new employee could not perform adequately. The company had to find a replacement, but by that time it was already late in delivering the work. It finally completed the contract, weeks late, and received no additional work from the customer.

Contrast that example with this one:

A start-up limousine service in New Jersey conducted a survey of customers and potential customers to discover what they wanted from such a service. Topping the list were punctuality and a positive driver attitude. The company decided to hire executives who had retired early (there were many in the area) for half-day shifts. The drivers understood the customers' concerns about punctuality, and were able to converse intelligently. The company rapidly expanded.

Do You Have a System, or Is Hiring a Good Employee an Accident?

Adding a new employee to your workforce is one of the most significant decisions—for good or for ill—that a small-business person can make, yet owners and managers often make it with little planning and less thought to its ramifications. That this is the case, however, should not be a surprise. Many people achieve management positions or start companies without any training in interviewing and selecting employees. Once in those positions, they assume or are assigned the responsibility of selecting employees. Under the circumstances, they fall back on their own experience as a guide or delegate this key activity to someone else—often someone who also lacks knowledge of how to interview and select employees.

Think back on your own experience as a candidate for a job. Were you always treated considerately? Did you always receive replies to your letters or résumés? Did interviewers honor the appointment times for the interviews? Did you feel that the companies had thoroughly reviewed your qualifications? Were your interviewers knowledgeable about the requirements of the job? If you answered no to any of these questions, your experience is similar to that of many job seekers, and those and other negative models may be the only ones you have to follow.

This book can help you avoid or correct such situations. It can help you make the most of your hiring opportunities by providing a system for selection and retention of the right employees. The system's basic steps are these:

■ **Deciding when to hire**
■ **Defining the job**
■ **Obtaining qualified candidates**
■ **Preparing for and conducting interviews**
■ **Making the decision**
■ **Offering the job**
■ **Starting employment**
■ **Keeping employees**

In the process, you may question the need to perform each step, but if you want to find and retain good employees, you need to be engaged in this vital activity. It is one that deserves your full attention.

This book details each of these steps and provides practical ways for you to implement them. Each chapter describes specific techniques, offers additional resources, and contains checklists—a convenient method to refer back to specific contents when the need arises. Many brief cases drawn from business life illustrate the points made.

The last two chapters of the book examine the conditions that will not only help you attract good employees, but help you keep them, too.

Also, the Appendix provides sample forms that you can copy or use as a basis for the creation of your own forms.

The book presents all of this information in a practical and flexible format that you can adapt to the specific conditions of your business.

Operating a successful small business requires many integrated activities. Although finding and keeping good employees is one of the most important activities, it depends on others, including business planning, good supervision and management, and use of proper financial controls. This book refers to those and related activities as appropriate, but only to the extent necessary for understanding their relationship to the selection process.

What Are the Essential Elements of Any Plan of Hiring?

AMA president Appley also felt that planning and controlling were the two basic activities of management, and that they had to receive equal time and attention. To a large extent, his point of view is reflected in this book, which stresses the need to plan and prepare for whatever you wish to accomplish, and to implement the plan so that your objective is properly met.

Let's take a closer look at the basic planning and controlling elements emphasized through this book:

This book can help you make the most of your hiring opportunities by providing a *system* for selection and retention of the right employees.

PLANNING. There is no substitute for good planning, yet it is one of the most neglected of all management activities. Businesspeople are more prone to action than preparation, but action without direction often leads to chaos. Too often decisions represent *Ready! Fire! Aim!* Correct planning consists of four steps:

1. Defining an objective
2. Identifying activities
3. Scheduling completion
4. Documenting the process

You should begin every management task with a clear understanding and description of what you wish to accomplish. Once you have established an objective, you can identify the activities required to accomplish it and develop a schedule with completion times. This is the basic approach the book suggests for each step taken to hire and retain good employees.

If you record your plan, you gain an additional benefit—the possibility of reusing it later. Unfortunately, owners and managers often ignore this step. They make plans and decisions but neglect to keep records of them. When they establish similar objectives, they have no way to reuse the work already done. Making a record of the hiring process and the information gained therein also helps to avoid, or makes it easier to resolve, unpleasant situations, especially legal ones, later on.

In hiring employees, you should always remember that the cost, both in time and money, of a mistaken hire far exceeds the cost of planning—in time and money—to avoid such a situation. Likewise, the unnecessary loss of a good employee far exceeds the cost of planning a program to retain employees.

JOB RELATEDNESS. Over the years, employers have complained about government regulations regarding what they can and cannot do in hiring. However, most such regulations merely require you, in all search activities, to stay focused on what's relevant to the job, and in the long run that is what is best for your company.

Obtaining an employment attorney's advice on your plans can save you much money, time, and unpleasantness.

Asking questions that have nothing to do with a job, hiring people using personal biases, and basing decisions on qualifications not related to a specific job are missteps that may sometimes occur, but this book will demonstrate that such actions are self-defeating.

Staying with job-related information in all employment decisions will contribute to hiring better employees and avoiding legal problems.

INFORMATION. We continually hear that we live in the information age, but consider this idea:

> *"Information is facts and figures in a format that is needed. Otherwise, they are just facts and figures."* –FERDINAND J. SETARO

To be sure you obtain information and not data, you need to describe the information required. What is it you need to know? That is the point of planning and focusing on job-relatedness. Decide in advance what you need, and then get that information to hire the right people.

As for keeping employees, you must constantly work to ensure that employment with your company meets your employees' expectations and needs. That means you need to have information about how your employees perceive things, regardless of whether their perceptions are correct. You or your managers and supervisors need to maintain open communications, and you need to remember that change is ever with us. What may appear acceptable one year may be unacceptable the next. I don't mean to imply that you must always meet employees' requests, but you do need to know what they want and expect, and respond truthfully to them.

LEGAL AND OTHER EMPLOYMENT ADVICE. This book emphasizes the importance of seeking expert advice. Because state and federal laws affect almost every aspect of hiring, you need to make sure that you are operating as required. Failure to do so can cost you—a lot. This book provides general guidance, but you need to obtain advice for specific actions from professionals such as accountants, attorneys, and employment or human resources consultants (see Chapter 4 for more details on hiring employment assistance and Chapter 10 for more on finding and hiring an employment lawyer).

In addition to general federal and state requirements, there may be industry requirements, individual contracts, and labor agreements that affect what you can do. If you do not have an employment attorney, obtain one. Obtaining an employment attorney's advice on your plans can save you much money, time, and unpleasantness.

DELEGATION OF ROUTINE TASKS. This book also emphasizes that you may not be able personally to take on all the duties associated with hiring and retaining employees. But many small-business owners have difficulty delegating this activity.

> *Tom was a successful plumber in the Chicago area. He was one of 10 plumbers working for a local contractor, but he was the one most requested. Tom finally decided to go into business for himself. As people learned of his decision, his business grew. Within a year he was working 14 hours a day on jobs and 2 hours a night on office work.*
>
> *Tom recognized that he needed another person to help him. Because he was most skilled in plumbing, he decided to hire an office person. Unfortunately, he could not bring himself to delegate to her the authority that she required to do the*

work. She constantly had to check all decisions with him. He still spent 2 hours a night on office work.

The second year Tom hired a another plumber, but again he couldn't delegate. He insisted on checking every job. "After all, it's my name on the truck," he said.

Within three years, Tom had closed his business and returned to work for his former employer. His business was a casualty of his inability to delegate.

Many small-business owners are excellent individual operators; they know what to do and how to get it done. But if your business is to grow, you must get things done through other people. That means delegating to them some of what you could otherwise do. You need to recognize when to delegate, whom to delegate to, and what to delegate.

Be sure the individual to whom you delegate has the skills to properly select qualified employees.

You'll know when to delegate when you discover that you can no longer perform all the activities that are required. Whom you will delegate to will depend on what duties are to be delegated. However, be careful. Be sure to keep for yourself those tasks that require your level of authority and ability.

Selecting new employees may be one of the activities that you should delegate. If so, be sure the individual to whom you delegate has the skills to properly select qualified employees. If you lack such an employee, you may need to hire someone or contract with an external source to perform such duties. (Later chapters discuss this option at length.)

CUSTOMER ORIENTATION. In the 1930s a sign common in many small businesses was, *The customer is always right.* That sign is seen less often nowadays, but in the past several years the concept has come back into vogue. Today, numerous books and consultants promote "quality" customer relations, and companies that are most successful in such efforts annually receive a number of prestigious business and industry awards.

This book stresses the opportunities you have to improve your customer base by always considering current employees and candidates for employment as customers or potential customers. Perhaps your sign should read, The customer is always right and everybody is a customer.

Can You Find and Keep the Right Employees in Today's Market?

Although the job market has always had its ups and downs, two factors in today's job market make the strategies and techniques for hiring and keeping people more essential than ever for your success.

More Frequent Turnover

At one time employers and employees seemed to favor long-term associations and loyalty was often spoken of, but that is no longer the case. Today people speak of the desirability of changing jobs at least every 10 to 15 years—if not every 3 to 5 years, among younger employees—and employers feel that regular (although not excessive) turnover brings them new ideas. Benefits such as individual company pension plans with 10 years' vesting, designed to retain employees, have been replaced by portable or convertible 401k's with three-year vesting.

For many smaller companies long-term employment is still desirable. Recall our earlier examples of the effects of adding employees to a large company and a small one. The same consideration can be given to the effects of employees' departure. A large company of 10,000 employees may lay off 200 employees with little effect on its operations, but a small company of 5 employees can be severely hurt by the loss of one employee—a 20% "reduction in force."

This is also the era of the two-income family and of frequent relocation by large companies. One spouse may be transferred to another part of the country, and the other (your employee) will follow.

Full Employment

As this book is being written, the United States is experiencing one of the lowest unemployment rates in its history. Opportunity abounds, and employees are taking advantage of it to improve their wages, benefits, working conditions, experience, skills, and status. One employer's gain of a good employee is almost always another's loss, and the competition among employers to find and keep the right employee in a vacated or newly created position is intense.

This book takes all these conditions into account, and it is my belief that good employees can always be hired and retained if your company goes about the process in a thorough and professional manner. Follow the steps in this book. They constitute a system that works in all job markets. Read the book carefully and then adapt the system to your company's needs.

Now, it's time to begin to learn how to find and keep good employees for your business.

Deciding When to Hire

"Before everything else, getting ready is the secret of success." —HENRY FORD

O FIND AND KEEP GOOD PEOPLE, THIS IS THE MOST important question you need to answer: When do I need to hire a new employee?

Hiring someone too early can create unnecessary expense. Hiring someone too late can result in work undone. Having too many employees can increase operating costs, and having too few can reduce income. How do you know when it's the right time to hire someone?

The answer to that question depends on the type of employee you think you need to hire and on your business plan. Let's begin by examining each of these areas.

Types of Employees

For our purposes employees are divided into two basic types: direct and indirect, or line and staff, which are the terms more often used in large organizations to refer to the classic positions on a traditional organization chart. Line jobs are those in the direct line of authority—the jobs that perform the primary mission of the organization. For example, in a manufacturing company, production workers occupy line jobs; in a retail store, the sales clerks; in a real estate office, the brokers. Staff jobs are the support positions that branch off from the lines of authority. In a manufacturing company, the shipping and maintenance workers fill staff jobs; in a retail store, the accounting and human resources people; in the real estate office, the receptionists and paralegals.

Adding a direct employee may increase your profit, while adding an indirect employee definitely increases your overhead.

Direct employees are the same as line employees. They perform the basic tasks of the business. In an electrical contracting firm they are the electricians, and in a restaurant they are the waitpeople and cooks. Indirect employees support those activities but do not perform the business's primary tasks. In an electrical contracting firm they could be schedulers, and in a restaurant they could be bookkeepers.

Why should you consider the difference? Because adding a direct employee may increase your profit, while adding an indirect employee definitely increases your overhead.

> One hotel manager justifies hiring only direct employees by saying, "If there is no direct relationship between what an employee does and the mission of our hotel, we don't need that employee. We subcontract support jobs such as maintenance and laundry to firms where those people are direct employees of the subcontractors. A small business should hire only direct employees!"

Direct Employees

Because direct employees perform the primary tasks of the business, it usually quite obvious when you do not have enough of them. For example, if customers walk out of your store because they cannot find a sales clerk, if your electricians consistently work overtime, or if your restaurant experiences low table turnover because of slow service, you are receiving signals that you may need additional direct employees. Before you decide to hire, however, you should examine the situation and assure yourself that the need is not just temporary. You should address temporary needs as such (covered later in this chapter). You want to avoid the expensive mistake of adding a permanent employee when you really require one for only a short period.

First, determine the correct number of direct employees for your business. To do this, you need two pieces of information:

■ **The total volume of work** that your business must perform
■ **The amount of work** a typical direct employee performs

To determine the total volume of work to be performed, you need to project into the future. The difficulty of this exercise will depend on the nature of your business. For example, an electrical contracting firm has work orders for 120 jobs that it must complete over eight months with an average job duration of four days. In such a case, the contractor knows the minimum amount of work his company must perform, and he can add to that an estimate of how much more work he can normally expect to obtain during the same period.

Before you decide to hire, however, you should examine the situation and assure yourself that the need is not just temporary.

Unfortunately, most small businesses do not have the luxury of knowing exactly how much future work they will receive; in most cases, they must estimate future work. You may need to answer questions such as these:

■ **How many customers will probably shop** in your store over the next year?
■ **How many lunch and dinner guests do you estimate will visit** your restaurant each day?
■ **How many people do you project will want to look** at new homes each month?

You can base your answers to such questions on your personal knowledge and experience, on the previous results of the business, and on local economic and sales projections. The point is that you need to have some idea of the future volume of work your business will have to perform.

To determine the amount of work that a typical direct

employee will perform, you must answer such questions as the following:

- **How many sales transactions does a sales clerk** typically handle during a day?
- **How many jobs can an electrician complete** each day or each week?
- **How many tables can a waitperson handle** during the lunch or dinner period?

You should be able to answer such a quantifying question because it is basic to your business, but your answer needn't be overly detailed. Employees are individuals. They work at different speeds and with different degrees of efficiency. So, just answer for an average employee—neither an excellent performer nor a poor performer.

Let's just deal with determining the basic number of direct employees you require. Later we can adjust for such things as absences, vacations, and turnover, to ensure that you always have the correct amount of employees.

Once you have determined how much work your business must perform and how much work a typical direct employee performs, it is relatively easy to determine the number of direct employees you require. Simply divide the total amount of work you are projecting for your business by the amount of work a typical direct employee can accomplish. For example, let's assume that you own a restaurant. You know from experience that your waitpeople can provide the level of service that you want if each handles six tables of four during a dinner period. You project that your business will average 30 tables of four at dinner time, so you need five waitpeople (30 tables divided by 6 tables per waitperson).

But what about absent employees? What about vacations? What about employee turnover? What about slow nights? Well, those considerations are all important and should be part of your business-planning activity; they are examined later in this chapter. At this point, let's just deal with determining the basic number of direct employees you require. Later we can make the necessary adjustments to ensure that you always have the correct amount of employees.

Now, let's turn our attention to the conditions that necessitate hiring additional indirect employees.

Indirect Employees

The need to add indirect employees is harder to recognize. If you already have people in those types of jobs, some of the same signals will apply: consistent overtime, and late or slow support services. However, you should examine such factors closely before deciding to add someone. Again, you may discover that the problem is just temporary or could be solved by another approach.

Indirect employees support the direct employees who perform the primary tasks of your business.

Keep in mind that indirect employees do not perform the primary tasks of your business. They support the employees who do—the direct employees. In very small or start-up businesses, the owner-manager often performs indirect activities. For example, a man opening a new service station might initially hire a mechanic and a pump attendant and assume for himself the duties of counterperson and book-keeper; or a woman opening a hair-styling shop may hire a shampoo person and three haircutter-stylists and assume for herself the duties of receptionist and bookkeeper. Later, as their businesses grow, each can hire indirect employees for those positions.

Whatever your business or its size, certain basic indirect jobs must be performed, whether by you (as in our above example), an employee, or an external service. A janitorial service could provide office cleaning; a landscaping company, lawn maintenance; and an accountant, record keeping and tax preparation. You need to make this decision and revisit it each time you feel the need to hire an indirect employee.

Perhaps you can measure your need for indirect employees by using a simple calculation. For example, you may know from experience that your real estate office requires one receptionist for every eight brokers, or that your grocery store requires one bagger for every four check-out locations. However, the decision is not always that simple.

Have you considered how your business will absorb the cost of adding indirect employees? As mentioned earlier, adding an indirect employee will not necessarily increase your income, but it will increase your overhead costs—and overhead reduces profit. For example, an additional bookkeeper may benefit the business by increasing record-keeping speed and reporting, but it will not increase sales, and you must allocate the cost of the employee to all transactions.

In contrast, direct-employee costs are a key part of the prices your business charges. A sales clerk's costs are part of each sale, an electrician's costs are part of each job performed, and a waitperson's costs are part of each meal served. If you add another direct employee, that employee's services should contribute to increased business income, and his or her costs should help generate that increased income.

One successful small-business owner has remarked, "A small business must continually fight overhead. Overhead kills many small businesses, and indirect employees are overhead. You should add an indirect employee only when you are absolutely sure one is required."

Before You Hire Any Employee

When considering the addition of any employee—direct or indirect—ask questions such as these:

- **Is all the work** now being completed on time?
- **Is all the work** now being completed as well as you wish?
- **Is the lack of another employee** affecting sales?
- **By how much will adding a new support employee** increase overhead and reduce profit?
- **Is the need temporary?**
- **Can you reorganize or reassign the work** instead of hiring a new employee?
- **Can you solve the problem with overtime?**
- **Can someone else perform these duties?**
- **Should you contract with an outside service** to do the work?

Some jobs combine elements of direct and indirect positions. For example, stock people in retail stores are basically indirect—support—employees, but their work—getting adequate merchandise to the right place at the right time—contributes to the success of the salespeople (the direct employees). The dispatcher for an electrical contracting firm and the busperson in a restaurant are in similar positions. When evaluating support positions, don't overlook their direct contribution.

A good question to ask is, What will happen if I don't hire an employee?

Alternatives to Hiring a New Employee

If you've decided that you must have additional help, perhaps you can avoid hiring full-time, permanent employees through the means described in this section:

Temporary Employees

One approach to solving a temporary need is to hire temporary employees. For example, temporary needs can be caused by seasonal fluctuations in business (Christmas retail-store sales), a particular contract, or the temporary absence of employees because of illness, vacations or family leaves. Don't hire a permanent employee when you require someone for a short period only. Hiring a permanent employee is a significant decision—for you and for the person accepting the job—so you want to hire only when necessary.

You can employ temporary employees directly or contract for them with a temporary employment agency (listed in the *Yellow Pages* under "Employment Contractors, Temporary"). If you hire temporary employees on your own, you need to tell them up front that the positions are temporary.

A small manufacturing firm recruited a number of people who were looking for part-time work. The company kept these people's files on hand and called them whenever it had a temporary need. Some of the temps could work only in the summer, and others could work only certain days of the week. The firm favored this approach—an on-call pool of temporary employees—because these people developed knowledge of the company and its operations that contributed to productivity.

If the employment period is short enough, you can hire without paying some voluntary benefits (see Chapter 10 for more details). You will still incur hiring costs and be obliged to provide legislated benefits (such as social security, worker's compensation insurance, and unemployment insurance), and it still takes time to locate and interview these prospective employees. A temporary agency can usually provide an employee in a short time (sometimes within hours), and the only cost is payment to the agency. The person is an employee of the agency, and the agency is responsible for benefits and other costs.

Whether you use an agency or hire temporary employees yourself, temporary employment provides an excellent way to preview a person's performance. If you decide that the temp is someone you want to hire permanently, you can make an offer, but be forewarned that permanent jobs often don't interest temps. Moreover, most temporary agencies charge a fee if you want to hire the temp.

Payrolling

A few businesses employ temporary-agency employees almost exclusively. They have arranged with an agency for a procedure referred to as "payrolling," whereby the agency employs the "temps," pays them, and supplies all of their benefits, whether legally required or voluntarily provided by the agency. The agency charges the employer for the employees' pay, benefit costs, and an administration fee.

Companies usually resort to payrolling temporarily. It generally costs more than hiring employees, and often results in considerable employee turnover. Even so, some small businesses feel it is advantageous not to have any employees of their own.

┌───┐
│ CHECKLIST │ **Considering Additional Employees**   │
└───┘

■ **If a shortage of direct employees** is preventing your business from carrying out its primary tasks or mission of your business, don't hesitate: you should consider adding a new employee.

■ **If you are considering the addition of a direct employee,** calculate how much increase in income the employee will produce.

■ **If it appears that you may need to hire an indirect employee,** carefully assess the reason for the need, as well as the cost and its impact on profits. Add indirect employees only when it is absolutely necessary to operate the business as you desire.

■ **Distinguish between indirect** jobs you should fill with employees and indirect jobs, if any, you can contract with external services to fill.

■ **Recognize when the need for an employee is temporary** and deal with it on a temporary basis.

■ **When an employee leaves,** do not automatically replace him or her. Examine your entire organization to find out whether you need a replacement or whether you can reconfigure current jobs.

■ **Always keep in mind the primary mission or purpose of your business.** As with the previous guideline, you always want to have enough employees to accomplish your primary mission or purpose.

Overtime

Sometimes paying for overtime (working longer hours and weekend days), rather than hiring, can solve a temporary problem, and it is usually less expensive than permanently hiring a new employee. However, overtime won't help all businesses. In some cases, paying the same number of "bodies" to work longer will help, say, to increase manufacturing production or enable a business to meet a deadline, but other situations simply require more bodies. For instance, paying overtime won't help a restaurant serve more people during a fixed lunch period.

Even when overtime is applicable, it produces the best results on a short-term basis. Studies indicate that long-term overtime tends to become increasingly less productive because employees begin to accept the longer hours as their normal schedule, instead of as an exception. Also, employees begin to view overtime pay as part of their regular income and raise their living standards accordingly. Then, when the overtime ceases, they have difficulty adjusting to the lesser income, and this situation can lead to wage pressure and low morale. As a rule, overtime for four or more consecutive weeks fits this description.

Replacement Employees

When an employee leaves, it may seem that you should immediately fill the vacated position, but a better approach is to question the need for the position. Ask yourself the questions outlined on page 16 again. An employee's departure provides an opportunity for you to review the need for that specific position, as well as to consider the possibilities for reorganizing or reassigning work or for transferring people.

Business Planning: The Bigger Picture

"To succeed, a business must have a plan—a direction for where it is going. Otherwise, how will it know when it has lost its way? But the plan does not have to be an elaborate document. I have seen excellent plans on the back of an envelope."
—JAMES L. HAYES

Most business owners had a plan when they began, but many do not continue planning once they've established the business. This can be a crucial mistake. To succeed, every business requires continual planning to identify the key objectives, assumptions, and information for its operation over the next time period (usually a year).

Your business plan should tell you where you are going, what you want to accomplish, where you will be spending your money, and what your probable income and profit will be. Without such information your decisions are likely to be guesswork, and success, an accident.

The information you need for a basic business plan is this:

The primary purpose or mission and objectives of the business for the next year. (What does your company want to accomplish?)

Projections of income from sales over the next year. (How much product or service do you anticipate selling and how much money will those sales produce?)

A budget to meet sales projections with expenses by major category, including:

■ **Operating costs** to produce sales and deliver your service or product

■ **Identification of capital expenditures** for equipment, inventory, or buildings to better produce the projected sales and income

Cash flow projections for the next year. (How much money will be coming in and going out, and when?)

At a minimum, you should develop this plan for the next year, but ideally you should project out for three to five years, to get a general idea of future possibilities and directions.

Total business planning is the subject for a separate book. For our purposes, we need only examine the portion of the business plan that deals with workforce planning. That will provide the information needed to identify your employee requirements—both in numbers and types of employees—and to know when to hire people based on projected increases or decreases in business volume.

Workforce Planning: The Specific Issue

E arlier we looked at two types of information about workforce planning: The total amount of work that your business must produce, and the amount of work that a typical direct employee performs.

In workforce planning you must consider those two types of information for both the present and the future. Then you can calculate how many direct employees you need at specific times. You should not take into account any current employees, pretending for this purpose that you have none (a form of "zero-based" planning). Ultimately, you will need to consider them and their skills, but for now, you should decide on the ideal number and types of employees your business requires. Otherwise, you'll tend to adjust your needs to your current staff, and doing that will undermine your workforce planning.

You may discover that you have too many employees with the wrong skills and too few with the right ones.

Once you have identified your need for direct employees, then you should identify your need for indirect employees. Some needs, such as the real estate office receptionist and the grocery store bagger, may be relative easy to determine, but some others may require you to rethink your operations.

For example, do you need to hire a bookkeeper or can you use an outside professional? Do you need to hire a purchasing agent, or will you or your manager handle those tasks? You know you need administrative assistance for the office, but how many assistants do you require? Can you combine two jobs, such as a human resources person and a bookkeeper, if you have need for only "half a person" in each position?

If you base your plan solely on your projected volume of business, without considering the number of people you already have, you will produce a workforce plan that reflects your business's true needs. You can then compare those needs with your current workforce. You may find you need to hire more people or to change employees' assignments. In some cases you may even discover that you have too many employees with the wrong skills and too few with the right ones.

Once you have calculated how many direct and indirect employees you need to meet your goals, you should adjust for reality. No matter how good your selection techniques, the required number of employees will rarely be at work all the time. Employees will leave, be sick, and go on vacation; you need to anticipate and account for those situations in your workforce plan.

Accounting for Employee Turnover

Employee turnover refers to the number of employees you lose each year, whether you ask them to leave or they quit. Most

businesses use turnover as a basis for their employment projections. To calculate turnover, divide the number of employees leaving the business over the course of a year by the average total number of employees during the year and then mul-
tiply that answer by 100. The result is a percentage.

For example, assume that last year you had an average of
50 employees. If over the course of that year five left, you have
a 10% turnover (5 departing employees ÷ 50
employees x 100). This indicates that you
need to hire 10% more employees than you
require just to stay even, but not necessarily
all at once; you will also have to consider
what types of employees have left and when,
and how much time you will need to train a
new employee.

Generally, employers calculate turnover
monthly and annually. You may discover
that most employees leave in March and
September, and only a few leave during the
other months. You may also discover that
most employees who leave do so within
their first three months of employment and
that only certain types of employees leave.

**You will learn when
you're likely to lose
people, so that you
can hire *before* your
projected needs—
an often critical
ability with respect
to direct employees,
whose presence
or absence affect
your ability to
make money.**

For example, maybe you have a 10% turnover at your
restaurant, but it is almost exclusively buspeople. Buspeople
don't require much training, so you probably wouldn't need to
hire much in advance of your anticipated need. But suppose
your company performs warranty repair for a small-engine
manufacturer. If you don't anticipate finding a repair person
who has experience with that manufacturer's engines, you will
have to train someone. If the training will take six to eight
weeks, you will need to hire someone six to eight weeks before
your projected need.

If you can factor such information into your workforce
planning, you will learn when you're likely to lose people, so
that you can hire before your projected needs—an often critical ability with respect to direct employees, whose presence or
absence directly affects your ability to make money. For example, if your employment turnover experience indicates that

you generally lose several employees in December, you can begin looking for new employees in November (or however early your local job market necessitates), or if someone happens to apply at that time, you can consider the application more seriously in light of your probable need.

Accounting for Absences

You also need to adjust your plan for absences and vacations in line with your experience and the terms of your benefit plans. First, estimate the average number of days that employees are likely to be absent because of illness and personal time off. Generally, the previous year's record of time off is a good guide to the future, so review those records. Add to this number the total number of days of vacation for which employees are eligible in the coming year. To get the estimated average number of days off per employee for the coming year, divide the total number of days off by the total number of your employees.

Employees generally do not spread their days off evenly throughout the year, so you must also consider when they take time off.

For example, assume that you have 10 employees, and you perform the foregoing calculations. You discover that, last year, employees were absent a total of 46 days due to illness and 22 days for personal reasons, and that next year they will be eligible for a total of 120 days of vacation. That adds up to a total of 188 days that your employees are likely to be away from their jobs this coming year. When you consider that there are only about 200 working days a year (52 weeks of five workdays each, minus holidays and other time off), the business appears to be, in effect, short one employee almost every working day. Assuming that the time off is distributed pretty evenly throughout the year, the business owner might choose to hire one more full-time employee to make up the difference.

However, that probably isn't literally the case. Employees generally do not spread their days off evenly throughout the year, so you must also consider when they take time off. They may take vacations mostly in the summer and suffer illnesses mostly during the winter. Perhaps the employer would be better off, in this case, to plan to hire temporary employees during those periods.

With this information you can calculate how many employees are away from work at all times during the year. You can then adjust your calculation of employee needs to reflect this reality. (Workforce planning may also reveal a need to adjust time-off policies to ensure that not too many employees are away at one time or at crucial times. For example, few retail stores or hairdressers allow vacations during the winter holiday season.)

You may discover that you need more employees than you initially thought. Whatever the case, you need to adjust your planning to ensure that you have the correct number and types of employees at all times.

Other Considerations

Employee turnover and absences are important considerations in workforce planning. A number of other measures of employment that supply useful planning information are described in this section:

THE PROPORTION OF DIRECT EMPLOYEES TO INDIRECT EMPLOYEES. Keep in mind that the cost of indirect employees adds to your overhead, which you do not want to increase unnecessarily. Nor do you want to inadvertently understaff and deprive your direct employees of the support they need to accomplish your business's mission. By calculating the ratio of direct employees to indirect employees regularly, say monthly, you will quickly notice any increase or decrease. Any change will alert you to reexamine the number of indirect employees you have.

For example, assume you plan to have one indirect employee for four direct employees (a ratio of .25), and this calculation has been running between .24 and .28 per month for the past year, regardless of the total number of employees. Then one month it increases to .35. That is your signal to review what is happening. It could mean the number of indirect employees has increased or that the number of direct employees has decreased. The deviation could be temporary—

you may have hired a new, indirect employee to replace one who will be leaving shortly, or you may have not replaced a direct employee who quit.

PROPORTION OF MANAGEMENT EMPLOYEES TO NONMANAGEMENT EMPLOYEES. The ratio of management employees to nonmanagement employees, like the ratio for indirect to direct employees, provides insight into overhead costs and the efficient use of your managers. Because managers are generally indirect employees, the more managers, the more overhead. To control overhead and avoid having unnecessary employees, you want a low ratio of managers to direct employees, but as before, there is no correct number. A supervisor with employees at many job sites performing complicated tasks may be able to deal with only a few employees. On the other hand, a supervisor with employees all performing similar tasks in a large office may be able to manage many employees. As with the previous ratio, you can calculate this one regularly and use it as a signal to reexamine your employment number whenever there is a significant change.

OTHER MEASURES. Other calculations—such as absenteeism, sales per employee, and costs per employee—allow you to observe and quantify your employees' performance and absences and adjust your workforce planning accordingly:

$$\text{Absenteeism} = \frac{\text{total number of employee days absent}}{\text{total number of possible employee workdays}} \times 100$$

$$\text{Sales by employee} = \frac{\text{dollars of sales}}{\text{total number of employees}}$$

$$\text{Cost per employee} = \frac{\text{dollars of costs}}{\text{total number of employees}}$$

As was the case with the previous ratios, by regularly calculating these ratios you can quickly identify any change, that is, any exception to the norm. For example, if you calculate "sales per employee" monthly, and the result generally runs between $4,000 and $5,000 of sales per employee, you will notice any

```
┌─────────────────────────────────────────────────────────┐
│  ┌──────────┐  ┌───────────────────────┐                 │
│  │ CHECKLIST │  │  Workforce Planning   │                 │
│  └──────────┘  └───────────────────────┘                 │
```

Your workforce planning should at least answer the following questions:

■ **What are my business goals** for next year?

■ **What sales income** have I projected for next year?

■ **What type of expenses** must I incur (budget) to produce the projected sales income?

■ **What are the cash flow projections** for next year (the relationship of cash needs to cash receipts)? This will tell you when you will have the money to increase your payroll by hiring additional employees.

■ **What types and numbers of employees** do you require, based on your answers to the foregoing questions?

■ **What adjustments** to anticipated employment needs must you make on the basis of your experience with and estimates of turnover and absences?

■ **What adjustments** will you or won't you make to accommodate the number and skills of current employees?

■ **When do you need** to add employees?

month in which the figure is $2,000 or $8,000 and you will want to know what caused the exception.

Each of those measures can help you adjust your employee pool to meet the circumstances that arise. You can also use them to gain insight into how your business is performing over time, or in comparison with competitors or other employers in your community or industry. For example, some community groups publish employee turnover for companies in their region, and some industry associations publish sales-per-employee figures.

If you use these tools regularly, they will identify changes in the operation of your business.

Why Workforce Planning Is Important

Knowing when to hire and whom to hire is important for good decisions, and it requires proper planning. The planning requires relatively little time, and once done, it provides a guide for your hiring. If you do not have such a plan, you will be forced to devise one ad hoc whenever you consider adding an employee (even if you just do the thinking); hence time spent planning now will save you more time in the long run.

To ease the planning process for you, the Appendix includes a Workforce Planning form, which leads you through the various considerations covered in this chapter and can serve as a hiring guide for the next year.

Summary

"Why is it we never have enough time to plan, but we always have enough time to correct the problems caused by not planning?" —ARTHUR E. PEARSON

One message of this chapter is that the hiring of a new employee by a small business is a major decision, affecting income, costs, and profits. Because the decision can have a lasting effect on your business and on the employee, you should make it only after appropriate analysis and planning. This chapter also emphasizes the importance of planning to the small business. Planning helps to identify what types of employees your business requires and when you'll need them.

Defining the Job

"Many employees and employers do not know the requirements of a job until the employee quits for not knowing what was expected." —ALLAN HYDRICK

E ASSUME YOU HAVE DEVELOPED A WORKFORCE plan and from that plan have identified the type of positions your business requires to achieve its objectives. We also assume you have analyzed your current situation and have identified any need to hire additional employees for those positions. The next step is to describe exactly what the available job is and what qualifications a candidate for it should possess. The job title alone will not do that.

Describing the Job

There are many ways to describe a job, but the most common is to create a job description that outlines the relationship of the job to others in the organization, the purpose of the job, and the duties of the job holder.

Once you have properly described every position in your company, you have a basic document that you can use continually and revise as necessary. In every job interview, you will be able to correctly identify the qualifications required for the job and communicate what type of performance you seek from the employee. This is a part of operating your business professionally.

The box on the following page shows a job description for a sales manager. As we review the key elements for developing a job description, you may find it helpful to refer to the example. The Appendix also contains a model job description form.

In a study made a few years ago, the most common reasons employees gave for leaving small businesses (those with fewer than 100 employees) during their first six months of employment were as follows:

More money	25%
Job was not what I thought	22%
Did not know what was expected	18%
Unprofessional management	9%
Better benefits	8%
Return to school	7%
Personal reasons	4%
Did not like supervisor	3%
Moved	2%
Other	2%
Total	**100%**

Note that nearly half (40%) of all respondents cited "job was not what I thought" and "I did not know what was expected." That result reflects a failure of businesses to adequately describe and communicate jobs and their requirements. Many small-business owners are entrepreneurial and have a clear idea of what they are doing and what needs doing, but their employees may not share that characteristic. By telling your employees what their jobs require of them, you will greatly reduce the bother and cost of having to replace recently hired employees.

Title and Department

The job description begins with general descriptive information: the job's title and department, which, in our example, is the sales manager in the sales department. Some small businesses have no departments, so the description will omit this.

Job Description

Title: Sales manager
Department: Sales
Reports to: Store manager
Supervises: Eight salesclerks and two stockpeople
Objective: To manage the sales function of the store to meet income objectives.

RESPONSIBILITIES

■ Manage the sales function.
■ Establish and assign sales objectives to salespeople.
■ Maintain the necessary number of trained salespeople who must be available during all store operating hours.
■ Ensure adequate inventory of merchandise available for display and sale.
■ Approve all conditions of sale outside established procedures.
■ Resolve all customer complaints and approve returns outside established procedures.
■ Recommend operating budgets for the department and operate the department within approved budgets.
■ Counsel and coach employees to maximize their individual performance.
■ Prepare daily, weekly, and monthly sales reports.
■ Review performance of all department employees and recommend any activities necessary for improvement.

REQUIREMENTS

Education: Reading and mathematical skills at a twelfth-grade level. Management and or retail sales training desirable.
Experience: At least three years of successful retail-sales experience and at least three years of successful retail-sales management experience, including supervision of four to eight salespeople.
Special qualifications: Ability to operate a desktop computer with spreadsheet and word processing programs.

Since a job description is based on a number of organizational principles, the easiest way to learn how to prepare one is to understand those principles. These are not complicated theories but straightforward approaches to defining a job. The first organizational principle is reportability.

Reportability

Every job should have clear reporting relationships. That means every job should "report" to another, and you should

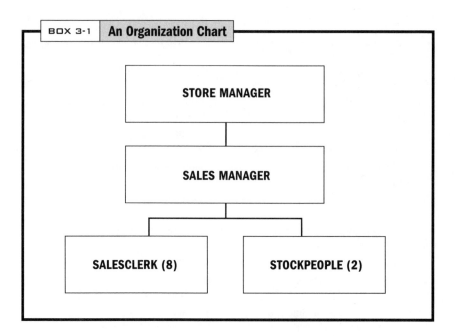

BOX 3-1 | **An Organization Chart**

STORE MANAGER

SALES MANAGER

SALESCLERK (8)

STOCKPEOPLE (2)

identify any jobs reporting to it. In the example, the sales manager reports to the store manager, and he or she supervises eight salesclerks and two stockpeople.

One way to consider reportability is to view a simple organization chart. The one shown above is for the sales manager.

Note that, on the chart, each position is represented by a box with the job's title written in it. If more than one of the same jobs exist, the chart includes that number in parentheses after the title. Each job has a vertical line from the center-top of its box to the bottom-center of another job box. Since the jobs appear in descending order of accountability, these lines indicate reporting relationships. For example, the salesclerks and the stockpeople all report to the sales manager, and the sales manager reports to the store manager. The line at the top of the store manager's box indicates that the manager also reports to someone else, probably the business owner.

Likewise, the chart shows who supervises whom. The vertical line from the bottom-center of a position box to the top of another indicates whom that person supervises. In our example, the sales manager supervises the salesclerks and the stockpeople, and the store manager supervises the sales manager.

With the information supplied by an organization chart it is possible to complete the rest of the job description heading *Reports to* and *Supervises*. Every job reports to another job. However, some jobs do not have other jobs reporting to them. For example, no one usually works for a busperson or a receptionist.

You may have seen dotted lines on an organization chart. Dotted lines indicate a relationship for some portion of a job. For example, in a typical solid-line relationship, a fast-food franchise may have a marketing manager who reports to the store manager. However, the same marketing manager may be accountable to the franchiser's director of marketing for the contents of all advertising. A dotted line could show that relationship.

Drawing a simple organization chart may cause you to clarify a number of existing job relationships.

The lines on an organization chart are called lines of authority, because they indicate how the business owner has delegated authority from one position to another. They are also called lines of communication, because they indicate how formal (as opposed to spontaneous or unofficial) communications flow through an organization.

If you are unsure of the reportability of a job, draw a simple organization chart. It should clearly indicate reportability, and the process may cause you to clarify a number of existing relationships. You may discover that some jobs that should have reporting relationships don't have them, or that others have several conflicting reporting relationships (more on this later).

Job Objective

The next organizational principal is the objective of the job. Every job in an organization should have a clear reason for existing—a reason that differentiates it from all other jobs in the organization and helps to avoid creating and paying for unnecessarily redundant positions.

Once you have identified reportabilities, you need to state each job's objective clearly and descriptively, to ensure that every job is different from all other jobs and, in so doing, to assess which jobs your business really needs. That will provide the basis for a detailed description of every job.

For example, assume that you hired a part-time janitor—say, a high school student to work two hours every night cleaning the offices, emptying the wastebaskets, and bundling the trash. If someone asked your part-time janitor what his job was, he would probably say, "To clean the offices." Very descriptive and clear. All job objectives should strive for such clarity.

If you cannot clearly define a job with an objective that differentiates it from all other jobs, perhaps there is no real need for the job.

A real estate broker's objective could be "to sell houses." A waitperson's objective could be "to provide prompt, efficient, and courteous table service," and an electrician's objective could be "to complete all assigned jobs within code and estimated time and cost."

If you cannot clearly define a job with an objective that differentiates it from all of your other jobs, perhaps there is no real need for the job. For example, an insurance agency employed several customer service coordinators. The owner decided to add an assistant customer service coordinator, but when she attempted to identify an objective for the new job, she discovered it was the same as that of the original jobs. She could not differentiate the new position, so, in effect, there was no such job or need for it.

A guideline: To simplify writing a job's objective, write it in one phrase beginning with the word "to": "To manage the sales function of the store to meet income objectives."

Responsibilities

Once you have established the job objective, you can identify the specifics tasks required to fulfill that objective. List those tasks in descending order of importance, from most to least important, to ensure that the first responsibility reads very much like the job's objective.

How many responsibilities should there be? It depends on what the job is and how detailed you want the job description to be. My experience suggests that between 6 and 12 responsibilities adequately describe most jobs and are about as many as most employees can accomplish well.

A guideline: Define each responsibility in one phrase beginning with an action word: "Manage the sales function" and "Establish and assign sales objectives to salespeople."

Other Factors to Consider

When you have identified all of the responsibilities of a job, you have completed the basic elements of a job description, but there are several additional principles of organization that you can use to further ensure the quality of the description.

Documentation

Describe every job in writing. Written job descriptions are less ambiguous than those communicated orally. They lay out the specifics of the job and eliminate the possibility of misunderstanding and confusion. Written job descriptions also provide a basis for identifying the level and type of performance required (more on this in Chapter 9).

Authority

For every responsibility assigned to a job, the appropriate authority should be delegated to accomplish that responsibility.

One of the most common complaints among employees is that their companies give them a great deal of responsibility (things to accomplish) but very little authority (the necessary power to get results), and then criticize them for not obtaining results. You can avoid this unproductive situation by giving your employees the necessary authority. For example, if an employee must pay invoices, you must delegate the power to approve payments and sign checks to the employee. If an employee must maintain inventory levels, you must give the employee the authority to purchase merchandise.

In the example, the sales manager's job description does not include a list of "authorities" delegated to it, but it could.

Authority and responsibility flow down the lines on an organization chart, and accountability flows up.

The sales manager's job description states: "Maintain the necessary number of trained salespeople during all store operating hours." To fulfill this responsibility, the sales manager must have the authority to hire salespeople, train salespeople, and schedule salespeople. Otherwise, the sales manager cannot accomplish the larger task.

Without authority, employees can accomplish their responsibilities by accident only, so you should review the responsibilities of every job to ensure that you have delegated the necessary authority to the correct degree.

The reverse—delegating authority without an accompanying responsibility—is also dangerous. For example, you do not want to give someone the authority to sign checks or remove inventory without also making that person responsible for how he or she uses that authority. And this gets into accountability.

Accountability

Employees must be accountable for using delegated authority to meet specific responsibilities.

Earlier we mentioned that the lines connecting the job boxes on the organizational chart represent the downward delegation of authority and related responsibilities. After you have assigned to a job the authorities and responsibilities required to fulfill its objective, whoever holds the job is then accountable for using the delegated authorities to accomplish the responsibilities. One way of looking at this is that authority and responsibility flow down the lines on an organization chart from one job to another, and accountability flows up the same lines. This concept can be expressed as a formula:

Accountability = Responsibility + Authority

Span of Control

Each employee should be accountable for as many "key result areas"—that is, major activities—as he or she can successfully handle. For example, a restaurant's major activities might be taking orders, delivering food, cleaning tables, and accepting money. Some restaurants assign all of those to waitpeople. Others make the waitpeople accountable only for taking orders and delivering food. No one way is correct for all businesses, but the way you assign the major activities in your business will determine the number and types of jobs you require.

You should review each job description to ensure that you have assigned to the employee the correct number of major activities—enough for an employee to be able to accomplish them successfully and be most productive, but not so many as to make success impossible.

The correct number of major activities for any job holder depends on many factors, such as location, type, and complexity of work. For example, the supervisor of data-entry clerks processing standard orders can probably handle several major activities. However, the laboratory supervisor for a research firm performing complicated experiments may be able to accomplish only the requirements of a single major activity. You need to use your knowledge of and experience in your business to determine how many major activities you can assign to each of your company's positions to achieve the required results.

Unity of Command

Every employee should report to only one other employee for each major activity. Nothing causes small businesses more problems than violating this principle of organization: requiring an employee to report to two or more people for the same key result area.

Earlier, we described a franchise's marketing manager who reported directly to a store manager but who was also responsible to the franchiser's marketing director for the contents of advertising. That arrangement is acceptable because the job holder is accountable to two different employees in two different major activities.

However, requiring a furniture salesperson to be accountable to a sales supervisor and to a store manager for sales volume, schedule, and work area is not acceptable because the salesperson may inadvertently receive conflicting directions.

Employees forced to report to two or more people for the same activity also quickly learn which person to approach for which type of decision, and how to use the dual-reporting relationship as a defense or an excuse. A good example of this can be seen in children, who quickly learn to which parent to address which request, and often develop approaches that play off the parents against each other.

Requirements

The job description can have one more element: a list of the requirements for the position. While important, this is not part of describing the job, but is part of determining qualifications.

CHECKLIST | Describing Jobs

You can create or review a job's description by answering the following questions, which are based on principles of organization. Have you:

■ **Documented** the job description in writing?

■ **Clearly identified** the reporting relationships of the job?

■ **Specifically stated** the job's objective—its reason for existing within the organization (preferably in a phrase beginning with the word "to")?

■ **Identified** the job's responsibilities (probably between 6 and 12 of them) and listed them in descending order of importance (each written as one thought beginning with a verb)?

■ **Reviewed** the job's responsibilities to ensure that you have provided the necessary authority to accomplish the job?

■ **Reviewed** the degree of authority that you have delegated to the job to ensure that there's enough, but not too much, based on the job's responsibilities?

■ **Reviewed** the job's reporting relationships to ensure that the employee won't be reporting to two different managers or supervisors for the same major activity?

■ **Reviewed** all aspects of the job to ensure that you have assigned the correct number of major activities to it?

Classifying the Job

Before you use the job description to determine the requirements that prospective employees must meet, consider how you will classify the job with respect to the federal Fair Labor Standards Act (FLSA). This act regulates a federal minimum wage and conditions for overtime payment. (Chapter 10 covers those in detail.)

This law doesn't cover all employees. There are exceptions for professional, administrative, and executive employees, as well as for independent contractors. However, there are specific requirements for exempting these employees. As a result, business owners often classify employees as "exempt" (exempt from the act) and "nonexempt" (covered by the act).

Exempt and Nonexempt Jobs

If a job is exempt, the law doesn't require specific working hours and payment of overtime. Most companies would like to exempt as many of their jobs as they can to avoid the added expense of paying overtime.

The federal government publishes rules to determine whether a job qualifies as exempt. You can obtain information about them from the U.S. Department of Labor by requesting a copy of the act and accompanying descriptive manuals or by visiting its Web site (U.S. Department of Labor, Employment Standards Administration, 200 Constitution Ave., N.W., Washington, DC 20210; 202-219-6666; www.dol.gov/dol/esa), or you can get it from one of the labor law services, which publish descriptions and analyses of employment laws (available at your public library or a law library; see Chapter 10).

CHECKLIST | **Job Classifications**

Have you:
- **Classified** your jobs as exempt or nonexempt?
- **Ensured** that all exempt jobs meet federal requirements?

- **Classified** any jobs as independent contractors, and if so, are you confident they qualify under federal law?

If you mistakenly classify a job as exempt when it is not, you may incur financial penalties, imposed by the federal government, which may include an obligation to make up for your employees' "lost" overtime wages in the form of back pay. If you are unsure whether a job qualifies as exempt, consult an employment attorney or consultant.

Independent Contractors

Independent contractors are firms or individuals who perform work for a company but are not employees of the company. Some companies see independent contractors as a desirable and less costly alternative to employees because they don't have to provide them with benefits, pay their social security, or adhere to the provisions of the FLSA.

If you give the person a goal to accomplish and allow the worker to pursue it as he or she sees fit, the person may qualify as an independent contractor.

Generally, if the independent contractor is another company supplying employees to perform work for you, it will meet the law's definition of a true independent contractor, but the situation is less clear with "self-employed" individuals, particularly if they work solely for your company.

Again, the law describes certain tests to determine whether a person qualifies as an independent contractor. One of the most important criteria concerns supervision. If you give the person a goal to accomplish and allow the worker to pursue it as he or she sees fit, the person may qualify as an independent contractor. Self-employed professional accountants, attorneys, salespeople, and consultants are likely to qualify. But if your company provides supervision (schedules and assigns work, and appraises and rewards performance), direction (advises on how to do each job), and control (sets starting and quitting times, location where work is to be performed, and time away from work), it is doubtful that the person will qualify as an independent contractor.

Other tests have to do with the following:

■ **Where the worker performs most or all of the work**—at your location, or, say, at the worker's home?

- **Does the worker have a "home" base** or office other than your's?
- **Whose equipment is used**—yours or the worker's?
- **How many firms the worker provides services to,** that is, is your company the only one for which services are provided, or services are provided for other companies?
- **How much time is devoted to your company?** Does your work represent full-time work and for how long, or does the worker simultaneously perform work for others?

The answer to any one of these questions does not necessarily confirm or deny independent contractor status, but along with amount and method of compensation the answers create a basis for determination.

If you are considering identifying someone as an independent contractor, you should obtain professional advice.

Identifying the Requirements for a Job

Now that you have described the job, you need to identify its requirements: What abilities, experiences, and special skills must someone possess to do that job? Generally, such qualifications are in the following areas:

- **Education.** What type and level of education does the job require of an employee to perform its responsibilities?
- **Experience.** What type and amount of experience does the position require?
- **Special training.** Does the job any require special training or licensing?
- **Management-supervision.** Does the job require management or supervisor training or experience?
- **Special qualifications.** Does the position require any special qualifications?

The best approach to establishing qualifications is to follow these two general rules:

1. **Establish the qualifications** for the type of person who will best fill the job.

2. Establish *only* the qualifications the job requires.

Those may at first sound obvious, but failing to follow them can lead to poor and unproductive hiring.

Rather than basing qualifications on an analysis of the job, employers sometimes establish the highest-possible level of qualifications, believing that they will thereby obtain the best possible candidates and employees. Sometimes employers pursue this strategy in reaction to a negative experience with an existing or former employee. Unfortunately, the strategy does not necessarily work in practice. You need to hire people who want the job and can handle it successfully, but are not so overqualified that the job soon bores them.

During the Depression it was possible to hire people with much higher levels of education than were required for a job. At that time postal clerks sorted all mail by hand. They had to memorize the various cubbyholes into which they put the mail. The postal service discovered that overqualified clerks learned the scheme very rapidly, but soon became bored by the repetitive nature of their jobs and began to think of other things as they sorted the mail. The number of delivery mistakes increased. When the postal service hired people with the correct qualifications for the position, those employees had to pay full attention to what they were doing and found the job interesting. Mail deliveries were far more accurate.

Some employers choose to hire overqualified people so that they can later promote them. That strategy works only if promotion is a certainty. When it is not, the result may be a poor work environment with dissatisfied or bored employees. Such a situation leads to low morale, loss of quality or productivity, and increased turnover.

Also, state and federal legislation and regulations governing nondiscrimination in hiring limits hiring overqualified people for later promotion unless such promotion is likely to occur. This area of law basically reiterates the two rules for hiring cited earlier, which we'll examine later. Depending on the size of your company, these laws may or may not apply, but the principle of establishing the "real" requirements of a position—not greater than needed—is a good one to follow anyway.

Education

Asking for a certain level of educational achievement is easy, but it's less effective than a more descriptive approach. For example, requiring a high school diploma will not yield similarly qualified candidates, because candidates may have pursued different courses of high school study and high schools vary in the quality of students they produce. Some school districts promote regardless of achievement. Other school districts may require passing a standardized test to graduate, but even that achievement won't guarantee that those candidates will possess the knowledge you require.

You need to hire people who want the job and can handle it successfully, but are not so overqualified that the job soon bores them.

You need to state exactly what knowledge and skills or specific course of study you require for the job. For example, "reading and mathematical skills at a twelfth-grade level" states the requirement more descriptively. But specifying "advanced reading skills and calculus" would be even better.

The same is true of college education, although more so. You should not require a college degree unless it is necessary to perform the job. If one is necessary, it probably means that a specific course of study is required; hence you should state that course of study. Always keep in mind that you want to obtain the candidate who most perfectly fits the job, not someone who is overqualified.

Don't overlook graduates of community colleges. Those two-year schools offer associate degrees in many disciplines and can often provide excellent candidates who have exactly the type of education and training you require for a position. If your area has a community college, you may find it quite productive to investigate what courses of study it offers. For

example, if you need a paralegal, you could require graduation from an accredited, two-year paralegal curriculum.

Experience

Employers often make three mistakes in this category of job
requirement: They state that a job requires previous work
experience when it really doesn't, they fail to describe the specific kind of work experience the job requires, and they arbi-
trarily describe work experience in terms of numbers of years
divisible by five.

If you want someone with work experience, try to state the
requirement in specific terms, for example:

> *Previous full-time work experience in a single job of at least
> six months' to a year's duration with satisfactory performance
> and reason for leaving. Will consider equivalent part-time
> and multijob experience.*

If you want specific job experience, you probably know
about how long it takes for someone to reach a certain level of
proficiency. But, remember, not all people learn and achieve at
the same rate, so that one person on the job for six months may
have acquired all the experience you require, while someone
else in the same time may have acquired only some of it.

What you are really looking for are certain skills. For an
automobile tire and wheel technician you might state:

CHECKLIST | **Qualifications**

Use this checklist to ensure that
you correctly establish qualifications for any position. Have you:
- **Identified** all the necessary
  qualifications?
- **Described** the qualifications
  necessary to perform the job
  satisfactorily?

- **Stated** all of the the qualifications specifically?
- **Listed** any qualifications that
  the job doesn't really require?
- **Described** requirements for education and experience?
- **Identified** the need for special
  training and qualifications?

Previous experience in replacing tires, repairing tires, and balancing wheels. Such experience should be for at least six months with a single employer, or one year with two to three employers, with satisfactory performance reviews and reasons for leaving.

Management or Supervision

If the job requires management or supervision of other employees, you need to specify related requirements, including certain training and experience:

Education or training in principles of supervision and experience as a supervisor of at least six employees, for at least one year with a single employer, and satisfactory performance.

Special Qualifications

This category covers any special requirements of the job. For example, if you want a singing waitperson, the candidates need to be able to sing. If you operate a translation service, the ability to speak Spanish may be required. If the worker regularly has to haul more than 50 pounds up a ladder, he or she must be able to lift that weight and have no fear of heights. You can fairly easily identify such special requirements as long as you stay with what is needed to successfully perform the job. Otherwise, you may eliminate good candidates for the job.

Some jobs by their very nature require special qualifications. For example, if you need a certified public accountant, that person must possess the proper certification. If you need an explosive technician, that person must have the proper federal and state licenses. If you need a real estate salesperson, that person must have a state license. In some instances, you may be willing to hire on the condition that the new employee obtain the qualification within a specified period of time. That's an option you might not wish to advertise, but can keep up your sleeve in case you have a candidate who otherwise perfectly meets your requirements.

Identifying the Standards of Performance for a Job

Finally, you must consider the job performance you desire. Descriptions of desired performance are given many names, such as results, goals, objectives, and standards of performance. For our purposes, we will use standards of performance. They complement a job description with an exact definition of what the employee must accomplish in that job.

Standards of performance are statements of the conditions that will exist when an employee successfully performs the job. For example, one of the responsibilities of a job holder may be:

Maintains a full inventory of needed parts at all times.

That generally describes what is to be done, but what exactly is a *full inventory?* What are *needed parts?* What does *at all times* mean? Standards of performance answer those questions. For example, a standard of performance for that responsibility could be:

There will be no instances during the year when listed repair parts are unavailable.

Full inventory means listed repair parts are available. *Needed parts* are listed repair parts, and *at all times* means no instances.

You might think that you should add standards of performance to the job description, but most organizations keep them separate, for a couple of reasons:

■ **Job descriptions do not change often,** but standards of performance are dynamic and tend to change at least annually.

■ **Employers may assign different levels (standards) of performance** to different employees in the same position because they have different levels of competency and experience.

Establishing standards of performance ultimately contributes to good management and better employee-and-employer understanding, but in hiring it serves another purpose: Standards of performance communicate in advance to candidates your expectations for performance.

| CHECKLIST | **Standards of Performance** |

Use this checklist to help you create a basic set of on-the-job, performance measurements that can also improve your hiring:

■ **Establish** at least one standard of performance—or as many as necessary—to define successful performance of each responsibility.

■ **Be sure** that each standard of performance includes a measure of accomplishment. Avoid vague words like adequate, enough, and some. Instead use specific words like all or none or use a specific number.

■ **Be sure** each standard of performance includes a completion date or a period of time in which the employee will accomplish the measure.

■ **Establish** standards of performance for an employee's first year or other training period, as well as standards for later, posttraining work, if you expect that they should or will change with training and experience.

In one seminar designed to teach people how to find a job, the seminar leader encourages the participants to ask prospective employers during an interview, "At the end of the first year, how will you and I both know if I have done a good job?" Many of the participants report that prospective employers cannot answer the question. Would you accept a job under those conditions?

Most employers write standards of performance as assertions of what they want and when. A positively stated standard of performance for an insurance office clerk might be:

To process a minimum of 24 insurance applications per day.

Sometimes, however, it is difficult to state what is wanted, and easier to state what is not wanted. For example a production foreman may be responsible for:

Operating a safe department.

The easiest way to express a standard of performance for that responsibility may be to state what should not happen:

There will be no employee injuries during the year as a result of a lack of safety guards on machines.

Summary

You are now armed with three pieces of information that form an accurate and sound base for hiring: a job description, requirements for the job, and standards of performance. They will not only assist you in hiring, but will also provide you with means for measuring the performance of employees. Next, you will use this information to obtain candidates and assess their qualifications.

Obtaining Qualified Candidates

"Surround yourself with the highest caliber people. Remember that first-rate people hire first-rate people—while second-rate people hire third-rate people."—RICHARD M. WHITE, JR.

OU HAVE IDENTIFIED A JOB THAT YOU NEED TO FILL and have pinpointed its responsibilities, qualifications, and standards of performance. Now you're ready to obtain candidates.

Note the use of the word candidate, as opposed to the more frequently used applicant. *The Random House Dictionary of the English Language* differentiates between the two words (somewhat paraphrased) as follows:

Applicant—a person who applies for something
Candidate—one who seeks and is deserving of something

The difference may seem subtle, but it's important: You'll more likely find the right person if, right from the start, you seek candidates who really want the job and are qualified (deserving), rather than wasting your time and resources on applicants who are just going along for the ride. Seeking candidates can also contribute to your having a more positive view of the people you consider. This chapter shows you how to find the candidates you need.

There are many sources of candidates but basically two

types: *internal* and *external*. Internal refers to sources already available within your company, and external, to sources outside your company. Which is better? Both have advantages and disadvantages. It depends on your objective in filling the position, and the conditions within your company.

Internal Sources of Candidates

Internal sources include promotions and transfers of current employees, and use of techniques such as job posting, employee referrals, succession plans, job families, and existing files of information. Job posting and employee-referral programs can identify candidates you might otherwise have overlooked. If your company has a workforce plan or a succession plan, you may have already identified internal candidates for jobs. Or you may have identified job families, that is, a hierarchy of positions through which a typical employee can grow. Finally, candidate files (with unsolicited résumés, applications, and employment inquiry letters) can be a good source because they represent people already interested in your company, if not the specific job. This section discusses the pros and cons of each of those strategies.

Promotions and Transfers

The first step in obtaining candidates for a position is to consider your current employees. Can you promote or transfer someone? Will such a move contribute to the company's and to the employee's success?

You can improve morale and reduce your hiring costs if your company has enough employees to consider promoting or transferring them. From a morale viewpoint, promotions (a move to a different job at a higher level or pay) demonstrate opportunities for development and advancement. Employees also generally view transfers (a move to a different job at the same level or pay) as signs of a growth opportunity.

From the viewpoint of cost, promotions and transfers provide candidates who already know your company and its operation. Because they may even know some elements of the job, they will need less on-the-job learning time. You can fill the job faster and at a lower cost because you do not have to locate, interview, decide upon, and await the arrival of external candidates.

Moving a productive employee to a new job does not always guarantee success.

The major disadvantage of promotions and transfers is that you may end up getting the skills immediately available instead of the ones actually required. For example, if you need to bring new experiences and ideas to the position, promoting and transferring a current employee is probably not the best approach. Likewise, moving a productive employee to a new job does not always guarantee success. You may only lose a good employee in one job and gain a poor employee in another. And of course, the employee's move affects the job and organization left behind because generally you must fill the vacated position.

Sometimes a slavish adherence to a policy of promotion from within can create a different set of problems, as, for example, when companies move employees before they are ready to move.

A few years ago, a Pennsylvania insurance company was experiencing rapid growth, doubling its number of employees within two years. The company had a strong policy of promotion from within, so it transferred or promoted most employees before they had spent even a year in a position. Time in entry-level positions averaged less than six months.

As a result, the company never had an experienced group of employees in place. Under the circumstances, employees made mistakes, and their expectations became unrealistic. Some employees (those under 25 years old with less than two years' experience in their first job) quit when they did not "make" supervisor within that time.

The company eventually chose to suspend its promotion-from-within policy until it had established a strong base of experienced employees. When that occurred, the company also discovered that it required fewer employees.

Job Posting

Job posting is a method of communicating job opportunities to all employees, so that those who are interested and qualified may apply. If you have few employees and are well acquainted with their qualifications and career plans, this tactic is probably unnecessary, but as your company grows, job posting can identify employees-candidates whom you might not otherwise consider. Even if your company is not ready for job posting, you should be aware of the procedure and its possibilities.

To be successful, job posting needs to have clear and well-communicated rules. Typically, you should designate a bulletin board, company intranet site, or employee newsletter as the location for job posting. When you post a job, you should describe its responsibilities, qualifications, and salary or job grade (salary level within the company), and give a date by when you must receive applications. (The Appendix provides a sample job-posting notice and application forms.)

Typical requirements for employees who wish to apply for posted positions are these:

- **A minimum amount of time** in the current job
- **Evidence** that the employee possesses all job requirements
- **A current performance rating** of "good" or better
- **No record** of detrimental performance, such as excessive absenteeism or tardiness
- **No record** of having applied for more than (number) of posted jobs within the past 12 months

When you receive the applications, immediately notify any employees who don't meet the qualifications and identify their deficiencies. Then consider the remaining, qualified candidates.

You could interview all of the qualified candidates; such a practice will be good for morale because employees will see that as fair. You could rank them by degree of qualifications, from most to least, and interview them in that order. Or you could rank the candidates first by job qualifications and then by seniority within the company. Whichever approach you choose, be sure to respond to all candidates as soon as you make a decision.

Most companies that use job posting do not guarantee to post all jobs. They retain the right to seek external candidates in accordance with the requirements of a job. But when companies seldom use job posting, employees feel slighted and poor morale results.

Employee Referrals

You can also encourage your employees to refer external people for jobs. The reasoning here is that employees will only recommend people they believe will do well and be an asset to the company. After all, no one wants to injure his or her own reputation by recommending someone who turns out to be a poor employee. If the company hires someone recommended by an employee, the employee receives a reward, usually cash, though it could be a free lunch, extra time off, or some other noncash motivator. Some companies limit their employee referral programs to nonexempt employees only.

No one wants to injure his or her own reputation by recommending someone who turns out to be a poor employee.

Employee referrals, too, require communication of open positions and qualifications to employees and clear rules. You can use the same communication methods as for job posting, including bulletin boards, newsletters, intranet sites, or a memo to all employees. Employees can then recommend someone by submitting an employee recommendation form with the candidate's completed application or résumé. (The Appendix contains a typical employee recommendation form.)

Some organizations encourage employees to refer people at any time, while others seek referrals only for announced positions. Either way, you need to establish rules so that the process is fair and perceived by your employees as such. Some of the more common rules follow, but you need to determine which ones apply to your company:

No one may recommend a relative. Many companies impose this rule to avoid issues such as conflict of interest and favoritism. If you desire this rule, you'll have to define who is a relative, for example, does it include a spouse or other immediate family member, or extended-family member, such as a cousin?

Anyone involved in hiring may not refer anyone. That group includes supervisors, managers, and human resources personnel. Many companies believe that helping to fill jobs is part of the responsibilities of every supervisor and manager, particularly of human resources personnel, and thus they should not be paid extra for referrals. Some companies allow supervisors to recommend persons for jobs only outside their department.

You will keep referral materials on file for six months (or some other stated period). People recommended for a specific job must have the stated qualifications and they must not have applied or been referred previously within the past six months (or some other time period). If they have already applied or been referred within that period of time, their résumés are on file for consideration. Accepting a second referral raises the question of who should receive payment if the person is hired.

Don't presume that candidates know that they've been referred. One employer says that about half of his referred candidates are unaware of the referral. So you may have to winnow out those candidates who are truly interested from those who aren't.

Two rules for payment of the reward are common:
- **The new hire must remain with the company** for at least six months.
- **The recommending employee must still be employed** by the company at the end of the six months.

Reward amounts of $50, $100, $250, and $500 are common. Generally, the greater the difficulty of obtaining candidates for the job, the greater the reward. One small company with difficult job requirements offers $1,000. Some companies change the amount from time to time, depending on their difficulty in obtaining qualified candidates. In a hot job market, where suitable—or any—candidates may be hard to come by, for a company that can afford it (or that thinks it can't afford not to), a reward of $2,000 might not seem too much.

Succession Planning

Large organizations often include succession planning in their workforce planning. For them the process of developing such plans is a formal one, performed regularly and with an established structure, but even the smallest company can benefit from the basic process.

In succession planning, you determine how you will fill jobs if their incumbents leave. You identify who, if anyone, within the organization is qualified to move into a vacated job, how much training he or she will need, and whether you also require an external candidate. For example, in a restaurant a key position may be shift supervisor. In a succession plan it might appear as:

SHIFT SUPERVISOR

1. **Bill Allison,** waiter, 1 year of experience, 1 month of training
2. **Alice Blennor,** waitress, 6 months of experience, 2 months of training
3. _____

Here the plan identifies two internal candidates for shift supervisor with their current jobs, the extent of experience, and the amount of training each would require. The business owner will consider them in order of greatest experience and least need for training. This plan requests three candidates, so the owner will have to obtain a third candidate elsewhere.

You can acquire information for a succession plan from annual performance reviews, your knowledge of employees, and input from your supervisors and managers. If such plans are to be useful, you will need to keep them current and realistic by updating them annually or whenever your organization experiences significant employee or structural changes. They should indicate logical choices of internal candidates who are qualified for the job, but should identify no one if no one is qualified. It should provide a real plan of action if a position is vacated.

A secondary advantage of succession planning is that the process will help you identify areas of vulnerability. You may discover that your company has no backup for key positions. So, although this process is most important for large companies, small companies also can benefit from it, and it requires relatively little time to complete.

A succession plan should help you assess the strength of your organization and identify internally qualified candidates, but it should not guarantee that any particular employee will actually get the job. When an opening occurs, the conditions at the time should be the basis for filling the job, but you should consider any candidates identified by the succession plan.

Often, particularly in larger companies, succession plans become a formality. Managers prepare them as required, but no one ever refers to them. If you make one, use it.

Job Families

A job family consists of a series of jobs that form a natural progression upward in the organization. Identifying a job family appeals to candidates and employees because it provides a road-map for their careers with your company. A small organization may not have enough different jobs for this to occur, but you should be aware of the concept.

For example, a typical job family, from top to bottom, within an insurance company might be:

- **Claims supervisor**
- **Claims investigator**
- **Claims receipt clerk**
- **Claims file clerk**

In this case, the company hires an inexperienced employee as a claims file clerk, and with experience and good performance, he or she works up through the various jobs.

When communicating job families and their potential career paths to your employees, you must describe the minimum accomplishments necessary to move to the next position. For example:

- **Claims supervisor**—at least one year as a senior claims investigator and completion of a supervisory-management course of study

■ **Senior claims investigator**—at least one year as a claims investigator

■ **Claims investigator**—at least six months as a claims receipt clerk and completion of a claims investigator course at the community college

■ **Claims receipt clerk**—at least six months as a claims file clerk

■ **Claims file clerk**—entry-level position in claims department

The requirements have been simplified somewhat here, but in actual use, they should be very specific, so that no one misunderstands.

Job families can be effective tools for attracting employees, helping them develop, and retaining them. Job families tend to create good morale and company loyalty, but they are not applicable to very small businesses. However, even if you use them, you should retain the right to hire externally if a current employee is not ready for a move, and you should promote an employee to the next job only when it is open—not just when the employee has met the requirements. For example, if you had a salesperson who was attending night school, obtained a law degree, and passed the state bar exam, that employee would then be a qualified lawyer. However, even if you had a law department, would you automatically promote the employee to an attorney's position? Let's hope not—not unless you *needed* another attorney.

You must describe the minimum accomplishments necessary to move to the next position in a job family.

There is an exception. Some organizations base jobs and promotion on acquiring the qualifications for a job, instead of a job vacancy, but they generally have unusual situations and job structures. For example:

A financial services firm in Utah has a position of credit analyst, for which it has continuous openings, and it has found it difficult to find candidates with the required training and experience. The firm has found that the typical new employee needs six months to gain the desired level of skill.

The company has subdivided the job into three positions: assistant credit analyst, credit analyst, and senior credit analyst, and it has established the required skill level for each position. New employees begin as assistant credit analysts, and the company informs them of the skill requirements for the next two positions. As soon as an employee has demonstrated the required skill level, the company promotes the employee.

In this case the company desires that all of the employees in this "job family" perform at the senior credit analyst level, but it recognizes that employees can only obtain the required competencies on the job. It also acknowledges individual differences in learning speed. So it allows employees to move as fast as they can.

Existing Files of Information

Most companies receive unsolicited applications, résumés, and letters of inquiry. Once you have received them, they become a good source of candidates. Ideally, you accept such documents and maintain them in a current and readily accessible file. When a job opportunity arises that you can't fill with a current employee or referral, you can review those files before seeking other candidates. The advantages to that? The files may speed up your hiring, and they represent people who have already indicated an interest in your company and who will cost you nothing to contact.

These files are most helpful if you organize them by job, but in many cases, particularly for entry-level jobs, that is difficult. Some companies' applications ask what job or type of job the person is applying for, and résumés usually state the type of jobs the person desires. Lacking such information, you can ascribe a job for which the person appears qualified, or you can maintain some type of general file.

There are two other considerations regarding the maintenance and use of such information: legal and public relations.

LEGAL CONSIDERATIONS. As with other considerations of employment, unsolicited résumés and applications need to be dealt with fairly and without bias. The appropriate laws are usually in the area of nondiscrimination. This is another subject to be reviewed with a local employment attorney or consultant (described in more detail later).

Unless a law or regulation requires you to do otherwise, a good rule is to maintain completed applications, résumés, and letters for at least six months. This includes unsolicited documents as well as those received in response to ads or from external sources such as employment agencies or online services.

Good record keeping can prevent and protect you from unjustified claims of discrimination in hiring.

You should time-stamp all applications upon receipt, and identify the job being applied for or that job for which the applicants' qualifications make them eligible. File the applications for that job in order of receipt: applications, résumés, and letters combined. (In some cases there may be no job in your company for which an applicant qualifies. You can keep those separately.) If six months is your retention period, it is probably a good idea to purge the documents after seven months. Such a practice eliminates arguments about exactly when a six-month period ended.

Whenever you do consider or contact someone on file, make a note of the action and attach it to the document. Otherwise, you may find yourself contacting people who have already declined an interview or trying to prove without documentation that you really did consider someone for a job. Such documentation is crucial in making and defending employment decisions.

Some companies maintain a log of applications and résumés. It consists of a chronological listing by date and time of receipt. It includes the person's name and, in some instances, other identifying information, as well as the date you removed the document from the file and discarded it.

You may be wondering, why all this record keeping? There are two reasons. It can be a good and inexpensive source of candidates if the information is well organized and accessible when you need it. And it can prevent and protect you from unjustified claims of discrimination in hiring.

We all know the United States to be a litigious society. It is no longer uncommon for candidates to sue employers that fail to offer them jobs (though this is less likely if there has been no interview), and for employees to sue employers that fail to promote or appropriately compensate them, or that "unfairly" fire them—in fact, for just about any possible condition of employment. In many cases, but not all, such claims are unjustified and easily dismissed if appropriate records are available. Unfortunately, employers sometimes fail to keep records. When that is the case, the employer may have little defense.

> *A motel regularly accepted applications from "walk-ins," but it rarely referred to them. It generally threw away the applications in a week if it had no openings. Over a six-month period, the motel hired three desk clerks—all male. The motel then received a complaint filed with the state equal employment agency by a woman. She had applied during the same six months and had excellent credentials (both education and experience), but the motel had never contacted her. She claimed sexual discrimination in hiring. The motel had no defense; it could not prove fair hiring practices because of its lack of documentation. The woman won her case.*

This book continually recommends keeping thorough records, and suggests relatively easy ways to do it. However, this is also an area to review with an employment attorney or consultant, to ensure that the records you keep are applicable to your business.

PUBLIC RELATIONS CONSIDERATIONS. "The worse public relations I know is for a company to post an external sign reading, 'No Help Wanted,'" said Frank Oakes. Oakes was a young man during the Great Depression, and he recalled encountering such notices as he attempted to find employment. He later became senior vice president of human resources for one of the country's major manufacturing firms. He never forgot how he felt when he saw such signs, and he made it a practice for his company never to post them. Also, his human resources department always accepted applications and he, himself, made it a practice not to do business with firms that posted such signs. The message is to always treat people—including candidates—as customers or potential customers.

Many times people will approach your company for work because, in their customer roles, they have developed a high regard for you. Don't destroy that impression. An employment inquiry is an opportunity for you to create or reinforce a favorable image of your company.

If someone enters your establishment to leave a résumé, complete an application or inquire about employment opportunities, be sure that you or anyone else treats that person with respect and consideration. Follow these guidelines:

- **Always greet the person politely.**
- **Tell the truth.** If there are no current openings, say so. If you will accept an application, say so and tell the person how long you will maintain it.
- **Encourage completion of applications on your premises,** but allow for completion at home and return. (A good rule, as you will discover later, is always to have it completed on site.)
- **Provide privacy** so that the applicant doesn't have to complete your application in an area with the general public. The candidates may not want someone they know to discover that they are seeking new employment.
- **Someone with greater authority than the receptionist** should accept the application and say a few words.
- **Train all your employees who may meet the candidate** in how you want candidates treated.
- **Always assume that any prospective employee** is a customer or a prospective customer. Remember that seeking a job can be very stressful and treat the person as you would like to be treated if your roles were reversed.

A consulting firm in California employs numerous professionals who travel a great deal. For years, one of the major credit card companies had attempted to sign up that firm to use its card. The firm always remained with a less-well-known card company.

Finally, a vice president of the credit card company called the consulting firm's managing director and asked what he could do to get the company's business. The answer was, "Nothing."

The managing director explained that during his senior year in college, when he was seeking summer employment, he approached one of the credit card company's local offices. In front of numerous people in the waiting area, the receptionist told him that the company would not take an application or his résumé. He felt humiliated.

He also approached a bank, the one that sponsors the credit card his firm now uses. The bank did not hire him but treated him with respect, accepted his résumé, and later called him for an interview.

How should you respond to mailed-in résumés, letters and applications? If the sender has addressed the material to you

---

CHECKLIST | **Internal Sources of Candidates**

Have you:

- **Considered** current employees for promotion or transfer?
- **Established** a procedure, such as job posting, to identify employees who may be interested in and qualified for open positions?
- **Established** a procedure that encourages your employees to recommend people they know for jobs with your company?
- **Identified** logical progressions for promotion or transfer within job families (if you have a variety of positions in your company)?
- **Identified** any key jobs for which internal backup does not exist (succession planning)?
- **Used** your succession plans when filling jobs?
- **Dated,** time-stamped, and recorded the receipt of all applications and résumés, solicited or not?
- **Kept** all applications and résumés for a specific period of time?
- **Referred** to application and résumé files before seeking external candidates?
- **Responded** to all employment inquiries?
- **Treated** people seeking employment in a professional and considerate manner?
- **Trained** your employees to recognize the public relations benefits of dealing well with applicants and candidates?
- **Discovered** what legal requirements may apply to your files of résumés and applications?

---

or your company, you or an associate should answer it. Sometimes you will receive general mailings—those obviously mailed to a list of companies, with no letter addressed specifically to you or your organization. You probably don't need to respond to such letters, but you may choose to anyway because it's a public relations opportunity. Besides, word processing makes generating a "boilerplate" response very easy. Write something similar to this:

> *We have received your résumé and appreciate your interest in our company. Unfortunately, at this time we do not have any opportunities that match your qualifications. However, we will keep your résumé for at least six months and reconsider it if an appropriate opportunity develops. In the meantime we wish you every success in obtaining the position you desire and thank you for considering our organization.*

So what does it take to create such a letter? If it exists in an easily accessed computer file, five minutes at the most—a small price to pay for excellent public relations. If you are replying to e-mailed material, you can respond even more quickly and possibly even automatically. Whichever route you choose, your response will generate or reinforce the candidate's positive image of you and your company, and provide you with a possible candidate for future openings.

External Sources

We have considered the internal sources of job candidates—generally the ones to exhaust first before seeking external candidates. Now let's turn our attention to external sources.

If you can't fill a job internally—say, because you don't have anyone ready to promote or you're looking for different skills or experience—you'll have to look outside. External candidates can bring new ideas and experience to your organization; they can show you how other companies might be accomplishing similar activities to better effect. They allow you to insist on specific qualifications rather than accepting less for convenience' sake. Hiring someone from outside prevents disruption of your current staffing.

External candidates, however, generally cost more to locate, require more time to select and hire, and take longer to get up to speed on the job. As a result, they are more costly than internal candidates. Also, external hires are more likely to leave the job after only a short time (more on this later).

Consistently hiring from outside to fill higher positions can breed resentment and a lack of cooperation.

When companies regularly select employees from outside the company, particularly for higher-paying and supervisory positions, current employees find it demoralizing as they see their hopes for rising through the ranks repeatedly quashed. This practice can breed resentment among current employees and a lack of cooperation with the newly hired.

> *A retail clothing store consistently hired department supervisors from outside. The current sales clerks grew increasingly resentful because they could discern no particular skill or knowledge that the new hires brought to the store. They soon developed a malicious obedience.*
>
> *All new employees require time to learn the unique processes of a company and their jobs. Before they learn those, they often make mistakes. In this case, newly hired supervisors would suggest approaches that current employees knew would cause problems. However, the employees took the approach, "If that's what you want, that's what we'll do," and created innumerable problems following the directions to the letter.*

It's probably best to have a policy similar to this:

> *Promote from within whenever possible, but retain the right to hire from outside the company to meet specific requirements.*

You should promote from within when such a practice will best meet the needs of the job, benefit your company, and help it fulfill its mission. You should not promote from within if the practice will cause internal problems and will not meet specific job requirements. Moreover, you need to carefully consider and recognize how you have filled jobs over time. If you have filled too many non–entry-level jobs externally without specific reasons, you should review the situation.

But you should not promote from within if the practice will cause internal problems and will not meet specific job requirements.

How do you locate external candidates? If you have time or staff, you can do it in-house, but if not, you can hire individuals or organizations to do the work for you. They can save time, but they cost money. Let's begin by reviewing how your company can conduct its own search for qualified external candidates.

Advertisements in Print

The most common method is to advertise. Not so long ago, where to place an advertisement was basically a matter of which publication to choose. With the advent of Web sites on the Internet dedicated to classified listings and career advice, you have the online option, too. Let's start with a discussion of advertising in print media. Many of the considerations there apply to advertising on the Internet, and that discussion follows shortly.

Where and when to place an advertisement in print media depends on answers to several questions: What publication will reach the group of people from which I am most likely to obtain qualified candidates? What day is best to advertise? What type of ad and what content should I choose?

WHICH PUBLICATION? Publications can be newspapers or magazines. Which to use depends on whom you wish to reach, which depends on what type of job you wish to fill and how wide you wish to cast your net. Some publications appeal more to one group than another, and there are publications directed to specific groups.

For example, the *Wall Street Journal* probably won't help you find a mechanic or bartender. Its ads tend to be aimed at managers and professionals. The *Wall Street Journal* also publishes the

National Business Employment Weekly, a newspaper devoted to such jobs. (The *Wall Street Journal* will accept ads for specific geographic areas as well as the nation.)

On the other hand, managers and professionals tend to not read community newspapers. Those are more often read by people seeking local, nonexempt, and technical jobs.

Some newspapers offer specific sections of advertising for various occupations. The *New York Times* offers a Sunday section devoted to educational and medical opportunities. The *Detroit News* has a separate section of classified ads for salespeople.

Even if you discover a magazine devoted to your industry, you may do better with a local newspaper.

Sometimes there's a regional magazine (whether it's of general interest or focused on a particular lifestyle or interest) that is useful.

Or there may be a magazine or trade journal devoted to your industry or profession. (There probably is one, and if you don't know about it, you should.)

To survey the publications in your area or industry, go to your public library and ask the reference librarian what's available locally, regionally, or nationally. Look at the most recent copy of the publication to get a sense of whom it is written for and read by. Check the masthead (usually on the editorial page or on the table of contents page) for circulation figures (how many copies are printed and distributed) and the telephone number of its advertising sales department. Sometimes the advertising rates will be printed on the masthead or at the beginning of the classified section, but you may have to call to ask.

If you read all the local publications for a week (a week without a holiday in it), the number and type of ads will tell you which newspaper attracts the most advertisements for the type of job you wish to fill. For newspapers that aren't published daily, read at least two weeks of editions. The whole purpose of this exercise is to determine which newspapers are most read by the type of people you are seeking.

The main problems with magazines are circulation and frequency. Regional magazines that will reach and appeal to job seekers only in your local area may be hard to find. And the odds are, the cost of advertising in it or in a national magazine will be much higher than in a local newspaper.

Moreover, magazines usually have longer lead times than newspapers and rarely appear weekly, let alone daily. It may take up to two months (and possibly longer in a trade journal that's published only four to six times a year) before a submitted ad appears. You may not be able to wait that long.

Even if you discover a magazine devoted to your industry, you may do better with a local newspaper. For example, if you operate a small amusement park in the summer, you can use a national publication such as *Amusement Business* for obtaining qualified candidates with specific skills and experience. Most professional park people read that publication. However, if you are attempting to fill only summer jobs, the type of candidates you are seeking may not read *Amusement Business*. The local Sunday newspaper may be a more effective way to obtain candidates.

WHEN TO ADVERTISE? In most areas, Sunday is the best day to advertise in the newspaper, but there is usually a second "good" day. It differs by community, but Thursday appears to be the most common. If you are unsure, ask the newspaper or just check the number of employment ads each day. You will soon discover which days most advertisers believe to be the best days.

Usually, advertising salespeople at newspapers will tell you the best day of the week to run your ad, but they also may attempt to sell you a full week for a better per-day price. In most areas, however, only one or two editions a week attract serious job seekers. Advertising all week generally gains little and costs more in total.

With a magazine, it might be easier to call its ad sales department and ask which month's issue is most popular for advertising jobs in the industry. For example, in some trades, employers like to advertise right before the industry's annual trade show or convention.

WHAT TYPE OF AD (AND RELATED ISSUES)? There are basically two types of ads: classified and display. Classified ads are the ones that appear in tiny type in running columns of ads. Here you purchase as many "column inches" of space as you desire.

Display ads allow you to create your own ad using whatever wording, design, and illustration that you choose, including your company's artwork or logo. Newspapers sell space for display ads in terms of number of columns wide by number of inches long. Magazines generally allow you to choose from pre-designated blocks of space, usually expressed as a fraction of a page, such as an eighth-, a fourth-, or a half-page.

Because display ads cost more than classified ads, employers usually buy them to reach higher-paid employees, such as managers and professionals. They usually direct less-expensive classified ads at nonmanagers and nonprofessionals. Consequently, managers and professionals tend to read display ads, while other employees tend to focus in on the classifieds.

Design and arrangement of classified ads. Because classified ads appear in large groups, which can add up to an eye-glazing mass of gray type, advertisers tend to design them to stand out. They use large or bold type, extra white space around the type, and unique fonts to catch the eye. Of course, you'll probably pay extra for the privilege.

Some newspapers arrange classified ads by the first letter of the job title. Sometimes the arrangement is alphabetical by the first letter of the first word, and sometimes it is by a selected classification regardless of job title.

It's smart to be aware of the publication's approach to placement and use it to your advantage. For example, if the publication arranges ads alphabetically by the first letter of the first word, to have your ad appear near the beginning of the listed ads, you might begin it with: *AAA opportunity* . . .

If the publication organizes the ads by classification, it will print the ad with all other ads assigned the same classification, and arrange the classifications alphabetically. Be sure that *you* assign the classification, not the newspaper, lest it misidentify and misplace your ad. At the same time, it's smart to choose the classification from among those most commonly used in the classifieds section, so that your ad will appear where frequent readers will expect to find it.

For example, you may be seeking a human resources inter-viewer, but when you review the newspaper ads you discover that most human resources jobs are classified as "Personnel." That being the case, you will want to classify your job the same. Your ad might read:

Personnel

**HUMAN
RESOURCES
INTERVIEWER**

Excellent opportunity for
experiencedinterviewer to
join human resources
department...

One caution: Pay attention to the submission deadline for ads. These vary by newspaper, as do placement rules. In some cases, the paper will place ads by classification if it receives them only by a certain time. It may include late ads in a mis-cellaneous section at the end of all other ads, where the candi-dates that you seek may overlook it.

Considerations for display ads: Some newspapers group display ads by type of job, but many do not. Some allow you to pur-chase a specific location, but not all offer this option. Ask the newspaper what options it offers and their costs. If possible, locate your ad in the section of the newspaper you feel your potential candidates are most likely to read. If you can select a location on the page, the best spot is the upper-right corner of an odd-numbered page ("under the right thumb" in newspa-per jargon). Next best is the upper-left corner of an even-numbered page, and you always want to be on the top half of the page ("above the fold"). In a multipage section of ads, the nearer your ad appears to the beginning, the better.

One other consideration for display ads: People who aren't actively job-hunting frequently read these ads, so you should view them as a type of advertising and public relations activity. One national organization uses its display ads both to obtain candidates and to communicate an impression of a growing, state-of-the-art company.

AD CONTENT? Once you've decided on the publication, date, and type of ad, what should the ad say?

Keep in mind your main objective: *To obtain qualified candidates for a specific job.*

You will be more successful in meeting this objective if you clearly state your requirements and provide a general job description. If there is anything you specifically require to evaluate candidates—salary history or résumé, for example—state it to avoid wasting your time and theirs. If you have properly identified the position, you know the qualifications (see Chapter 3); you do not have to state them all, but list the most important ones. Also, list any unusual ones or ones that are likely to reduce responses from people who would not accept the job under those conditions, such as night-shift work, heavy overtime, considerable travel, or relocation.

Some firms give a telephone number. When prospective candidates call, the firm conducts a brief interview to prequalify them. If qualified, the firm sends an application for completion or invites the individual for an in-person interview.

Some employers advertise open houses. Those can be quite effective for multiple entry-level openings, but many people decline to apply for a job in a group setting.

HOW NOT TO DO IT. What follows is the wording from a display ad that appeared in a major Sunday newspaper:

RETAIL SALES MANAGER
Upscale furniture store with 10 sales people seeks an experienced sales manager. We require at least five years of furniture sales experience and at least two years of sales management experience. Send résumé with salary history to:

Box 1256

Would you answer an ad like that?

If you already have a job, you probably would not. It offers no real information about the job. You would have no idea to whom you were sending a great deal of personal information, and you might even be sending a résumé to your own company.

When companies use a box number, they generally are attempting to limit the replies they will have to make. They reason that if a person does not know to whom the résumé is sent, the applicant can't hold it against the company when it doesn't respond. This can be self-defeating. Many qualified candidates will not respond to box numbers. Furthermore, this approach does not recognize the potential positive public relations value of your ad. Contrast the preceding ad with the following one, from the same Sunday paper.

Using a post office box number doesn't take advantage of the positive public relations value of your ad.

OFFICE MANAGER

Ralton Company, a fast-growing, direct-marketing firm, has an opportunity for an experienced office manager to manage a staff of six clerks and order processors. The position reports to the general manager. We require three or more years of office experience and at least two years of experience in office management. PC Windows experience a plus. Excellent benefits and opportunity for advancement with an initial salary of $40,000. Send a résumé to:

Ms. Jill Page, Human Resources Manager
Ralton Company

Our employees know of this opportunity and this ad.
An Equal Opportunity Employer

What a difference. This ad tells you about the job and the employer. You're impressed that the company treats its employees fairly, because the ad advises you that they know of the ad. In other words, if you were an employee of the company, you would know about the job opportunity.

The same is true for classified ads. Below are two classified ads from the same section of the same newspaper. To which ad would you most likely respond?

WAITPERSON
Wanted for lunch shift.
6 days a week. Some
experience required.
Send letter or résumé
to Box 235.

WAITPERSON
Casual Italian bar and
restaurant has a full-
time opening for a lunch
waitperson. Good salary
and benefits. Some
experience required.
Apply in person to Jim
Mason, manager, between
2:00 P.M. and 4:30 P.M.
Monday through Thursday.
Mario's, 123 Elm St. An
equal opportunity employer.

Probably the longer one. It provides some detail and identifies the company. The short ad reads more like a fishing expedition.

ARE YOU AN EQUAL OPPORTUNITY EMPLOYER? In the next chapter we examine the legal requirements of hiring, but we need to deal with some of them here. You have probably noted that the ad examples included: *An Equal Opportunity Employer.*

The federal government initiated use of this statement in the 1960s to assist in ensuring fair treatment in hiring for all groups. Some firms in certain industries and below a certain size may not be required to include the statement. Also, there may be local or state requirements regarding the use of such a statement.

The best approach is to include it, even if the requirement does not apply to your company. Because most ads will have it, prospective employees may perceive your failure to include it as an admission that you are not an equal opportunity employer— that you do not treat all groups equally. You don't wish to project that image.

You should also exclude any requirements, such as gender, that have nothing to do with ability to perform the job (more on this in the following chapter). For example, advertising for a "Girl Friday" or "Mail Boy" in most instances would be illegal.

Advertising Online

The Internet is a recent, fast-developing addition to external recruiting sources. Just imagine: Instead of having to run out on Sunday morning to get the Sunday classifieds, prospective employees can log on to any of the job-related Web sites—any time of day or night, any day of the week to find your ad.

Here are some examples of the Internet in use:

An Indiana computer services firm has made its past 11 hires through the Internet.

A California search firm uses the Internet to obtain candidates to present to clients.

An Alabama bank has a Web site describing current employment opportunities and how to apply for them.

Unfortunately, the Internet does not have a single method for referring you to sites of potential candidates or employment advertising, so you may have to explore awhile before you find sites appropriate to your purpose. However, if you are familiar with the Internet or someone in your company is, it is worth examining.

Your favorite search engine, such as Yahoo or Altavista, is likely to offer a jobs feature on its home page. Click on it to see which online classifieds service it connects you to. Or you can use the search engine to search by key words—such as a specific job title, a generic job title, the name of your industry, or the words *employment* or *classifieds*—in order to find likely Web sites. *Monster.com, topjob.com, careerbuilder.com,* and *hotjob.com* are just a few of such sites currently available. *Careerpath.com* features job ads pulled from the Help Wanted ads of dozens of U.S. newspapers.

Each site operates differently, but typically you pay a fee that is based on the number of jobs you wish to advertise, the length of time you want the ads to appear online, and the number and choice of affiliated Web sites where your ad will appear. You could pay $150 to advertise one job for a month, or several thousand dollars to post unlimited jobs for some time.

If you would rather pay (or perhaps not even have to pay) to reach a more focused pool of candidates, you might consider the following avenues:

Does your industry's membership association or other related professional or trade organizations allow members to post job listings on their Web sites? This approach could be a cost-effective way to reach the candidates you desire.

Many city newspapers now maintain their own classified-ad Web sites. Print ads don't necessarily appear online, and vice versa, but some newspapers may offer a "two for one" price to advertise both in print and online. You're sure to reach local candidates, as well as people who may be interested in relocating to your area.

Is there a university known for producing people in your field? Would you be interested in advertising your jobs to recent graduates or alumni of your alma mater? Check its Web site to see whether it offers a classifieds feature. (See also the discussion of schools, below.)

If you know people in your area or industry who have used the Internet to fill a job, talk to them. Which online classified service did they use? How satisfied or dissatisfied are they? How many useful responses did they receive? The ease with which people can respond and send their résumés electronically may invite an e-mail flood of unqualified responses.

If you think you've found the source for you, take a closer look at the site to see the types of jobs offered and to obtain a description of the charges. Then, prepare a description of the job with qualifications and submit it for posting, following the same guidelines outlined earlier; some sites will provide online forms for you to fill out. Just as you would if you were advertising in the newspaper, be sure to peruse the Web site to see how the job listings are organized and choose the category that you think is most appropriate and that contains ads similar to your own. Check whether the online service will discount its fee if you wish to post your ad in multiple categories.

If you have an e-mail address, you can expect to receive many responses in that manner. As always, remember that this is a public relations opportunity; make sure to reply to all submissions with a note of thanks for their interest and whatever other information you want to provide.

If your business has its own Web site, don't forget to post job listings there.

Is the Internet right for you? It depends mostly on what type of job you have available, and whom you are trying to reach. You can assume that computer-related jobs will do well on the Internet, but so do some others. What does not appear to do so well are jobs for which older people apply and nontechnical entry-level jobs. However, with the growing acceptance of the Internet, that situation may soon change.

If your business has its own Web site, don't forget to post job listings there, where you can describe them more fully at no extra cost. Even if your business is quite small, a job-seeker who is searching the Internet by key words that are relevant to your business or to jobs you are advertising may still find you.

Alternative Advertising Opportunities

There are other ways to advertise your job. Some firms post Help Wanted signs. Some describe job opportunities in mailings to customers and suppliers, and some post notices in their lobbies and public areas. For example:

- **Certain trades traditionally seek employees** through Help Wanted signs. Businesses usually post them near a street where passers-by can view them, and they usually list the types of jobs available.
- **Retail stores often include job opportunities** as a separate item in monthly charge account statements, and chain restaurants regularly post open jobs near their service counter.

Whatever your industry and the job you're advertising,

you want to use whatever medium gets your opportunity to the most likely source of candidates, so be creative. You may discover a new one that no one else has used.

Companies That Are Downsizing

Other possible sources of candidates are local firms that are downsizing, going out of business, or laying off employees. A Los Angeles aerospace firm established an internal department to place its people during a downsizing. Other firms hire so-called outplacement companies to counsel and assist their downsized employees in locating other jobs. If you know of a company that is reducing employment, call its human resources department, or if it's a small firm, call the owner or manager. You can also call local outplacement firms to find out whether they are counseling people who may be candidates for your job openings.

Associations and Schools

Other possible external sources of candidates are associations and schools.

Associations range from unions to professional associations, and what they do varies. Some will post job opportunities in their offices or on telephone "job lines," and publish them in their newsletters or on their Web sites. Some keep member résumés on file for your review, and some have staff members assigned to work with companies to place members. Call the association or organization most relevant to your business and ask about its employment services, including any fees or deadlines, or check its Web site.

Almost the same can be said about schools. Some post jobs in their career centers, some publish jobs for students, some have employment counselors, and some do nothing. Some schools help only recent or upcoming graduates. Others deal with alumni. In situations where the school does little, individual professors, teachers, or counselors who take a personal interest in their students may be a source of recommendations.

A small firm in Atlanta developed an excellent relationship with a computer instructor at a local community college. As they worked together, the instructor acquired knowledge of the company's requirements, and the company gained confidence in the instructor's recommendations.

As a result, the instructor regularly recommended graduating students to the company, and the company generally hired them. It was not a formal program, but one that developed through a continuing and mutually beneficial relationship.

In Chapter 2, we discussed the advantages of hiring temporary employees. It can also be beneficial to develop work-study programs with local schools. Hiring students in appropriate fields of study during their vacations or part-time during the school year can be an excellent way of obtaining good employees. The students receive pay and gain experience, while you have an opportunity to preview their performance. If you hire them, you owe no placement fee and they already know your company.

CHECKLIST | **Advertising**

Have you:
- **Determined** which advertising outlet is most likely to reach the candidates you desire?
- **Decided** which day of the week, month, or season is best for your advertisement?
- **Decided** whether to use a display ad or a classified ad in a publication?
- **Obtained** the publication's rules for ad placement and designed your ad to take maximum benefit of those rules?
- **Written** an ad that is complete in its description of the job and its requirements?

- **Identified** your company in your ad?
- **Considered** the public relations aspects of your ad's wording?
- **Included** "An Equal Opportunity Employer" in your ad?
- **Identified** Web sites that will help you reach prospective candidates?
- **Found** the most cost-effective online advertising plan?
- **Considered** alternative media such as "Help Wanted" signs, public postings, and letters to customers and suppliers?
- **Developed** relationships with schools that can provide qualified candidates?

If this idea interests you, check with schools that provide the type of education your jobs require. For example, if you hire people for entry-level jobs who have graduated from a specific curriculum, ask the schools offering such courses of study whether they have work-study programs. Even if they don't, you may want to ask how you can invite students to visit your company and submit applications for part-time work, independent of their schooling or on graduation.

Some schools offer employment orientation programs and job fairs for graduating students. Depending on the number and type of jobs you have open, you may want to consider attending one of these.

Professional Assistance

If you are not staffed to obtain candidates or you prefer to have someone else do the work, you can hire a professional service. The four basic types are consultants, search firms, employment agencies, and government agencies.

CONSULTANTS. There have always been consulting firms willing to provide companies with just about any human resources service desired. Traditionally, only larger companies have used them, but in the past few years a new type of consultant has appeared. Often individual practitioners, they sell their time by the hour or job to smaller organizations. Instead of having a few major clients, they have many smaller ones.

Hourly charges vary by region and type of service. Consulting is a highly competitive business that is governed by supply and demand. Telephone calls to several nationwide firms specializing in services to small companies obtained hourly rates from $50 to $250 (though you might encounter rates of $400 to $500 an hour in large metropolitan areas). That may sound expensive, but in the long run, a few hours of a good consultant's time could save you a great deal of wasted time and unnecessary cost. In any event, regularly using a consultant should also get you a reduced rate.

One such firm, based in Louisville, Kentucky, and headed

by a former senior human-resources executive for a major financial corporation, provides services for both large and small organizations. For smaller companies, it serves as the company's human resources professional and performs all such tasks as needed. Assisting in screening and interviewing of job candidates are common assignments.

Most human resources consulting firms do business locally, so you should consult the *Yellow Pages* to find them in your area. Generally, they are listed under "Consultants," "Management Consultants," or "Personnel Consultants" (the classifications seem to differ by geographic area). However, it's best to get a referral from someone who has used such a service. Call another small company that you may know has recently done some hiring and ask what sources it used.

A new type of human resources consultant has appeared. Those firms, often individual practitioners, sell their time by the hour or job to smaller organizations.

You can also check *The Directory of Executive Recruiters,* published by Kennedy Information Publishers (One Kennedy Place, Route 12 South, Fitzwilliam, NH 03447). It is primarily a listing of larger search firms, but you may discover a local consultant whom you can contact. Your local library may also have lists of local consultants, and you can search online for individual recruiters' and consultants' Web sites.

SEARCH FIRMS. Search firms tend to concentrate on higher-paying professional and management positions. For locating qualified candidates, companies generally pay in accordance with the job's projected or actual compensation. Typical fees are in the 30% range, paid in two or three installments. In addition, search firms require reimbursement for out-of-pocket expenses, such as travel and telephone calls.

Some search firms specialize in certain industries and types of jobs, or limit themselves to jobs paying within certain salary ranges or to certain geographic areas, while others will accept just about any assignment. Some firms are large and national in scope, while others are individual practitioners operating locally.

Use *The Directory of Executive Recruiters* (mentioned earlier) in combination with your local *Yellow Pages* to locate such firms. Also check the display ads in the local newspaper (generally on Sunday) to identify search firms in your area. Companies similar to yours in size or type of industry may be a source of referrals.

If you consider using a search firm, attempt to obtain a recommendation from another company. If that is not possible, be sure to contact two or three recent clients of the search firm. To discover how well the search firm handled the assignments, ask these questions:

- **Did the firm refer qualified candidates?**
- **Did it properly check candidate qualifications?**
- **Were they able to fill the job within the desired time?**
- **Would the company use the search firm again?**

Regarding the firm's fee, you need to ask specific questions:

- **On what compensation does the firm calculate its fee:** base salary, base salary and bonus, projected or actual?
- **How and when must I pay?** Can I pay in installments? Can I pay part now and the rest later?
- **Must I pay the search firm if** it doesn't find a qualified candidate within my time requirements?
- **What do I owe if** the search firm fails to recommend any qualified candidates?
- **What do I owe if** none of the referred candidates accept the position?
- **Will I receive a refund if** the newly hired employee leaves within a specific time?
- **Can I approve out-of-pocket, billable expenses before** the search firm incurs them?
- **Will the search firm guarantee not to** attempt to recruit candidates from my company for a period of time?

If you're running a small business, you may need to use a search firm only occasionally. Since these firms operate on supply and demand, you will probably have less bargaining power than a larger company that uses its services regularly. Even so, ask questions and get the best fee arrangement that you can.

You may find that an individual practitioner will give you better service than a large firm.

Some search firms will develop a list of probable candidates for a fixed fee. They agree to provide the list within a specific period of time. If you decide to have the search firm interview those candidates, the search firm applies its regular fee structure, and you receive credit for the fee already paid. Search firms generally charge a percentage of normal charges for limited work. For example, a search firm that charges 30% of a job's compensation for referring candidates, may charge only 15% or 20% for a list of candidates, but you must negotiate that arrangement with the search firm because there are no standard prices.

> **The better candidates will often not interview with companies that refuse to pay an agency's fee, so it is to your advantage to do so.**

Find out who will do your work, and be sure that you are comfortable working with that person. Because that person will represent your company, you will want him or her to project the image you desire.

EMPLOYMENT AGENCIES. Employment agencies tend to deal with lower management and nonmanagement positions. As with search firms, some specialize and some do not. Most *Yellow Pages* list employment agencies under that heading. As with search firms, a study of newspaper classifieds often indicates the types of jobs or industry in which an agency specializes.

Employment agencies generally charge a percentage of compensation. The size of the fee varies by region and often by type of job, though these agencies generally charge less than search firms. However, you usually need not pay the fee until you have hired someone. Most candidates from an employment agency have signed an agreement to pay the fee themselves, but the employment agency will still ask you, as the employer, to pay it. Should you? Probably, yes. The better candidates will often not interview with companies that refuse to pay the fee, so it is to your advantage to do so.

Employment agencies generally request these two things of employers:

| CHECKLIST | **Using Professional Assistance** |

Have you:

- **Analyzed** whether you are staffed to seek candidates or should use professional assistance?
- **Decided** which type of professional assistance is most appropriate for the position you wish to fill (consultant, search firm, employment agency, government agencies, association, or school)?
- **Sought** references and recommendations from other companies for any professional assistance you are considering?
- **Asked** all the appropriate questions about type of service, fees, payments, and limitations before contracting for professional assistance?
- **Talked** to at least two professional assistance organizations before making a decision to hire one?

---

1. You will give them an exclusive right to fill the position. If you have worked with the employment agency and its performance has satisfied you, you might consider an exclusive arrangement. Another approach is to tell the agency that you will not place the position with another agency, but that you will consider unsolicited candidates from other agencies that call you.

2. You will pay the agency if you hire someone recommended by them, even if you do so at a later date or for another job. That's fair, but the arrangement should include a time duration. Three to six months from the time the agency first recommended the person is usual, but this arrangement requires you to keep a record of where you have obtained candidates. An employment agency may recommend a person who has applied to your company independent of the agency. If this happens, you should immediately let the agency know so that it doesn't charge you a fee if you eventually hire the person.

As with search firms, you should try to obtain recommendations and ask the same questions about fees. Some states require employee agencies to be licensed, primarily to protect individual job seekers. But you can call your state's labor department to see whether it requires licensing and ask a prospective agency to show you its license. You can also call the Better Business Bureau to check the employment agency's record of customer complaints.

A final word about employment agencies and search firms. When you select one, it becomes your representative. Any action you authorize it to take is your responsibility. For example, assume that you want to hire only Christians for your company. Your reason is that, because you are a Christian, you want to treat your fellow Christians preferentially, but there is no specific job-related reason for the requirement. If you give those instructions to the employment agency and it follows them, you are not an equal opportunity employer. If rejected candidates later initiate legal action, you will probably be liable.

STATE EMPLOYMENT/UNEMPLOYMENT SERVICES. In some states, unemployment services have become employment services that attempt to find jobs for recipients of unemployment benefits. Do not overlook them. Their degree of effectiveness varies, but many provide excellent service for some types of positions, especially nonmanagement and trade positions.

Investigate the state employment services in your area. You might start by talking with other employers who have used them. Make an appointment with the employer liaison person to ask about services and benefits. Some state unemployment services offer incentives for using them. For instance, they may check references or verify qualifications for you, or they may even pay for some new-employee training. If their services sound correct for the jobs you need to fill, give them a try. You will learn whether or not it is a relationship you wish to develop. You may find working with your state's employment services is an efficient and cost-effective method for obtaining candidates.

Summary

This chapter has introduced a variety of sources for candidates and described the advantages and disadvantages of each. You need to choose the source that best fits the needs of the position, and your time and cost requirements.

If you decide to use professional assistance to fill positions, try to locate an organization that should be able to assist your company on a continuing basis. Developing such a relationship should lead to more productive candidates.

A key point: All candidate searches are public relations opportunities, and all candidates are customers or prospective customers. If you fail to treat candidate searches with appropriate care, you will miss out on a fine opportunity to generate good will and future business.

Preparing for and Conducting Interviews

"The best person you interview isn't necessarily the best person for the job." –ROBERT HALF

 OU HAVE IDENTIFIED THE JOB AND ITS REQUIRE-ments, and selected sources of candidates. Once those candidates respond, you need to evaluate their individual qualifications in terms of the job's requirements. That means you interview them. This chapter deals with preparing for and conducting interviews, and it examines the laws governing such activities. When you actually become involved with candidates, many requirements guide your dealings, so we begin by considering them. Again this book is a general guide, and you should consult your attorney with specific legal questions.

Understanding the Legal Requirements in Hiring

Here are a series of questions that an employer might ask on an application or in an interview. Which ones do you think you could or should ask? Which ones do you think are legal to ask?

- Are you married?
- How old are you?
- Do you have a car to get to work?
- Do you have a sitter or day care for your child?
- Where were you born?
- Will you please send a recent photograph with your application?
- Of what organizations are you a member?
- Do you have any physical limitations?

Well, the correct answer is none of these questions should be asked, with the exceptions that are noted below. Federal and state laws designed to prevent employment discrimination prohibit you from asking those questions (more on this in Chapter 9) and from making hiring decisions based on non–work-related criteria. But as the following discussion shows, those questions are typically irrelevant to most jobs anyway, and you'll have no reason to ask them.

Are you married? Does this question have anything to do with the job? Probably not. Some prospective employers might say they need to know marital status for insurance purposes. That isn't necessary until *after* you've hired the person. Then it's okay.

How old are you? Again, what does this have to do with the job? You can ask if you suspect that a person is underage for certain requirements of the job. For example, some states have laws that prohibit anyone under a certain age from operating moving equipment. If that age is 16, you can ask if the person is at least 16 years old. Otherwise, you must not ask.

Do you have a car to get to work? You can ask this question if the job requires use of a personal car, say, for making deliveries. Otherwise, how a person gets to work has nothing to do with the job. If you're concerned because no public transportation serves your company's location, you may say:

> *No public transportation serves this area. Our hours are 8:30 A.M. to 5:00 P.M. Will you be able to get to and from work for those hours?*

Do you have a sitter or day care for your child? First, you should not ask the person if he or she has a child, and second, how the child is cared for during the workday is not your concern. Refocus your question to pertain to the job. Here is a better question, similar to the previous example:

> *Our hours are 8:30 A.M. to 5:00 P.M., Monday through Friday. Can you be here during those times?*

Where were you born, or, What was your birth name? Candidates may view those questions as an attempt to determine their national origin. If that has nothing to do with the job, do not ask about it.

Will you please send a recent photograph with your application? When hiring for some jobs, such as modeling and casting a play's role, you might justify this request. But in the vast majority of cases, you cannot, and candidates can view your request as an attempt to determine sex, national origin, age, color, and race—all conditions that you cannot use for employment decisions.

Of what organizations are you a member? Such a broad question covers possible associations—such as religious, national, or sexual—that may have nothing to do with the job. If you want to know whether a person is a member of an organization when such membership is required for a job, typically an accrediting organization, ask that question. For example,

> *Are you a member of the state bar association?*

That is a legitimate question if the job requires such membership. Or you could ask more generally:

> *What organizations are you a member of that are relevant to this job?*

Do you have any physical limitations? You cannot ask job applicants about the existence, nature, or severity of a disability. But you can always ask questions to determine if a candidate has the qualifications required by the job. For example, if a job requires the employee to work with or around produce, you can ask a candidate if he or she is allergic to it. If the job requires the employee to regularly walk aerial catwalks, you can ask the candidate if she or he is able to do that.

Now, here comes the main exception. If you can show that any of the foregoing questions truly relate to the job, you can ask them. For example, if you are operating a restaurant designed to reproduce an authentic Japanese teahouse experience, and you wish to hire people who look and speak Japanese, you can probably justify questions to determine those characteristics.

You can ask questions to determine if a candidate has the physical qualifications required by the job.

However, an English-style pub in New Jersey wanted to hire English employees only, but when pressured to justify that position, its owners had to admit that they really wanted only people with English accents.

If you believe you have an unusual job that requires you to ask about a characteristic that would otherwise generally be prohibited, you should first contact an employment attorney or consultant before making it a job requirement.

Notices

In the physical area where you greet candidates or they complete applications, you should have a bulletin board on which required notices are posted. Those include federal notices regarding minimum wage, overtime, equal employment, and occupational health and safety. Your state or locality may require other notices. It is important to discover what the law requires of your company, to obtain the notices, to post them, and to keep them current.

Many companies place such notices on a bulletin board with a locked, glass front. Then they regularly (usually once a year) check to ensure that all notices there are current. If you use an employment attorney or consultant, subscribe to some type of service, or belong to a professional organization, you may automatically receive updated posters. Because it is your responsibility to post and keep them current, you need to establish a system to ensure that occurs.

Notices required by federal law include the following:
- **Fair Labor Standards Act**
- **Family and Medical Leave Act**
- **Job Safety and Health Protection**
- **EEO Is the Law**
- **Employee Polygraph Protection Act**
- **Occupational Safety and Health Act**

Those typically required by state law include the following:
- **Workers' Compensation and Disability**
- **Unemployment Compensation**

To find out specifically what federal and state law requires of your company, you can consult any of the following sources: the U.S. Department of Labor (see page 39), your state's department of labor, any local employers' association (if you're not aware of any, check with your local chamber of commerce), an employment attorney or consultant, a CPA, or labor-law service books at your public library. (Chapter 10 provides more details on those resources and how to locate them.)

Applications

You will generally receive applications that you have designed and given candidates to complete, but occasionally you may receive an application produced by an employment agency, school, or professional association. Whatever the source, you must consider how the equal employment laws apply to such forms.

Most companies use a single application, but some use two—one for nonmanagers and one for managers and professionals. With the flexibility of customization provided by personal computers, some firms now store a basic application form that they customize for the requirements of specific jobs. For example, if the job is for a bookkeeper, specific questions regarding related knowledge and experience can be included. If the job is for a delivery person, questions regarding driving experience, type of license, and familiarity with different vehicles are appropriate. Whatever your situation, ensure that your application requests the information you need to fill the job requirements, but does not ask illegal or non–job-related questions.

The elements of a standard employment application are listed here. (The Appendix contains a sample employment application, but you may want to develop one specifically for your company and the type of jobs for which you hire.) The suggested "statements" highlighted at the end of this discussion are designed to provide you, the employer, with a layer of legal protection, but they must be reviewed by an employment attorney for your use.

Contact Information: Including name, address, telephone number(s), e-mail address(es), and a second (permanent) contact

Job title or titles, or type of job desired

Education: high school, community college, college or university, graduate school, trade school, graduation date, degrees granted, courses of study completed, majors, awards, grade-point average or class position, dates of completion, and any specific accomplishments

Work experiences: employer, dates, job title(s), job duties, accomplishments, starting compensation, current or previous compensation, current department, current supervisor, location, and reason for leaving or wanting to leave

Related experiences: any other experiences relating to the desired job(s) with dates and description

Related skills: any other skills relating to the type of jobs with description and amount

Limitations relating to jobs: any limitations to successfully meeting the job requirements

Personal references: two, with names, addresses, telephone numbers, e-mail addresses, and nature of relationship

Professional references: two, with names, addresses, telephone numbers, e-mail addresses, and nature of relationship

A signature and date of completion

You might also wish to include any or all of the following statements.

Statement regarding accuracy of information. This paragraph is meant to help ensure the accuracy of information. It notifies the candidate that the employer can use any incorrect information to discharge the employee. Most applications include a statement similar to this:

> *The applicant certifies that all information provided in this application is true and complete, and recognizes that in submitting this application, authorization is given for the investigation of all information. Furthermore, the applicant understands and agrees that any misrepresentations or omissions will be sufficient cause for cancellation of the application or termination of employment if already employed.*

A release for references. This paragraph anticipates that some organizations and individuals will require a release from the candidate before they will provide a reference. It also obtains the candidate's permission for such checks. Employers and "references" also see it as providing some protection in case a candidate disputes the content of a reference and its effect on a hiring decision. The application may include a statement similar to this:

> *The applicant also grants the company the right to contact any or all places and people mentioned on this application (with the exception of the current employer) and any institution, school, or agency for information about the applicant with respect to the applicant's qualifications, and hereby discharges and exonerates the company, its agents and representatives, and any person supplying information.*

Statement about job requirements. Many companies state on their applications that employment is contingent upon the successful completion by the candidate of any other company requirements, such as a preemployment physical. This is meant to notify candidates in advance of such requirements.

Statement regarding no guarantee of employment. A company may state that completion of an application does not guarantee employment and that the application is not an employment contract. Companies including such a statement do so to prohibit later claims of implied or promised employment upon completion of an application.

Statement regarding life of the application. In some cases, the application states that the company will hold it for six months from the date of submission, but be careful with such language: If the candidate considers such a statement to be a promise and believes that your company has failed to live up to it (in this case, prematurely taking the candidate out of the running), he or she could sue your company for breach of an implied contract (maintaining it for six months). Therefore, you should also make an affirmative statement that holding the application is no assurance of a future job.

Statement regarding employment at will. Many companies hire under the terms of employment at will, which is also the legal presumption in many jurisdictions. That means that the company has the right to terminate employment at any time, and the employee may do likewise with proper notification. Some applications include a statement to this effect. The following statement is from a Florida company's employment application:

> *(Company name) hires all employees under an employment-at-will policy. The terms of this policy allow any employee to be terminated by the company at any time (unless otherwise covered by the terms and conditions of a specific employment agreement with the employee), and an employee may terminate employment at any time by providing proper notice (one full pay period).*

> *Any statements regarding discharge, promotion, or other aspect of employment shall be interpreted consistent with an employment-at-will relationship between the company and its employees, regardless of whether such statements are in written form or transmitted orally to employees.*
>
> *The policy of at-will employment shall be applied consistently for all employees without regard to their position, length of service, and standards of performance.*
>
> *The policy may be varied in the case of an individual only by written agreement with the employee and signed by an officer of the company.*
>
> *Your signature to this application indicates your understanding of this policy, and in the event that you are hired by the company, you agree to sign an employment-at-will policy recognizing your understanding of and agreement to the employment-at-will policy.*

If you wish to include an employment-at-will statement on your company's application, you need to first talk with an employment attorney or consultant. You need to be confident that it is legal in your state, and you need to develop specific wording for your company. *(Note:* Any separately negotiated employment agreement, such as a union contract or an individual employment contract for senior management) may invalidate the principles of employment at will.)

CHECKLIST | **Legal Requirements**

Have you:
- **Checked** to determine the specific laws regarding hiring to which your company is subject?
- **Reviewed** your application form to ensure that it meets legal requirements and requests the type of job-related information you require?
- **Ensured** that your application makes no promises and cannot be considered an employment contract?
- **Considered** the possibility of customizing applications for specific positions?
- **Identified** the legal notices that you must post in the candidates' reception area?
- **Obtained** all required notices, posted them, and arranged to keep them current?

Processing Applications, Résumés, and Letters

Your next step before interviewing is to process all the materials submitted by applicants. First, you'll evaluate and sort the applications, résumés, and letters in terms of the job's requirements. Later, you will respond to unqualified and qualified candidates.

Initial Classification of Résumés and Applications

What do you look for in a résumé? First, find out whether the person meets the requirements of the job. This evaluation will probably result in a three-category sort:

- **Those who clearly meet the requirements**
- **Those of whom you are unsure**
- **Those who clearly don't meet the requirements**

You can then concentrate on the ones that make the grade, and go to the second category only if there are too few of the first ones or if they do not work out.

Some job seekers have a single résumé and send it for all jobs. Ideally, they will include a cover letter that relates the résumé information to the job requirements and helps you evaluate their qualifications, but often you will receive no letter or just a form letter. You will have the most difficulty classifying those submissions, and you may have to consign them to the unclear pile.

Then there are applicants whose qualifications do not even come close to the job's requirements, and you have to wonder why they bothered to submit a résumé. Perhaps they assume that if they apply for everything, they will get something sooner or later. Unqualified résumés are the easiest to classify.

Educators have traditionally used a type of résumé called a *curriculum vitae* (or CV). Some noneducators have labeled their résumés the same, possibly to attract a prospective employer's attention, to affect an intellectual or scholarly air, or just to be different. If you receive a CV, treat it as a résumé.

Sometimes you will receive a letter of qualification rather

than a résumé. Such a letter summarizes a person's qualifications with respect to the job's requirements. You should treat this, too, as a résumé.

Finally, you will have to sort through completed applications, which candidates generally have picked up in person or obtained by an earlier letter, a telephone call, or a visit to your Web site. Since you designed the application, you will more easily evaluate it, but, again, your first evaluation should be a three-category sort according to the job qualifications.

Once you have evaluated the basic facts, review the applicant's materials for what else they can tell you.

You must also consider who will perform this initial classification. If you delegate the task to someone else, be sure that he or she truly understands the job and its requirements. Otherwise you stand a good chance of losing some excellent candidates in the shuffle.

WHAT DO YOU LOOK FOR IN THE INITIAL EVALUATION? Aside from the basic qualifications, consider the applicant's salary history or requirements. In the process you may identify additional information that you need to know but the résumé doesn't provide. If so, make note of it, but never mark the actual résumé, application, or letter. Those materials may someday be reviewed by others, say, in a legal situation, and often the type of shorthand notes most of us make could easily be misinterpreted with negative consequences to you. Make any notes on a separate sheet of paper, but retain it with the application, résumé, and letter.

Once you have evaluated the basic facts, review the candidate's materials for what else they can tell you. For example:

- **Is there a logical progression** of jobs?
- **Is there a pattern** in the reasons for changing jobs and the time spent on jobs?
- **Are there unexplained gaps** in the background?
- **Does the person provide all the information** you requested or require?
- **Does it appear that the candidate provided all the information** without unexplained exceptions?

How do you discover these things? By considering the entire application. If you receive a sloppy, dirty application, you have to wonder if the candidate will demonstrate the same style on the job. If the job qualifications include written communication with customers, you'll want to review candidates' materials for spelling and grammatical errors and the ability to write clearly and simply. Depending on your requirements, materials that are a mess may compel you to immediately consign the candidate to the "thanks, but no thanks" pile. Make notes of anything that needs explaining. Those notes will help you prepare for an interview.

Be cautious if you allow candidates to complete their applications off-site; they may not have filled them out themselves.

A Kansas company was having problems with the performance of a newly hired employee. After discussions with him, the company discovered he was illiterate and could not read the documents he received in his work. His application, however, was well written. His sister had completed it for him. Though most companies would have fired the employee for being unqualified and for having falsified his application, this one moved him to another position and gave him one year in which to take remedial reading.

With résumés, you may find that you receive information you did not request. Pay attention to what the person has chosen to tell you. You may gain unexpected insights, for good or bad.

The candidate may also have sent you inappropriate information, such as a photograph, a birth date, or religious affiliation. If the item is separate, such as a photograph, remove it, throw it out, or return it, and make note of the removal. If it's part of the document, black it out. Some firms return such documents with a request for the candidate to resubmit it without the unnecessary information.

Response

Once you have sorted and classified all the résumés, letters, and applications that you have received, you can move forward with the qualified candidates, conclude involvement with the unqualified candidates, and hold the materials for candidates with uncertain qualifications for possible consideration later.

As soon as possible, conclude communication with the unqualified candidates by sending each one a letter. If the candidate has provided an e-mail address, you can use it. However, be careful, because often the e-mail is on the current employer's system. As previously mentioned, employers who used a post office box in their advertisements may feel that this step is unnecessary because the candidates do not know to

> **Studies indicate that the few firms that treat applicants with respect and consideration are long remembered in a favorable light.**

whom they applied. Other employers believe you need reply only to those candidates who included a letter specifically written for the job or addressed to the company.

That's okay, but recall the importance of using the job search as a public relations tool. Most often, job seekers find the experience very emotional and stressful, and they suffer a great deal of rejection. Studies indicate that the few firms that treat individuals with respect and consideration are long remembered in a favorable light, so write a letter.

With desktop computers it is simple to have a boilerplate letter on hand, ready for addressing and signing. In replying to unqualified candidates you can use a variation of the earlier letter that you wrote for unsolicited applications. For example:

> *We have received your résumé. Thank you for responding to our recent advertisement for a merchandising supervisor. We appreciate your interest in our company. Your qualifications, although well described, do not match our requirements for that position. However, we will keep your résumé for at least six months and reconsider it if an appropriate opportunity develops. Meanwhile, we wish you success in obtaining the job you desire and thank you for considering our organization.*

You need not reply, however, to candidates submitted by employment agencies and search firms unless you have had contact with the candidates. Otherwise, it is up to the employment agency or search firm to maintain its positive image by appropriately communicating with the candidate.

You also needn't respond to candidates in the middle, "wait and see" category until you have exhausted the qualified group or hired someone. Then you can send them a concluding letter, or you can request more information. Between one and two months is as long as you should delay before sending an acknowledgment.

Qualified Candidates

The rest of this chapter focuses on dealing with qualified candidates. The first step is to ensure that you have all the required information. Then sort the candidates in the order of their qualifications, say, from most to least qualified. You may be able to accomplish this simply by reading each application, but it may be easier and clearer to use a simple rating system. It isn't scientific, but it will help you organize yourself to interview the most promising candidates first. Start by listing the qualification categories for the job, such as:

- **Education**
- **Type of experience**
- **Length of experience**
- **Special qualifications**

Next, rate each applicant's qualifications in each category using this simple scale:

- **1 point**—Less than required
- **2 points**—As much as required
- **3 points**—More than required

Every employer must define what each rating means for itself and the job at hand. Consider these examples, in which the category of qualification is flexibility:

- **A Colorado manufacturing company** has a very authoritarian management approach. It has detailed rules and regulations, and expects its supervisors not to deviate from them.
- **A California Web site design company** believes its supervisors

must constantly deal with rapidly changing conditions and requirements from both customers and employees.

What happens when someone with low flexibility applies to each company? The Colorado company would assign that person 2 points for having just the right amount of flexibility, while the California company would assign the same person 1 point for having less flexibility than required.

What happens when someone with high flexibility applies? The Colorado company would assign the person 3 points for having more flexibility than required, and the California company would assign the candidate 2 points for having just the right amount.

You might expect to total or average the points, but that result would be misleading. If you correctly identified the requirements for the job, someone who is assigned 2 points in each category has received the ideal evaluation—exactly the amount of each qualification you want. So, first consider those candidates who earned all 2's. If you have enough of them, you can move ahead and hold the others for later consideration.

However, if you have too few all 2's or none, you must proceed in light of your knowledge of the job and its requirements:

In some jobs, you might absolutely require a 2 in every category so you would have to obtain additional candidates.

CHECKLIST | **Received Candidate Documents**

Have you:
- **Established** a procedure for initially classifying applications, résumés, and letters?
- **Educated** whomever will preview those materials for you about the job and its requirements?
- **Set** guidelines for classifying candidate qualifications?
- **Created** a procedure for responding to all applications, résumés, and letters that you receive?

Will you:
- **Respond** as soon as possible to unqualified candidates?
- **Respond** to qualified and possibly qualified candidates within at least two months of receiving their materials?

But if you have some flexibility in the degree of skills and experience that might suffice—that is, a 1 or a 3 in certain categories might be okay—you can revisit the remaining résumés or applications.

Sort them by the number of 2's received, from most 2's received to least 2's received, and evaluate them by individual category. For example, someone with nearly all 2's might be expected to be at the top of the pile, but if that person is over- or underqualified in a critical category, he or she would fall back to the bottom of the pile.

All candidates will want enough information to decide whether this is the type of company for which they want to work. Prepare to provide that information.

Next, consider when the résumé was received (see the earlier discussion of date and time-stamping incoming materials). All else being the same, use first received as first considered.

With your basic evaluation completed, have the person to whom the candidate will report, if it is not you, conduct a similar, but independent evaluation. Use his or her input to prepare a final ranking of candidates, and use that ranking to determine the order in which you will interview candidates.

Preparing to Interview

Good interviews do not just happen. They result from preparation—of the questions, the candidates, and the environment. But to be fully successful, an interview must be a two-way gathering of information. Preparation to conduct a job interview often concentrates only on collecting the information the company needs, without allowing for the candidates' needs. All candidates will want enough information to decide whether this is the type of company for which they want to work. Do not prepare only to obtain information, but also to provide it.

PREPARATION OF QUESTIONS. You should design interview questions to obtain information you can evaluate in terms of the job requirements. You must develop them from those requirements and then adjust them to each person's background. A good way to start is to list the job requirements in order of importance. Then after each item, write two or three questions that you believe will solicit the necessary insights and information.

In writing questions, follow these guidelines:

Questions should not be answerable in single words. For example:

Can you describe your most difficult past assignment?

If you ask a question that can be answered in a single word, yes or no, you will have to follow it up with a probing question, and that can begin to feel like an inquisition. So, ask questions that require longer, more explanatory or evaluatory answers. For example:

What were the most difficult assignments you were asked to complete in your last job?

Ask questions that require reference to previous experience, because past performance tends to be an excellent predictor of future performance. For example:

When you were faced with a complaining customer in your last job, how did you handle the situation?

Don't reveal the answer you desire. Candidates want to do well in their interviews. They want to get the job, so they look to their surroundings and your statements for signs of what you want to hear. For example, a candidate may have no interest in bowling, but if you have bowling trophies in your office, the candidate may talk about how much he or she likes bowling.

You can also communicate through your questions what you want to hear. For example, don't ask:

Here at our company we believe leadership is an important attribute. What type of leader are you?

Instead, ask something similar to this:

*In the past, how have you motivated employees (or yourself)
to do the required work to the best of their (or your) abilities?*

Ask practical questions. You are concerned with discovering how
someone will perform on the job, so ask questions that require
the application of knowledge and not the regurgitation of facts.
For example, don't ask:

What is a good definition of decision-making?

Instead ask:

*If you were asked to create a third-shift operation from a two-
shift operation, how would you decide which employees would
be assigned to which shifts?*

Ask "scenario" or situational questions. For example:

*Assume that I hire you as one of our real estate salespersons.
You have shown a number of houses to a couple. They have
finally decided to make an offer on one of those homes.
Knowing their financial condition, you doubt their ability to
obtain a large-enough mortgage commitment. How would
you deal with such a situation?*

**Arrange your questions so that you begin the interview with easily
answered ones.** This approach will contribute to full and open
communication by not immediately intimidating the candidate
with difficult questions. Once you have developed a set of basic
questions, you can use your questions time and again as you
need to fill the same job. You can file them with the job description, so that they are available the next time the job opens.

Preparation for Multiple Interviews

Separate interviews of one candidate by more than one
employee of the company can be very effective if the interviews are coordinated. Questioning by more than one interviewer can add to the thoroughness of evaluation. If someone

other than you will supervise the new person, the supervisor should have an opportunity to interview candidates.

> *A small appliance store in Montana had the supervisor of the job, the store manager, and the human resources person conduct separate interviews of each candidate.*
>
> *The human resources person asked questions about the candidate's general background and experience, and gave an overall view of the store. The supervisor asked specific questions related to the job's requirements, and described the job in detail. The store manager asked questions about the candidate's goals and career plans and described the overall direction and mission of the store.*
>
> *As soon as possible afterward, the interviewers met briefly to compare results. They looked for consistency in the candidate's responses and similarity in their evaluations of qualifications. If they identified areas about which they needed more information, a follow-up interview was conducted.*

It is important for the interviewers to decide in advance who will ask what. You don't want to ask duplicate questions, and each of you may be better qualified to question in different areas.

> *A West Virginia company sent all of its managers to an interview training course. Its objective was to ensure that all of the managers possessed similar interviewing skills. Unfortunately, they all learned to ask the same questions.*
>
> *A candidate who was interviewed by three of the company's managers remarked, "The first interview was interesting, and it taught me how to answer questions in the next two. By the third interview, my answers were excellent."*

Although multiple interviews that are coordinated and conducted individually are quite effective, interviews conducted by a panel of interviewers are far less effective. Candidates generally perceive them as a form of interrogation. Imagine three or four people sitting at a table, maybe all of them on the same side of the table, firing questions at the lone candidate. The candidate may do well in the interview, but will often decline a later job offer simply for having been put through such an experience. Also, candidates sometimes remove themselves from consideration if requested to attend a panel interview.

Finally, identify any facts a candidate has not provided or any questions that are particularly appropriate for him or her. You then have your questions prepared.

Creating an Interview Question-and-Report Form

You can facilitate the interview and accurate note taking by preparing an interview question-and-report form, which presents each question followed by note-taking space. For example:

> *Q. There are times that a supervisor must request employees to perform unpopular duties. From your experience, what is the most effective way to obtain the desired performance?*
> *A.* _____
> _____
> _____
> _____
>
> *Q. How do you react when your decisions are challenged?*
> *A.* _____
> _____
> _____
> _____

Prepare an original set of questions for the job in this format and reproduce it as often as necessary. Allow space to add customized questions and notes under each key area of the job; education and work experience almost always invite individualized questions.

Preparation of an interview question-and-report form may take a few extra minutes the first time you prepare to interview for a position, but you will save a great deal of time thereafter. The form will provide you with a structure for taking accurate notes and for evaluating the results. It will impose consistency on your questioning that will help you better compare the candidates' interviews and individual responses.

This approach will also benefit others in your company who conduct interviews by facilitating the coordination of questions for multiple interviews. It also provides documentation for later comparison.

Inclusion of a Reference and Fact-Checking Release

You should obtain permission from every candidate to check the information and references that he or she provides. If the candidate has completed an application, it probably contains a release, but if you are working from a résumé or an application furnished by an employment agency or search firm, you may not have one. Instead, you should obtain the release at the interview. For an example of the language you might use in a release, see page 91. The candidate should sign and date the release form. (The Appendix contains a sample release form.)

Preparation of Company Information

You should consider two questions:

1. What do you want the candidate to learn about the job and your company?

2. What do you think the candidate may ask?

You certainly want to present your company in the best possible light. After all, you want to persuade the selected candidate to join you, and you want to take advantage of this excellent public relations opportunity even with candidates you do not hire.

Begin by making a list of the advantages of working for your company. Consider such things as these:

■ **Your company's size (small versus large)**
■ **Your plans for growth (or other goals)**
■ **An exciting industry**
■ **Increased responsibility ("everyone in our company wears more than one hat")**
■ **Potential for advancement**
■ **The opportunity to know everyone**
■ **Competitive compensation**

- ■ **Unusual benefits**
- ■ **Flexible scheduling of work**
- ■ **The opportunity to telecommute from home**

Then rank these advantages from most to least significant from your point of view.

Next, identify any disadvantages, such as limits of compensation, location, and hours. If you can't think of any disadvantages in working for your company, you are either fortunate or unrealistic. Perhaps you haven't been staying in touch with your employees or your competitors. (See Chapter 9 for more discussion of both subjects.) Rank the disadvantages as you did the advantages. Then develop a compensating (or offsetting) factor for each disadvantage:

True, we are not near public transportation, but we have a free parking lot for employees who drive, and we can be flexible as to starting and quitting times.

Yes, we do work long hours, but we also pay more than our competitors.

Correct, our pay schedule is slightly lower than that of some similar companies in the area, but we offer flexible hours and short days for employees with children in school.

The point is to prepare to stress your strengths, and acknowledge and counter your weaknesses. With this accomplished for the company, do the same for the specific job.

Keep in mind that your perception of the pros and cons of your company and the job may differ from each candidate's. Be prepared to stress the positives, but wait for the candidate to ask about the negatives.

Most important, tell the truth. If you avoid the truth when asked a direct question, the candidate will discover it sooner or later, and a good relationship with the candidate or employee may be damaged.

It's also a good idea to prepare a package of materials for the candidate. Those materials can include the following:

- A job description (see Chapter 3)
- A company mission statement, which defines the company's primary purpose
- Copies of recent media stories on the company
- Any company-published materials (such as brochures, catalogs, annual reports)

All of these will contribute to preparing a candidate for making a good decision if you make a job offer.

Alternatively, you may want to look for evidence that the candidates have prepared themselves for the interview by learning about your company beforehand. This is easier than ever to do because of the Internet. If your company has a Web site, even if you're not using it to solicit candidates online, candidates at a certain level probably have visited it before the interview. They may also have searched the Internet for any recent news about your company.

Preparation of an Interview Schedule

When you have prepared your questions and company information, it is time to notify the candidates and schedule interviews. Select a time that will be convenient for you and each candidate. If a candidate is employed, give that some consideration. He or she may be available only before or after work or at lunchtime; you may even have to schedule the interview for the weekend if the candidate must travel from a distance. Schedule the interview when you can ensure uninterrupted time, and most important of all, schedule enough time. The last thing you want to do is hurry the interview or conclude it before you or the candidate obtains all the required information. If more than one person will interview the candidate, be sure that person will be available, too.

When planning an interview, be sure to allow time at its beginning and end to answer any questions from the candidate. Not only will this give the candidate information, but the candidate's questions will provide you with feedback on his or her understanding of your company and the job. Questions asked at the beginning may give you clues about what you need to cover in your overview, and those asked at the end will let you know whether you succeeded in your presentation and how you might need to amend it for the next interview.

One other consideration in scheduling your interviews: note taking. Notes taken during an interview will be relatively brief and you'll need to clarify and organize them. The best time to do that is immediately after the interview, before other activities contribute to your forgetting some of what occurred. Generally, a half-hour is adequate, so when you schedule the interview, schedule that additional time for yourself.

Your first consideration in choosing a location should be for privacy: no lobbies, open work areas, or cubicles allowed.

As always, this is a public-relations opportunity for your company. Even if you don't select the candidate, you want everyone to leave feeling that he or she was treated with consideration and that your company is an excellent one.

Preparing the Interview Environment

Where should you conduct the job interview?

It is obvious when a two-person conversation is a job interview. You have probably seen people being interviewed in airport lounges, restaurants, and hotel lobbies. You immediately know you're witnessing a job interview, and it's easy to tell who the interviewer is and who the interviewee is. That is not a good situation for sharing the kind of information asked for in an interview.

Your first consideration in choosing a location should be for privacy. An office with a door is ideal, but if one is not available, find another private location, even if you have to use a conference room or go off to a hotel meeting room, private club, or similar location. Whatever you do, never interview candidates in the lobby, an open work area surrounded by employees (and that includes an office cubicle), or a lunch room with employees eating or on break.

Keeping the need for privacy in mind, you also want to avoid interruptions. If you use your office, arrange to receive no telephone calls or visits. That arrangement communicates to the candidate that the interview is important and that you are giving it your full attention.

Another factor that can contribute to the correct environment is a clean desk or table. It projects your preparation for the interview and its importance to you and your company. The interview is part of a selling of the company to candidates, so image counts. What kind of image do you want to convey? Organized and on top of things? Or messy and behind the eight ball?

Because the point of the interview is to exchange information, you want the environment to contribute to that process. You will obtain the most information in the shortest time when the candidate is at ease and does not feel threatened. One way to promote this result is to not sit behind your desk with the candidate on a chair in front of you. In such a setting the desk becomes a communication barrier. Instead, consider sitting in similar chairs around a neutral table or working over the corner of your desk.

Finally, remember to review the résumé or application and your notes before the candidate arrives. Be prepared.

Conducting the Interview

At last it is time for the interview. You have prepared the environment. The candidate is scheduled and prepared. You have your questions and company information, and you have reviewed the candidate's information.

The first step is for you to be on time. Do not keep the candidate waiting. A study found that at somewhere between five and ten minutes of waiting a candidate begins to form a negative view of the process and the company. If you cannot help being a few minutes late, let the candidate know immediately.

Although employers take many different approaches to interviewing, the one suggested in this book is based on two-way communication to determine a candidate's qualifications and supply the candidate with company and job information.

If you want to conduct a different type of interview (a brief initial interview, a structured interview, an informal interview over lunch, a hostile interview) you need to establish the reasons and objectives for such an approach. Because there are so many possible interviewing strategies, you may want to consult with your human resources staff or consultant to choose the best one for your situation. If you have properly prepared and seek to exchange accurate information for a hiring decision, the following approach is effective.

Greeting and Introduction

Greet the candidate. State your name. Ask the candidate to take a seat. If possible, shut the door.

Tell the candidate who you are and what the schedule is. Then state the objective of the interview. The opening dialogue might go something like this:

> *"Good morning, Ms. Anderson. I'm George Benson, the store manager. Please have a seat.*
>
> *"We have invited you to this interview to discuss a position with our firm. It is for a salesperson in our women's shoe department. This will give us an opportunity to learn about each other, so that we can both make an informed decision."*

Because this is probably your initial meeting with the candidate, it will be the first time you have seen him or her. While meeting face-to-face provides the opportunity to experience the candidate's interpersonal skills, such as communication, you're also bound to be aware of the candidate's physical appearance.

You should note any unusual physical appearance. Candidates should be trying to project their best image, so if one arrives unshaven, dirty, or with ripped clothing, at the least you will want to attempt to discover why.

Some jobs require excellent personal hygiene or attractive style. For example, someone with extremely poor personal hygiene is not likely to succeed in a face-to-face sales job; nor is a cosmetic clerk who wears an unattractive hairstyle or displays clumsy use of makeup.

In most cases, however, appearance is not the key issue. Do not let the candidate's physical appearance—such things as clothes, hair, and weight—distract you from focusing on the job's requirements and the candidate's ability to meet them.

An Alabama company was having difficulty hiring successful people to take insurance claims over the telephone. The majority of people hired quit within the first month. In desperation the company hired a consultant to identify the problem.

The consultant discovered that the hiring decision was based to a great degree on the candidate's physical appearance—the better groomed the candidate, the more likely a job offer. However, the consultant also discovered that there was no correlation between physical appearance and success on the job.

The company introduced a new hiring system, which restricted the people making the decision to reviewing the candidate's application and to conducting a telephone interview. Not only retention but also performance increased, and many managers confided that they would never have hired some of these exceptional performers if they had been allowed to see them.

Candidate Questions
Open with:

"Before we begin, do you have any questions about our company, the job, or this interview?"

If you are asked questions, answer them. They are important to the candidate, and to some extent the questions will communicate to you the candidate's thoughts and preparation.

You may be asked a question that is best left for a later answer, such as, "What happens if you decide you want to hire me?" If this happens, say that you'll address that subject later and be sure to follow up. That type of question is better answered at the end of the interview.

Do not hurry this step. Allow the candidate to ask all of his or her questions before moving on to your questions.

Note Taking

Tell the candidate that you will take notes. Studies indicate that candidates *prefer* that the interviewer take notes; it makes them feel that the interviewer has captured what they have said. But as was recommended previously, don't make notes on résumés or applications. At least use a separate sheet of paper. An ideal technique is to make notes beside your prepared questions (see the discussion on page 104).

What if the candidate wants to take notes? Great. It demonstrates thoroughness.

What if the candidate wants to tape-record the interview? Neither you nor the candidate should ever tape-record interviews. If you were to tape-record interviews without telling the candidates, sooner or later your practice *will* become known. Employees and anyone else who learns of it will usually view it as improper or untruthful, and sometimes it is illegal. If you do tell candidates, they will tend to change the quality of their answers because they now realize that unknown others will listen to them.

Questioning of the Candidate

Now, it's time to ask your prepared questions. Ask a question, focus your attention on the candidate, and listen to the complete answer. When you have heard the answer, make a brief note. Complete the note before asking your next question.

All candidates will respond differently. Some will supply short answers, and others, long ones. Some will respond immediately, while others will pause before answering. Allow each candidate to answer in his or her own style.

As a general rule, you should remain silent after you have asked a question. Wait for the candidate to answer it. In the unlikely event that a minute or two passes, ask the question again. If you still receive no answer, ask whether the candidate understands the question. If not, try rewording the question, and if that doesn't help, move on. If more than one applicant fails to understand the same question, you probably need to rewrite it.

Even though you have prepared questions, you will receive

answers that will require you to create new, follow-up questions on the spot. Just keep in mind the purpose of the interview and the general guidelines.

■ **To exchange information needed for a hiring decision**
■ **To obtain information related to the job only**

Something may occur during an interview that suggests a humorous response or a personal comment. Generally, you should avoid those. For example, asking candidates if you have seen them attending your church may seem like a friendly question, but they can easily misinterpret your query, as they can jokes.

Some interviewers prefer to end their interviews by allowing candidates to summarize their qualifications, using questions similar to:

"All things considered, what do you believe are your strongest qualifications for this position?"

"How well do you feel that your qualifications match the requirements of this job?"

"What three words best describe your qualifications for this position?"

If you conclude this way, accept whatever answer you receive, regardless of whether you agree. If you ask candidates for explanations of their answers to such summary questions, you may appear to be challenging their answers. Because you asked for a personal opinion—not a fact—and received it, accept it.

Final Candidate Questions

When you have asked all your questions, ask the candidate again if he or she has any questions and answer them. He may ask you whether he will receive a job offer. Answer truthfully. If you are prepared to hire him, say so. If not, use the following advice.

Conclusion

The last step is to conclude the interview. Tell the candidate what will happen next and when it will happen, and provide an ending statement. Remember that the candidate wants the job and is looking for cues from you as to how he or she did. Unless you are absolutely confident that you will offer this candidate a job, do not supply such cues. Instead, conclude with a supportive but neutral statement, such as:

"We have two more candidates scheduled for interviews. We will complete those by next Thursday. We plan to make a deci-

---

CHECKLIST | **Interviewing**

Have you:
- **Scheduled** enough time for the interview, and selected a time convenient for you and the candidates?
- **Scheduled** for multiple interviews with all of the appropriate people?
- **Arranged** for a private location for the interview?
- **Arranged** for no interruptions and a clean desk?
- **Arranged** to conduct the interview without a desk separating you from the candidate?
- **Prepared** your interview questions in line with the job requirements and information received from the candidate?
- **Developed** questions that cannot be answered in one word, are based on the candidate's experiences, do not communicate a desired answer, and require application of skill or knowledge?
- **Written** your questions with extra

space or accompanying paper for notes of the candidate's answers?
- **Coordinated** interview questions with all interviewers in the case of multiple interviews?
- **Analyzed** the advantages and disadvantages of working for your company and in the job?
- **Identified** an advantage to offset each possible disadvantage?
- **Prepared** a package of company and job information?

Will you:
- **Review** the candidate's information just before the interview?
- **Allow** the candidate to ask questions during the interview?
- **Tell** the candidate you will be taking notes?
- **Conclude** by telling the candidate what will happen next and when she or he will hear from you?
- **Schedule** time immediately after the interview to clarify and organize your notes?

---

sion the following week, so you will hear from us within two weeks.

"I've prepared a package of information about our company for you, and if you have any questions, feel free to call me. You will find a card in the package with my phone number.

"Thank you for meeting today. It's been a most interesting interview."

As soon as the interview is over, review your notes. Clarify and expand them as necessary. Identify any information that requires checking or additional information that you need.

Testing Candidates

At times you may want to learn more about candidates' specific abilities than you can determine in an interview. You may want to know whether and to what extent a candidate can use a specific software or database program, operate a wheel-balancing machine, or perform certain mathematical tasks. Asking the candidate to demonstrate his or her skill can be an excellent way to determine ability. However, this approach isn't standardized, and as the rest of this discussion shows, you should require the same "try-out" of every candidate applying for the same job.

Or you may choose to use measurement devices, such as tests. You can use certain simple skill tests, such as those that are available for typing and mathematics, but you must be careful that the test you choose measures a job-related ability.

A Michigan company required a minimum typing speed as measured by a standardized test. However, a study of the jobs for which the company required the test revealed that it never asked its employees to type at even half the required speed on the job. Instead, the company encouraged them to construct correspondence, type drafts, and type more accurately than fast. The company tested for an unnecessary skill, and it may have screened out the best employees.

Some companies use so-called general employment tests. Those tests, usually some form of intelligence or "learnability" test, often make unsupported claims. One test, with fewer than a hundred questions, claimed to identify suitable candidates for various standard jobs by scores differing by as little as one point. Companies that used this test often lost good people.

If you use a test improperly, you may find yourself having to defend it against charges by disgruntled job seekers, based on nondiscrimination law, that the given test is not relevant to the job or that it can't predict job performance. So you need evidence that the test works for your purpose. A company that uses a test only once or twice can probably base its use on the test publisher's validation statistics (assuming that such information was professionally obtained). However, once a company begins to use a test regularly, it needs to validate it for itself to demonstrate the test's accuracy relative to the company's jobs.

A defense that you had the test administered but did not use the results in the hiring decision is no defense. If you did not use the results, why did you require the test? Equally indefensible is to give the test to some candidates but not to all. Similarly, saying that an employment agency gave the test is not a defense if you knew the agency was using the test to screen candidates for your job or if you received the results.

If you think you need to use a test, select one that measures

---

CHECKLIST | **Measurement Devices**

Have you:
- **Determined** that the job requires abilities that you cannot discern through an interview?
- **Identified** tests that can measure those abilities?
- **Determined** whether you could measure ability by asking the candidate to perform a work sample?
- **Asked** a testing consultant or agency to prove a test's validity

(Will it measure what you want to measure?) and reliability (Will the process be free of errors that could distort the results?) in general and as it applies to your organization and the job in particular?
- **Made** the test or work sample a part of the procedures that you use to screen all similarly qualified candidates?
- **Reviewed** the legal considerations with your attorney?

a job requirement. Then make sure that it is an accurate and reliable measure of prospective employees' ability to meet that requirement—in your environment for your jobs.

The Equal Employment Opportunity Commission (EEOC) publishes guidelines regarding employers' use of such devices that require tests to be related to the job, accurate, and reliable. You can obtain specific information regarding psychological test requirements by requesting a copy of "Uniform Guidelines on Employment Selection Procedures" from the EEOC (1801 L St., N.W., Washington, DC 20507; 202-663-4900), or you can access the text online at www.eeoc.gov, in the section, "Law, Regulations and Policy Guidance."

Any test should accurately and reliably measure a candidate's ability to meet your requirements—in your environment for your jobs.

That means you probably must hire a professional, such as a psychologist or test consultant, to recommend appropriate tests, give them to candidates, ensure their accuracy, and evaluate the results. A good approach to obtaining such assistance is through an employment attorney or consultant, who can also advise you on what legal requirements apply to your company in this situation.

The poorest approach may be to purchase a test though direct mail or over the Internet from a test supplier that makes many claims but offers no supporting evidence.

Using Other Tests

Some companies require other types of tests, such as polygraph tests, physical examinations, and drug tests. You can require those tests only after you have made a job offer and the candidate has accepted it. The tests then become a condition of employment (see Chapter 9 for more on conditions of employment). Also, you must give such tests to all new employees. You cannot require them of selected employees only.

Whether to use such tests is a fairly controversial question. Polygraph tests are not completely accurate. Drug tests must be readministered when positive, and some normal foods affect their results. Physicals are difficult to justify except when the job has certain physical requirements. Also, be aware that candidates can readily obtain information and advice on how to "beat" all three of those tests.

Some firms want to test for HIV, but, by law, employers may impose this test only in situations where someone with HIV would pose a proven, on-the-job health risk to others (see the following discussion). The need for these tests vary greatly, depending on the nature of the job. It is illegal to require an HIV test under any circumstances before offering a job.

If you are considering requiring any such tests, be sure there is a valid, job-related reason for them. Is there a valid relationship between the job requirements and the test? How accurate is the test? If you are then convinced that the test will assist you and your employees, make sure that it is administered in a fair and legal manner. Otherwise, you may be initiating an expensive procedure that does little to improve your pool of employees or their performance. Also, you should obtain specific advice from an employment attorney or consultant on this subject. Drug and HIV testing is highly regulated.

You could follow the example of a New England–based company that wanted to ensure that its employees were drug-free without the expense of drug testing. It posted this sign in the area where it accepted applications:

This company operates a drug-free environment. All newly hired employees are subject to drug-testing.

CHECKLIST | Other Tests

Have you:
- **Identified** the specific reason for using a polygraph, drug, or HIV test or a physical examination as a condition of employment?
- **Compared** the test results with the job requirements to ensure that the test will test for the competency you require?
- **Asked** appropriate sources (employment attorney, consultant, psychologist, and so on) about how accurately the test will tell you what you want to know?
- **Identified** the legal requirements for your use of the test?
- **Established** a procedure for ensuring that the test is administered fairly and legally, whether in-house or by a testing agency?

Although the company never conducted drug tests, it noted that several people who had requested applications read the sign and left without submitting completed applications.

The Americans With Disabilities Act

The Americans With Disabilities Act (ADA) defines a disability as a substantial physical or mental impairment that limits one or more major life activities, such as walking, breathing, hearing, seeing, or learning. Acquired Immune Deficiency Syndrome (AIDS) and HIV infection are considered disabilities. ADA focuses its definition of physical requirements on the person's ability to do the job. Generally, you can refuse to consider disabled people only if they cannot perform essential job functions or if they will pose a safety threat to themselves or others. For example, you needn't consider someone who cannot walk for a job that requires ladder climbing. However, if the same person applied for a desk job for which he or she is otherwise qualified, an inability to walk wouldn't be a legal reason for not hiring that person.

ADA also covers employees who have no current disability, but had one in the past and are perceived by the employer to still be disabled. It also protects rehabilitated drug addicts and alcoholics who remain qualified to do their jobs. It does not protect current users of illegal drugs.

Employees with contagious diseases may not be denied work unless they are involved with preparing food or working closely with patients, or their disease is easily communicable to other employees. ADA probably prohibits refusing to consider someone who is HIV positive for a job as a telephone salesperson.

An employer can also refuse to hire a disabled person if the employer cannot eliminate or reduce the risk of substantial harm by reasonable accommodation—for instance, if the person would be required to work with a certain piece of machinery that's unsafe for him to operate as is and can't be modified.

If the disability does not disqualify the person from the job, you may need to revise your physical plant to accommodate the person. Accommodations can include: making existing facilities used by employees readily accessible to and usable by persons with disabilities, say, by installing entrance ramps as an alternative to stairs; restructuring jobs or modifying work schedules; acquiring or modifying equipment or devices, such as special computer keyboards or magnifying monitor screens; adjusting or modifying examinations, training materials, or policies; and providing readers or interpreters.

If it would cause you undue hardship or expense to bring your facilities into compliance, you may be exempted from doing so or from hiring the person who requires it. However, you may be required to comply when any revisions to your facilities are made. For example, a restaurant that did not have wheelchair access to its administrative offices was required to create such access when it remodeled the building. If your business rents or leases its space, you have to work with the building's owner to ensure that your facilities comply.

The Equal Employment Opportunity Commission can provide more information (page 212), but you should also obtain specific legal advice from an employment attorney or consultant.

Summary

This chapter stresses the importance of proper preparation for the interview and the need to make it an exchange of information. That approach will prepare you and the candidate to make an informed decision. Your next steps are to confirm the information you have, evaluate each candidate in terms of the job requirements, and make a decision. The next chapter deals with these subjects.

Making the Decision

"Decision-making isn't a matter of arriving at a right or wrong answer; it's a matter of selecting the most effective course of action." –PHILIP MARVIN

P EOPLE BASED THEIR JOB DECISIONS ON THEIR EXPERIence and on the information available to them. In the short run, you cannot do much to increase your experience, but you have great control over information. You can find out what information you require for a decision, and take the necessary steps to obtain it. The quality of your decisions will relate directly to the quality of the information you have and use.

The interview, along with the application and résumé, is designed to supply three categories of information:
1. Facts about background
2. Answers to specific questions
3. Observations of a candidate's interpersonal behavior

Information in category 1 may eliminate some candidates by revealing their lack of qualifications for the job. For example, if you discover in an interview that a candidate does not in fact have a required skill—or, with respect to category 2, if you learn in an interview that a candidate has a firm salary demand beyond what you can pay—you need not spend additional time considering either candidate. Instead, document the reasons for rejection and move on to other candidates.

If there are one or more candidates who appear qualified for the job and for whom you have all the necessary information, you can evaluate that information and make your final decisions. But what if there seem to be areas that require additional investigation—facts to be checked or other questions to be answered? In that case, you need to determine exactly what additional information you require.

Reviewing Your Notes and Identifying the Gaps

To determine just what information you have and what you still need, you should review your interview notes along with the application or résumé. Studies of trained interviewers, who work for companies that perform standardized management evaluation, found that they had difficulty keeping information about multiple candidates separate unless they immediately reviewed and organized their notes. After 24 hours, they could recall only part of the interview information without organized notes, and as time passed, they could recall less and less.

Notes made quickly or in a private shorthand can be difficult to interpret later. If you confine the notes you take during the interview to a few key words, reviewing and organizing them provides a method of expanding and clarifying them so that you capture their meaning.

Review the application or résumé, as well, and then make a list of any problems you need to resolve and any facts you need to check. Perhaps you failed to ask a question, or the candidate misunderstood your question and answered off the point. Perhaps conflicts emerged in different interview answers or between the candidate's interview answers and his or her application or résumé.

Whatever the case, list what you still need to know in terms of the job requirements. Such a list might include items like the following:

- **Training:** Did the candidate's computer training include *Excel?*
- **Work experience:** Did the candidate's parts-inventory experience include use of a computer-based classification system?
- **Education:** Did the candidate receive an associate degree in retail merchandising as he indicated on the application or in marketing as he stated in the interview?

You can easily obtain answers to questions such as those with a follow-up telephone call to the candidate, but be careful: Candidates typically interpret such calls as a positive sign. Some facts are not worth your time to check unless you are seriously considering the candidate for hire. If it appears the candidate is the one you wish to hire, you can check or clarify the facts before offering the job.

Do not allow unrelated information to sidetrack you.

> *A small department store in Michigan sought a new sales manager. It found a candidate who had all the qualifications it required, but its managers still had a concern. All of their sales people were short, and the candidate was six feet five inches tall. This extraneous information caused them to hesitate before making an offer. By the time they recognized that the candidate's height wasn't really relevant to the job's requirements, the candidate had accepted other employment with a competitive store.*

Discrepancies

What if you have identified conflicting information that, rather than just requiring clarification, indicates problems? Such a list could include the following:

> *Candidate indicated on résumé two years' experience in waitperson food preparation at tableside but couldn't describe dishes prepared in that manner.*

> *Candidate's application indicated five years as a successful men's suit salesperson but appeared for interview in a badly soiled shirt and suit.*

Candidate claimed that she knows WordPerfect but could not answer questions regarding the operation of that software.

Candidate stated that she had five years' experience selling real estate, but she could not describe the selling procedure that she used.

In those examples, the interview information didn't support the candidate's résumé or application information or was internally inconsistent and raised questions or concerns. Should you go to the trouble of resolving those apparent discrepancies? Only if you otherwise believe that the candidate qualifies for the position. If you have other candidates who appear qualified without such issues or concerns, you may wish to immediately eliminate this candidate. But of course, be sure to document your decision.

Facts to Be Checked

Some companies make it a practice to check every job-related fact offered by all qualified candidates, while others check them only for candidates to whom they plan to offer a job. Still others check facts only if they feel there is a discrepancy or problem, or they confirm only the employment and education dates. Some companies never check any facts. So what should you do?

You probably do not have to check all information and claims. If you are hiring a real estate salesperson, you probably have little, if any, need to check whether the candidate was a motion picture theater usher five years ago, as stated on the person's résumé. Some employers might counter that checking everything is a way of ensuring that someone is truthful. Maybe so, but it is not efficient to check every fact.

One employer said, "If I suspect a candidate is lying, I probably won't check the facts. He might be telling the truth, but even so, I would be very disturbed because he caused me to believe he was lying. I would concentrate on understanding why that occurred. If others might perceive him the same way, I won't want him representing my company."

Probably the best guideline is to always check crucial facts—those that represent absolute requirements for a job— but only for serious contenders for the job. If the job requires a truck-driving license, obtain evidence that the person has one. If the job requires U.S. citizenship, be sure the person is a U.S. citizen. If the job requires a health department certificate, obtain a copy or confirm that the person has qualified to receive one. Once you have confirmed such crucial facts, check any additional facts for which you require clarification.

Whatever policy you choose on fact-checking, it's best to put it in writing. That will help you ensure that you treat all candidates the same. A New Jersey direct-marketing company has adopted the following policy and gives a copy of it to all candidates as part of the company's information package:

We check information for all candidates before making a job offer. We check employment for the past five years (except the current employer), education and training directly related to the job, and any discrepancies in information provided by the candidate. We check the current employer after a candidate has been hired and has reported to work. We document all such checks.

CHECKLIST | **Additional Information**

Have you:
- **Scheduled** and used some time immediately after the interview for reviewing, organizing, and clarifying your notes?
- **Identified** any facts that clearly disqualify the candidate for the job? Have you documented them?
- **Obtained** all the necessary information for the candidate and decided that the person appears qualified?

- **Identified** any facts that require checking or confirming?
- **Identified** any disparities between the information from the interview and from other sources?
- **Asked** all other interviewers whether they perceived any additional need for information?
- **Compiled** a comprehensive follow-up list for the candidate?
- **Created** a company policy on reference checking?

Multiple Interviewers

If your company conducts multiple interviews of a candidate, ask the other interviewers whether they identified a need for any additional information. Sometimes you will discover that you can answer each other's questions. Other times, you may discover that you have all identified similar areas for checking. At the very least, you can compile a single list of your needs for each candidate.

Now that you have identified the additional information that you require, it's time to get answers by checking references.

Checking References

You already have a list of specific facts that you wish to check. Group them by employer, school, or any other source. You can get some of the answers you need by asking the candidate, but you may prefer to query third parties, starting with employment and education references and concluding with personal or professional references.

At one time checking references was relatively easy. You called a candidate's former employer or school, asked a series of questions, and usually received answers and recommendations. Times have changed. Now, employers and schools worry about their legal liability in providing such information. Candidates who did not get jobs have sued former employers and schools for providing information they believe cost them the jobs they wanted. They have claimed that the information was incorrect, private, or irrelevant to the job in question.

Whatever the actual laws or facts, many companies and schools refuse to provide any information without a signed release from the job applicant. Even with a release, some sources still will not provide information or they release only dates of employment, job title, location, major, and date of graduation.

You can get around this impediment to your information gathering in a couple of ways.

The Appendix provides a sample employment application

form that includes a release statement as well as a separate release form for use apart from an application. Many companies photocopy such a release with the candidate's signature and provide it to references when they request it.

You could also ask candidates to provide authenticated copies of employment and educational information. For example, candidates can obtain certified copies of their school records or a letter of class standing (if the school calculates it) from the school registrar; copies of training certifications; and signed letters from former employers indicating dates of employment, position, and salary. Some candidates may already possess some of these items.

Keep in mind that if you use the statement suggested on the sample application form, you can always discharge an employee for providing false information or claims that were relevant to your hiring decision.

Be careful about making informal requests.

The owner of a Denver-based company attended a monthly service-club meeting with other small-business owners. After the meeting, the owners regularly exchanged information about former employees who were prospective candidates for one another. They felt that this informal, personal, and undocumented approach would not cause difficulties. They were wrong.

One woman lost her job when her current employer discovered, while attending a meeting, that she had applied for employment at another company.

One man who had been job-hunting learned from his uncle, one of the small-business owners, that members had made derogatory remarks about him at a meeting. He felt that he had been, in effect, "blacklisted" from employment.

Both the woman and the nephew brought suit against their former employers and received out-of-court settlements.

The point is that checking references is harder than it once was. However, it can be done professionally and restricted to job-related issues. Be sure that there are no laws or other legal requirements that may limit your performing a reference check. As with all aspects of hiring, it is good for your employment attorney to approve your procedures.

You should not check a candidate's current employment—at least until after you have hired him—lest you harm his relationship with his employers, or even cost him his job.

Reference Checking Services

You can hire a service to check a candidate's references for you. Some employment agencies and search firms check references as a part of their usual service. Be careful. When another company performs this task for you, it acts as your representative, so you are probably ultimately responsible for whatever it does, unless you have a signed and comprehensive agreement that states otherwise.

> *A Florida firm had an employee who was a former private investigator and still maintained his state license. He suggested to the company president that he use his sources to check job candidates' references. The president agreed.*
>
> *In turn, the employee used a service typically used by private investigators. It delivered a great deal of information to the company about such things as traffic tickets, credit history, marital problems, religious and political affiliations, and medical records. Most of the information was not job-related and much of it violated the individual's right to privacy. Not surprisingly, a candidate who discovered this practice received a substantial out-of-court settlement.*

Some human resources information systems include functions for conducting reference checks, or you could use the Internet to investigate a candidate's background, whether you access public records or hire an investigative service online. You must be careful, however. Confine yourself to acquiring only the information required for an employment decision. As mentioned in the previous chapter, "We received the information but did not use it in our hiring decision," and "We needed that information for benefit purposes" are not legally defensible positions.

Once you have obtained information, you have no way to prove that you didn't consider it: Why did you obtain it if you did not use it? As for information needed for benefit purposes, you can ask all such questions after you have hired someone.

Employment References

Although prospective employers find it increasingly difficult to obtain from former employers information other than dates of employment and jobs held, certain techniques may produce more detailed results.

In many companies the owner and human resources people (if any) may have a policy of not providing detailed, prior employment information, but individual supervisors may not know of the policy. Call the supervisors first. That is why it is a good idea to ask, on the application or in the interview, to whom a candidate directly reported in previous jobs.

Begin by introducing yourself and ensuring that the supervisor can talk with you at this time. For example:

> *"Good morning. I am Joy Calvin, manager of Metro Distribution Company. Do you have a moment to talk, or have I caught you at a busy time?"*

If the person is busy, ask for a good time to call back. (Don't ask the supervisor to call you because it's unlikely that he or she will do so.) Try to do this without revealing your purpose. If pushed for a reason, say something similar to this:

> *"I am looking for some information about a job applicant. It will only take a few minutes."*

But do not lie. If pushed for details, tell the truth.

> *"One of your former employees has applied for a job with our company, and I have a couple of questions relevant to that."*

Once you have the supervisor's attention, whether on the first or second call, say something similar to this:

> *"Bill Robinson, who used to work for you, has applied to us for employment as an inventory-control clerk. He will be using an inventory-control program to enter inventory transactions and prepare inventory status reports. Most of the time he'll work with processed orders, but he'll spend about 20% of his time dealing with other employees on the telephone. In that regard, I have two questions for you.*
>
> *"How similar is this to the work Bill performed for you, and how well do you think this job fits his capabilities?"*

You have described the general situation and asked two specific questions. Most likely one of two things will occur. The supervisor may tell you to call the owner or human resources person for such information. If so, you are no worse off than before you called. Or you may receive an answer. If you do, wait for a full answer. Do not interrupt.

When the supervisor finishes, you can move on to even more specific and direct questions. Be careful not to ask "why" questions, which your source may perceive as requiring justification of his or her answers.

Instead, ask for examples or elaboration such as:

- *"What factors contributed to that performance?"*
- *"What can we do to help Bill succeed at this job?"*
- *"How do you rate Bill's overall performance?"*
- *"How well did Bill get along with other department employees?"*
- *"How well did Bill deal with customers and employees outside the department?"*
- *"Did you ever have to discipline Bill for any reason?"*
- *"How was Bill's punctuality and attendance?"*

Next, confirm Bill's position and employment dates. Ask whether your source can refer you to someone else for whom Bill worked who may be worth calling. If you need to verify salary, ask about it last. Then thank the person.

Again, do not lie when making such a call. Answer the source's questions truthfully—even if you lose the reference.

If, in your conversation with the supervisor, you failed to obtain all the information you desired, call the owner of the company or its human resources person. If it's a small business, always call the owner first; you'll have a better chance of success with that person. You can always call the human resources person later. Use the same basic approach that you used with the supervisor. Get as much needed information as you can.

Be careful not to ask "why" questions, which your source may perceive as requiring justification of his or her answers.

At any point in the process, be prepared to mail, e-mail, or fax a copy of the candidate's signed release statement.

When you have completed the employment reference check, make note of any questions that the personal and professional reverences may be able to answer.

The Appendix contains a copy of an employment reference check form. You can use it as a guide for such calls and for developing your own form.

Education References

Responses to requests for education references vary by school.

Most high schools have established specific procedures for obtaining information and specific guidelines for or limits to the specific information they will release. If possible, start with the candidate's teacher or, alternatively, a counselor. (In some cases the candidate may have given a teacher or counselor as a personal reference. You can approach the person as a personal reference, but you can ask for the educational information you desire, too.) If you have neither name, call the administrative office.

When calling a college or university, begin with the specific names of professors or others that the candidate has given you. Otherwise, call the school's registrar or office of records. Large universities may keep their records separately by discipline, for example, at the engineering school, college of education, or school of nursing. You will quickly learn what you can obtain and what procedure to follow.

Training organizations and trade schools are generally more eager to tell you who completed their courses of study.

The Appendix contains a form for checking educational references.

Personal and Professional References

Save the personal and professional references for last. Some of your earlier calls may have identified additional questions to ask the personal references.

Keep in mind that candidates usually select their personal and professional references on the assumption (though it's not always true) that they will provide excellent references, so personal references may not provide much negative information or resolve discrepancies.

Always try to determine the references' relationships to the candidates before calling. You can request that information on the application or ask the candidate at the interview. Knowing whether the references are from the candidate's school or former employer will help you identify the questions to ask. You may even obtain otherwise unavailable employment or educational information. For example, a former supervisor given as a personal reference may also supply work-related information, or a former teacher given as a personal reference may also provide educational information.

Have your questions ready. Start positively with easy questions. The initial conversation and flow of questions might be similar to this:

> *"Good evening. I am Jack Williams of Progressive Marketing Services. Jane Cooper has applied to us for the position of copywriter and has given you as a personal (or professional) reference.*
>
> *"I have a few questions.*
>
> *"First, how long have you known Jane?*
>
> *"What was the relationship?*
>
> *"What do you know of her professional skills?*
>
> *"We're a small agency. We have only six people. Jane will work with a senior copywriter in preparing catalog and newspaper ads. The majority of our clients are retail clothing*

stores. Jane will deal with their merchandising people and some manufacturers. How does this situation fit with what you know of Jane's abilities and interests?

"What are Jane's greatest strengths?

"In what areas do you think Jane requires some development?

"What else can you tell me that will help me select the right person for this job?"

When calling personal or professional references, use the telephone number provided by the candidate. If the candidate provided the references' home numbers, do not call them at their places of employment.

Call first the reference who appears able to provide the most appropriate information. He or she may request a letter from you. In such situations it is better to forget the reference, but if you have time and you need it, write something similar to this:

Dear Mr. Arnold:

As I described on the telephone, Susan Anderson has applied to our company for the position of receptionist. In that job she will receive and distribute incoming telephone calls for a five-person office and greet visitors.

Ms. Anderson has given your name as a personal reference, so we will appreciate any information that you can provide to help us make the right decision.

Sincerely,

You may want to include a photocopy of the signed release statement and the reference from the application. Because this is in writing, you may want to have standard wording for such letters approved by your employment attorney. Some companies send letters to all personal and professional references immediately after they hire a person in an attempt to confirm all information supplied by the candidate.

Document all reference checks in writing: Whom you called and when, what you asked, and what the reference said. Do not tape-record the call. In most instances, that is illegal without both parties' permission, and if you ask for it, the reference will probably either terminate the call or fail to give you the information you want.

Listen to what a person doesn't say. It can raise questions about the candidate's qualifications.

You may tend to do most of the talking in a reference check—after all, you have questions you want answered. A better approach is to frame the situation—describe your need and then listen. By just remaining quiet you might elicit information you could never get by direct questioning.

Finally, listen for what the person *doesn't* say. If you ask about punctuality, and the answer concerns absences, perhaps the person misunderstood the question, or perhaps the person is avoiding answering it. If you ask three times in various ways about the candidate's productivity and each time the reference fails to comment directly, that person may be telling you that he or she does not know the answer or does not want to give

---

CHECKLIST | **Reference Checking**

Have you:
- **Grouped** your questions by employer and school?
- **Eliminated** questions irrelevant to the job?
- **Obtained** the name of the candidate's former supervisor, teacher, or counselor?
- **Prepared** the appropriate information for your reference during the call (dates, activities, course of study, or job)?

Will you:
- **Identify** yourself and the reason for your call?

- **Reply** truthfully to questions?
- **Make** a written record of the call (the time, the person you spoke with, content)?
- **Relate** personal and professional references to the candidate's background and direct your questions accordingly?
- **Identify** any questions in checking educational and employment reference checks that personal and professional reference checks might answer?
- **Ask** the candidate any questions that remain after you've finished checking all references?

you an answer. This situation can raise questions about a candidate's qualifications that you need to try to answer through one of the other means available to you.

Your reference checks may generate additional questions to ask the candidate. If so, ask them by telephone or in a second interview. Remember, by following up, you may lead the candidate to misperceive that you will probably make a job offer or that you suspect falsification of facts. A good guideline is to not contact the candidate unless you want to schedule another interview and will offer a job if you resolve the additional questions.

Comparing Candidate Qualifications With Job Requirements

You should now have everything you need to select the new employee: the application and the résumé, as well as the results of the interview, any tests, interviews conducted by others, and reference checks. You now need to relate all of this information to the job requirements.

But before you do, you may have some unfinished business. You may have discovered facts in the reference checking that disqualify someone. If so, document the information and remove the candidate from further consideration.

Then complete the evaluation of the remaining candidates.

Chapter 5 introduced a simple rating scale for evaluating candidates' qualifications before their interviews. You can use the same scale for a final evaluation of qualifications:

- **1 point**—Less than required
- **2 points**—As much as required
- **3 points**—More than required

Begin by listing the categories of job requirements:
- **Education**
- **Type of experience**
- **Length of experience**
- **Special qualifications**

Within each category list any specifics, such as these:

Education
■ **Major: Retail marketing**
■ **Associate degree**
■ **Knows Excel**

Type and length of experience
■ **Retail sales experience** of at least two annual sales cycles for a single employer or at least three cycles for no more than three employers
■ **Retail merchandising** of at least two annual sales cycles for a single employer or at least three cycles for no more than three employers
■ **Inventory control experience** for one year's sales cycle for a single employer or at least two cycles for no more than two employers
■ **Experience in conducting supplier sales presentations**
■ **Additional employment experience**

Special qualifications
■ **Knowledge of retail advertising approaches**
■ **Knowledge of in-store display techniques**
■ **Knowledge of Internet and catalog sales techniques**

Considering everything you have learned about all the candidates you are considering for the job, rate each one on each qualification. If other people also interviewed the candidates, ask them to complete similar evaluations independently, with no input from you or other interviewers.

Meet to compare your evaluations. Where you have differences, discuss them to find out why you are evaluating the candidate differently. Use factual information from the application or résumé, and from the interview and reference-checking notes to resolve differences. In some instances, you may need more information from the candidate. What you want to obtain is a final evaluation of each candidate's qualifications.

In any event, whether the evaluation is the result of a discussion with others or is solely your evaluation, you will have at last evaluated all the candidates. You can then decide which of the candidates, if any, are qualified for the job and in what order, from most to least.

To discover who is the best candidate for the job, you can use a procedure similar to the one recommended for evaluating application and résumé information: Sort the candidates by the number of 2's received, and then consider them in descending order. Whoever has earned all 2's in the evaluation is a qualified candidate, followed by whoever earned the next highest number of 2's, and so on.

If no candidate meets the requirements, you may have to seek additional candidates or consider other solutions. You may decide to go with someone who isn't fully qualified in the belief that you can provide the necessary training within a reasonable period.

You will need to review all the candidates' ratings to determine whether they are acceptable or unacceptable. A 3 or a 1

When you have thus ranked the candidates or identified a single qualified candidate, review the results with anyone else involved, such as the supervisor of the position.

may be acceptable in some categories, but not in others. You must decide, based on your experience with the job, where you can afford to "give a little" in the job requirements.

When you have thus ranked the candidates or identified a single qualified candidate, review the results with anyone else involved, such as the supervisor of the position if it is someone other than you.

Make sure you have documented why you ranked the candidates as you did. This does not have to be an elaborately written statement. Notes should suffice.

Problems of underqualified and overqualified candidates were discussed in Chapter 3. Employers generally don't offer jobs to underqualified people, but they do tend to offer them to overqualified people.

A small appliance repair shop in Maine always hired the person with the greatest amount of experience and training even when the job required a junior repairperson. The owner once said, "Hey, I want the best, and if I can get an overqualified person, I will get a higher level of repair."

This shop did not experience the same problems as the post office in our earlier story (page 42), but it did have problems. Overqualified people accepted the lesser position, which required lesser skills and paid less, because they could not find something that better fit them, and they kept looking. As soon as they located a more desirable situation, they left to take it. The shop was constantly hiring and rarely had a full staff.

Assessing Strengths and Weaknesses

I f you now have a pool of qualified candidates from which to choose, the last step in the candidate evaluation is to determine each one's strengths and areas of needed improvement in terms of the job. Even candidates who earned all 2's will have individual strengths and weaknesses.

Identify up to three strengths and up to three areas in which improvement is needed, then describe any necessary training and development.

CHECKLIST | **Candidate Qualifications Versus Job Requirements**

Have you:
- **Used** a standard method, such as an evaluation scale, to evaluate each candidate's qualifications for the job?
- **Identified** all categories of job requirements and each one's specific requirements?
- **Ranked** in order of priority the categories of job requirements and the specific requirements within each category?
- **Evaluated** each candidate on the basis of all information you have?
- **Asked** other interviewers, if any,

to independently evaluate the candidate's qualifications?
- **Compared** your evaluations of candidates with those of other interviewers and resolved any differences?
- **Identified** any information that you still require from a candidate?
- **Ranked** the candidates in line with your evaluation of their qualifications?
- **Identified** any training that the candidate requires for job success?

Perhaps you can conduct the training as part of the job, for example:

■ **Needs WordPerfect training**
■ **Needs training in front-end alignments**
■ **Needs training in geographic areas of the county**

Or perhaps others (schools or manufacturers) can provide the training:

■ **Needs training in repair of portable generators as** offered by generator manufacturer
■ **Needs to attend basic budget preparation and variance analysis course** offered by community college
■ **Needs training in claims processing** as offered by worker's compensation carrier

Also indicate when the employee should accomplish the training, for example, during the first three months of employment.

The Danger of Indecision

Sometimes, even when you have identified a perfectly qualified candidate, you or one of the other interviewers may want to see additional candidates. The reasons given may be similar to the following:

> *I don't like to hire when I have seen only one person. How do I know there is not someone better available?*

> *I need to compare candidates to know which one to hire.*

Such statements indicate that the prospective employer does not know what he or she wants and hasn't properly identified the job requirements. Consequently, after seeing several additional candidates, the first one usually turns out to be the one to hire, but by that time, he or she may be unavailable.

> *A firm in Washington continually lost good candidates and increased its hiring costs because of the general manager's*

persistent requests to see additional candidates. The firm's owner finally established this policy: When you see a candidate, you must make a decision to hire or not hire that candidate before you can see another.

Did the policy work? Yes, but it was some time before the general manager was comfortable with it.

The solution? Once you have identified the job requirements and obtained candidates who meet them, make your hiring decision.

Making a Decision

The last step is to decide: Which candidate is best for your job? Sometimes you'll find only one who is qualified. This makes an easy decision, but poses a problem if the candidate does not accept the job offer. If, however, you have several qualified candidates, which one do you select?

The numerical evaluations you and others gave the candidates will help you, as will your assessment of each candidate's strengths and areas of needed improvement. In addition, you may have to consider such practicalities as how soon someone can start, how much training or compensation the person requires, and how well the person will fit with your existing team.

You have done everything possible to gather the necessary information for your decision. Selecting an employee is an individual activity, not something for a group vote. Groups can provide input and recommendations, but in the final analysis, an individual must make a decision—either you or the job's supervisor—preferably, whoever knows the job's requirements best, has interviewed the candidate, and has all the candidate's information. As a general rule, this should be the person to whom the new employee will directly report. At minimum, that person should concur with the decision. Whoever is chosen, everyone should support the decision until it is proved wrong.

Summary

Y ou now have a list of candidates (in order as they are most qualified for the job) and you have decided to whom you wish to offer the job. You have eliminated unqualified candidates. Now it's time to persuade the candidate you want to accept the job.

Offering the Job

"Most people want to be part of a team."

—CANDICE KASPERS

OU IDENTIFIED A PROBLEM TO SOLVE (HIRING A new employee); gathered the necessary information (defined the job, obtained candidates, and reviewed candidate information); and proposed a solution (decided which of the candidates you wish to hire). Now you become a salesperson; you want to sell the chosen candidate on accepting the position with your company.

A common adage of salespeople is that you cannot sell a person something that the person does not want. Your challenge is to prepare and present the job offer in such a way that the candidate will perceive it as meeting his or her needs.

Preparing the Offer

First, you must prepare the offer by considering all the appropriate elements: compensation, benefits, working relationships, schedule, and any special conditions. Second, you must present those factors most appealingly to the candidate. Let's examine these factors in detail.

Compensation

In our capitalistic society, money is how people keep score, so a worker's pay can be an indicator of self-worth and importance. But don't be misled. Although pay is a key factor in whether someone accepts or declines an employment offer, it is not the only factor or even necessarily the most important one. (An exception is the person who is work-

Pay is a key factor in whether someone accepts your job offer, but it isn't the only one.

ing solely for money, such as a part-time student or someone working for extra money to pay for holiday purchases, but even in those situations, money may not be everything.)

A number of years ago psychologist Frederick Herzberg, investigated the issue of what motivates employees. He distinguished between so-called hygiene factors and motiva-

tors. Herzberg described compensation and other contextual or environmental factors, such as benefits and security, as hygiene factors. His theory was that so long as the hygiene factors were sufficient, they were not motivators. Only when they were absent or less than anticipated did they become motivators. The only job factors that motivate are those that challenge an employee, such as the opportunity to advance and assignments that make maximum use of abilities.

Let's apply Herzberg's theory to candidates and job offers. So long as compensation meets the candidate's perceived needs or requirements, it is not the main factor in deciding whether to accept your offer. If you offer significantly less than anticipated, then pay becomes the most important factor unless you provide an offsetting factor. For example, someone may work for less money in exchange for a flexible schedule or a convenient location. Hence, you must think of compensation as only one part of a total employment package.

Each candidate has a notion of what you *should* pay him or her for your job, and you probably used that perception to qualify the person as a candidate when you asked for desired or current salary. You may also have told all candidates what the job pays, either as a specified amount or as a salary range. Thus, you probably eliminated candidates who did not wish to work for what you planned to pay.

But sometimes prospective employers and employees may interpret the same range differently. You have seen ads that state the following:

Salary: $40,000 to $50,000, depending on qualifications

How much do you think a candidate reading that ad will expect you to pay? Right, $50,000 or as close to it as possible. However, you may be planning to pay $40,000 or as close to it as possible.

Asking for each candidate's salary history along with a résumé and application will help you determine whether he or she is within the job's possible range of pay. Consider the following two points before you take this approach:

First, the earnings that candidates report may well be incorrect. A study made by a Detroit recruiting firm discovered that 80% of job candidates misreported their current earnings; on average, they overstated their salaries by 10%.

Second, numerous articles and books suggest that job seekers should change jobs only for a 20% to 25% increase in compensation. So, someone who is currently employed will probably seek an increase, whereas someone who is currently unemployed will probably accept less—unless he or she has received a competitive offer from another firm, which is a good possibility in a hot job market.

You know what the job is worth and what you can pay. Ideally, you have evaluated the job (see Chapter 10) and have established a salary or salary range for the job that you can adjust in accordance with the individual's qualifications.

Let's examine the factors that influence what compensation to offer the candidate.

CONSIDER CURRENT EMPLOYEES. If you have employees in the same job as the one you are filling or in jobs similar to it, you should consider what you will offer a new employee versus what you are paying current employees.

A medical laboratory in North Carolina hired laboratory technician graduates from a local community college. The college had an excellent program, and its graduates were in increasing demand. As a result, the lab offered the inexperienced technicians starting salaries that increased faster than the cost of living, but it paid its experienced technicians salaries that increased only about the same as the cost of living. This inequity created many morale problems, and the experienced technicians eventually left for higher starting salaries at other companies.

Even if you do not have employees in similar positions, you need to consider the relationship of the new employee's salary to those of your other employees, who will find out what the new person is earning—and quickly. Don't believe otherwise.

All this strongly suggests that you need an equitable salary program to attract and keep employees. (Chapter 10 describes creating such a program in more detail.)

CONSIDER OTHER FORMS OF COMPENSATION. So far we have considered base pay, whether an annual, monthly, or weekly salary, or an hourly wage, but you may wish to consider other forms of compensation.

Commission. The ideal form of compensation is directly related to job performance, and sales jobs naturally lend themselves to this type of compensation since individual results (sales) are easily determined and measured. Because money is how we keep score, commission directly and easily communicates how well a salesperson is doing.

Commission programs often include advances paid against future commissions, and pay new employees a starting salary, which may automatically decrease as commissions increase. If you pay commission and the job does not qualify as an independent contractor (see page 40), you must be sure that you comply with minimum wage and overtime laws by guaranteeing a minimum payment equal to the minimum wage. If you are not sure about how the law applies to your jobs, check with an employment attorney or consultant.

If you pay commissions, you should consider the same points as just mentioned about making sure that the pay for new employees is commensurate with the pay for current employees. Most important, you should give a copy of your written commission policy to the candidate when you make the job offer.

No single commission policy or set of rules for its implementation is correct. However, you should consider and address the following points:

- **The method of calculation of the commission,** whether on the individual's or the group's performance.
- **The amount of the commission** as a specific amount per sale item(s) or as a percentage of sales dollars. This should also include any variations in the commission as a result of such things as sales of different items or sales volume.
- **The basis on which you pay the commission,** such as gross sales dollars, net profit of sales, or sale of specific items.
- **Factors, if any, that reduce commission,** such as returns, specially priced items, or return of advances.
- **The period for which you calculate commission**—daily, weekly, monthly, or annually.
- **The time the commission is paid,** whether upon receipt of payment for a sale, on a specific date or regularly scheduled payday, or after a specific time period.
- **Your policies regarding advances,** that is, how much the employee can draw in advance, how often, and payback procedures.

Bonuses. The most common form of additional compensation is a bonus—annual, monthly, quarterly, and weekly. You can pay bonuses on the basis of individual performance, group performance, or company performance, or some combination of those factors.

The most common bonus is paid at year-end or holiday time. Employers generally pay two or three levels of bonus: executive or owner bonus, management bonus, and nonmanagement bonus. Sometimes they pay a separate sales bonus.

Ideally, bonuses relate to job performance, that is, what a person does determines the size of the bonus. But keep Herzberg's concept of hygiene factors in mind: If you pay the bonus annually and don't relate it to individual performance, and if the employee expects it, it probably has little motivating effect; and the more that the bonus depends on group or company performance and the less on individual performance, the less motivation it provides.

Like commissions, no single bonus policy and procedure is correct. However, candidates will want to know about the following points of your bonus plan:

- **How you determine the bonus amount.** Is it guaranteed? Is it based on company profit? Is it based on individual or group performance? Is it a fixed amount or a percentage of salary?
- **When you pay it**—monthly, quarterly, or annually—and the date you pay it.
- **Length of time with the company necessary for full or partial eligibility,** that is, the length of time a person must be employed to qualify for the bonus and the extent to which you prorate the bonus in accordance with partial service during the period.

Unless you guarantee a bonus and its amount, do not assure the candidate that he or she will receive one or quote a specific figure. If asked, you can describe what the bonus has averaged for the past year or two, but state that this is no guarantee of what the next bonus payment will be. However, if non-management employees receive fixed amounts, such as two weeks' pay at holiday time without a tie-in to performance, you can state the amount.

Signing-on bonuses. Sign-on bonuses have become an increasingly significant component of many companies' job offers. They provide a way of attracting people with a one-time payment that does not become part of base salary. The idea is to offset the employee's cost of changing or accepting a new job (moving, rescheduling, and so on). Sign-on bonuses may range from a few thousand dollars to 15% of annual base salary or more—a significant figure.

As always, no single approach to sign-on bonuses is correct, but you need to think about the following points:

- **What percentage of base salary** are you willing to pay as a sign-on bonus?

- **Must the employee pay back the sign-on bonus** if he or she leaves within a specified period?
- **Will you offer all new employees similar sign-on bonuses?** If not, what will be the basis for varying the policy?
- **What determines the amount of a sign-on bonus:** competition, cost of moving, loss of bonus at previous employer?

As with salary, do not assume that other employees will not know the amount of any sign-on bonus that you pay to a new employee. It is best to have a standard, communicated policy that treats everyone the same. If you feel compelled by an over-heated job market to offer more now than you might have had to in the past, be prepared to explain your policy to longer-term employees.

Overtime. Federal law requires employers to pay nonexempt employees overtime if they work more than 40 hours in any week (see page 39). Companies vary in how they meet that requirement.

> **As with salary, do not assume that other employees will not know the amount of any sign-on bonus.**

For example, the work schedule at some firms is 9:00 A.M. to 5:00 P.M. with a one-hour, unpaid lunch, so that the work week totals 35 hours in five days. Some firms pay overtime for a sixth or seventh day worked, but others do not pay overtime until after 40 hours of actual work. Those companies pay the first 5 hours of overtime as straight time.

Some companies pay overtime for more than 8 hours worked during any one day in a 40-hour workweek, or they pay overtime for more than 40 hours worked in any one week, but not both. Hence an employee might work 10 hours on Wednesday, but only 4 hours on Friday; the company would pay the employee for the 2 hours of overtime on Wednesday, because he worked more than 8 hours that day. If the employee then worked a couple of hours on Saturday, he or she would not be paid overtime for those. (Again, companies working a 7-hour day may have a different rule.)

Some firms pay double time for all holidays and for the seventh day worked in a week.

Compensatory time. Some firms provide compensatory ("comp") time—time off in lieu of overtime pay. Employees earn an equal amount of time off for overtime worked. For example, a company might allow an employee who worked four hours extra on a Monday to leave four hours early on Friday of the same workweek. For nonexempt employees (who are covered by the Fair Labor Standards Act; see page 39 for more on this) you cannot provide compensatory time in lieu of overtime pay unless the overtime and compensatory time occur in the same workweek. (In some situations, you can allow the nonexempt employee to take the comp time within a longer pay period, but your employment attorney should advise you on this subject.)

Small companies often ignore or perhaps just don't recognize the importance of federal overtime requirements, and many have suffered large fines and back payments of overtime as a result. Be absolutely sure to pay overtime as required and to classify employees as exempt from overtime only when they meet federal requirements for such status.

Georgina was an inventory-control clerk (a nonexempt job) for a small Long Island parts distributor. Her husband

---

CHECKLIST **Compensation**

Have you:
- **Determined** the candidate's starting salary?
- **Considered** the relationship of the starting salary to current employees' salaries?
- **Decided** whether you will give a sign-on bonus?
- **Identified** the conditions for giving a performance bonus?
- **Chosen** to pay a commission? If so, will you pay an advance or base salary?
- **Prepared** a written description of

your commission structure?
- **Communicated** when payday is, and when the new employee's first one will be?
- **Determined** whether this position is eligible for overtime?
- **Identified** and applied the rules regarding overtime pay to this job?
- **Provided** bank transfer (direct deposit) of pay? If so, have you instructed the person to bring bank account information on the first day of employment?

---

worked a few miles from Georgina's company, so he dropped her off every morning on his way to work, even though that meant that she arrived 45 minutes before she was scheduled to start work. Because she was there, she began working, so that she actually worked 8 hours and 45 minutes each day. However, the parts company paid her for just 8 hours per day.

Each morning as she was working the additional early 45 minutes, her supervisor would arrive. He always saw her at work, and at times even asked her to check items in inventory during that time.

One day a U.S. Department of Labor investigator visited the company. He talked to several employees including Georgina. His ruling, later upheld in court, was that the company owed Georgina back overtime pay for 6 years of working an additional 4 hours and 15 minutes overtime (at 45 minutes per day) plus interest and the company was required to pay a hefty fine. In addition, the government identified several other employees to whom the company owed back overtime.

The basis for the government's ruling was that the supervisor knew that Georgina was working overtime each morning and did nothing about it. The ruling held that the failure to tell her to stop represented approval of the overtime.

Payday. Finally, let the prospective new employee know how frequently you pay—weekly, every two weeks (26 checks per year), semi-monthly (24 checks per year), or monthly—and which day it is. Most important, be sure to mention when the person will receive his or her first pay. If you use direct deposits of pay to a bank account exclusively or make them available, so inform the person. You should advise someone who wants direct deposit of pay to be sure to bring bank, routing, and account number information on the first day of employment to avoid delay in making the arrangements necessary for payment.

Benefits

Most companies offer a common benefit plan for all employees, so that benefits are less likely to be individualized than compensation is. (An exception is the cafeteria plan of benefits, described in Chapter 10.) Ideally, you should present the candidate with a written description of the benefits that you offer. Then discuss the benefits, including the following information:

- **Which benefits are mandatory and which are optional**
- **Eligibility date**
- **Employee contributions** (the employee's share of the benefit's cost, if any)
- **Dependent coverages** (which of the employee's family members are eligible for benefit coverage and how much extra the employee must pay, if anything, for such coverage)
- **The amount of employer contributions, if any, to any plans of deferred compensation,** such as a 401(k), deferred-profit-sharing plan, pension plan, and employee stock-ownership plan

However, do not attempt to cover all benefits in detail. Give the candidate a general description and provide specifics when asked for them. The most common questions at this point concern any health coverages you offer (health, dental, eyeglasses, prescriptions, and so on). Candidates will want to know when coverage becomes effective, what type it is (HMO, major medical, or other), who is covered (employee and dependents), and how much it costs the employee.

The next subjects on which you may receive questions are vacation (how much and when eligible) and type of retirement. Otherwise, you will probably not be asked for too many details unless the candidate has a specific need. You should be prepared to respond to whatever is asked or to find the answer promptly.

CHECKLIST | **Benefits**

Have you:
- **Identified** mandatory and optional benefits?
- **Identified** all benefits for which this person is eligible?
- **Determined** the candidate's benefit eligibility date(s)?
- **Determined** the amount of any employee contribution that is required?
- **Determined** the total value of your benefit plan?

If you know that a good candidate has a need that you can address with a benefit, be sure to mention it. For example, tuition assistance will interest someone attending night school. Someone with a child who has a disability may be interested in knowing whether your medical insurance imposes any precondition requirements.

If you know you offer fewer benefits than the candidate's current employer or than other employers in your region or industry typically provide, be ready to counter with a compensating factor. For example:

> *We do not provide dental insurance, but our pay scale is higher than our competitors' and we provide a flexible-spending account that you can use to save pretax income for such expenses.*

> *We do not provide tuition assistance, but we will design your work hours around your school schedule.*

Whatever you do, though, do not indicate the possibility of additional benefits unless you will provide them. The candidate is likely to take the discussion as a promise.

Other Conditions of Employment

Besides compensation and benefits, you have numerous other items to cover in your offer. These will vary by company and job, but the most typical subjects to consider are discussed in this section.

ESSENTIALS, INCLUDING WORKING RELATIONSHIPS. This item may seem obvious, or you may think that you covered the subject of working relationships previously in the interview, but employers often do not properly cover this subject. Take this opportunity to reiterate:

■ The position title
■ The department or area he or she will work in
■ The location of the job
■ The name and title of the direct supervisor

■ **Any special conditions unique to the position,** for example, whether it is a management job, an exempt job, or a temporary position

SCHEDULE. Scheduling has been referred to already, but you should provide both the first day's work schedule and the regular work schedule.

The first day. There should be no surprises on day one. The first day's schedule includes when, where and to whom to report. You should include specific items that the employee should bring. For example, proof of citizenship status requires one of the following:
■ **A U.S. birth or naturalization certificate**
■ **A valid U.S. passport**
■ **A valid foreign passport with U.S. work authorization visa**
■ **A U.S. green card authorizing work in the United States**

or
■ **A social security card *and* a driver's license**

The need for bank information, if you provide direct deposit of pay, has already been discussed.

In addition, you should consider whether the new employee must show proof of having met other legal requirements of the job, such as a food-handling license, a commercial driver's license, or other kinds of licensing. Do you have any special requirements? You may want to allow time on the first day for the employee to take care of such business.

Some companies require a physical examination or drug test on the first day. If so, be prepared to advise the person what the test consists of and whether failure to pass such a test cancels the offer of employment.

If you provide an initial training or orientation program, describe it and its length.

Regular work schedule. This refers to the normal schedule the person will work. What you need to cover are:
■ **Starting time**

- ■ **Quitting time**
- ■ **Days of work each week**
- ■ **Any rotating schedule or shift schedule**
- ■ **Lunch periods**
- ■ **Breaks**
- ■ **Overtime requirements**

A relatively new concept in scheduling is that of flexible hours, which allows employers to adjust work hours (and location) to the individual needs of employees. Here are a few examples of how companies have standardized their approach to "flex time":

Employees may begin work anytime between 7:00 A.M. and 10:00 A.M. and leave anytime between 3:00 P.M. and 7:00 P.M., provided they work 8 hours per day, and take at least 30 minutes for lunch.

Employees must work at least 40 hours per week from Monday through Friday, but they can work as many as 13½ hours per day, thus completing their workweek in 3 days. Days on the job need not be consecutive.

Employees must work 40 hours per week. They must work a minimum of 3 days, of 6 hours each, on company premises, but they can work the rest of the time at home.

These examples show only a few possible approaches to a flexible schedule. In all cases the employee's supervisor must approve the schedule, and the schedule must agree with the company's business hours, allow the department and company to meet its objectives, and be available to all employees in similar jobs.

A retail store that is open from 10:00 A.M. to 6:00 P.M. must have its salespeople on the floor during its regular retail sales hours to serve customers; as a result, it cannot allow employees to come to work at any time they desire. Similarly, a financial services firm that deals with employees throughout the United States requires employees to be available for all time zones. However, writers or programmers may be able to work evenings and weekends without impeding their organization's progress.

FEE PAYMENT. If an outside agency, such as an employment agency, referred the candidate, he or she may owe a fee for that service and may have signed a guarantee of payment. If your company is willing to pay the fee, be sure the candidate knows that. Or you may offer the employee some type of assistance, such as a short-term loan, to pay the fee.

SPECIAL CONDITIONS. Finally, there may be conditions attached to the job that you should discuss:
- Clothing or uniforms
- Special equipment
- Travel
- Use of personal car
- Parking
- Relocation

In each case, specify what you require and whether you or the employee is to provide the item. If the employee is to assume the cost, consider whether you will reimburse him or her for at least part of the expense.

CHECKLIST | Other Conditions of Employment

Have you:
- **Identified** all of the working relationships?
- **Provided** a list of all identification and any other materials that you will require on the first day?
- **Identified** when, where and to whom the employee should report?
- **Alerted** the employee to any conditions of employment, such as drug testing?
- **Outlined** and explained any initial activities, such as orientation and training?
- **Offered** to pay or subsidize the employee's payment of an employment agency's fee?
- **Identified** all special conditions of employment?

Presenting the Offer

With your preparations complete, you are ready to make the offer. If there is more than one candidate, you may have to present the same offer in more than one way to address each candidate's differing needs and goals.

Begin by listing the items you need to cover. (The Appendix provides a job offer form that you can use as a checklist for making the offer.) The first three will probably be:

1. Offer of the position
2. Start date
3. Compensation

The candidate wishes to hear those critical items, and they may generate questions that could affect the rest of the offer. Some firms attempt to obtain an initial acceptance of those items before getting into additional details.

When you prepare to present the rest of your offer, deal first with those items that you believe are most important to the candidate, because those could influence acceptance. For example, if working hours or the amount of travel are of major concern, cover those topics.

The Best Approach

What approach is best: making the offer in person, in writing, or by telephone? Each has advantages and disadvantages. Writing is the most accurate means, but it allows for no questions or discussion. It also takes the longest unless you use e-mail or fax, but keep in mind that e-mails and faxes are subject to receipt by others. Avoid them unless the candidate has indicated that their use is acceptable. An offer in person requires the candidate to revisit your office, which may inconvenience or even pose a hardship for the candidate. An offer over the telephone may be misinterpreted.

Unless you need to see someone in person, most employers use a telephone call followed by written confirmation. So let's consider the steps in that approach.

An offer by phone. The first items you present are the three just stated—the job offer, start date, and compensation. When making an important telephone call, always begin by ensuring that the other party has the time and privacy to talk and that the time is convenient. Failure to do that can lead to misunderstanding and negative reactions. The initial conversation should probably go something like this:

> *"Hello, Mike (or Mr. Carlson). This is Sheila Jones from Anderson Catering. Do you have a few moments, so we can talk?"*

If the time or place is not good, find out when and where to call back and do so as scheduled. The candidate may prefer to speak after hours or from home, and you should be prepared to accommodate such a request.

Assuming that the time is convenient, let's resume the call:

> *"I am calling to tell you that we have reached our decision regarding the position of unit supervisor, and I am pleased to invite you to join our company in that job. (Pause.)*

> *"We would like you to start by the first of next month and, as we discussed, the compensation will be $45,000 a year with eligibility for a performance bonus at year-end. We base that bonus on the profitability of your unit, and it has averaged 15% of base compensation during the past few years."*

You have now covered the first three items, so it's time to stop and invite questions. If the candidate has none or you have answered all of them, attempt to obtain an initial decision. Usually it will be forthcoming without a prompt from you, but you might want to say, after answering any questions, something similar to:

> *"I want to go over other items such as benefits, but before I do that, what do you think about our offer?"*

The actual conversation is likely to differ from your script. The important point is to have developed in advance the specifics of what you want to say and accomplish. If those are written and in front of you, you can then adjust as the conversation develops and still achieve your objective.

A request for additional time. The candidate may ask for time to consider the offer, and that is a reasonable request. You have probably spent a day or two making your decision; give the candidate the same consideration. After all, he or she may be deciding among more than one offer. But someone who requests a great deal of time, generally will not accept the offer. What's reasonable will vary with the job and your circumstances. A practical guideline is up to two days for a nonexempt position and up to one week for professional and managerial positions. Anything longer requires a reason.

> **With the specifics of what you want to say and accomplish in front of you, you can adjust as the conversation develops and still achieve your objective.**

If the candidate requests additional time, ask for a specific reply date. If the candidate's choice of date doesn't meet your needs, negotiate one that does and confirm it. If the candidate does not call or otherwise reply by that date, call the candidate to obtain a decision. If the candidate requests additional time, you should probably not grant it unless he or she gives a good and specific reason for the delay.

If the candidate does not call back and you can not reach him or her by telephone, you need to bring the matter to closure and ensure that neither of you misunderstood the date. Either leave a voice-mail message or send an overnight letter stating that since you have not heard back and have been unable to contact him or her by telephone, the offer is good only through the date of your choice. In this case, you probably won't receive a reply, or if you do, it will probably be negative.

A request for a different start date. In some cases, during the offer, the candidate may attempt to negotiate a different, probably later, starting date. The candidate should provide a reason for the request.

Unless the starting date you have suggested is absolutely

necessary, it is better to allow the candidate to change to a more convenient date. Here are a couple of related considerations:

■ **A candidate who wishes to give proper notice to his or her current employer should probably be encouraged.** Such a desire indicates professionalism, and can lead you to expect that the candidate will treat *you* fairly if he or she later leaves your employment. What is proper notice? Some companies define proper notice and tie final reconciliation of benefits to it, as in the following example:

> *One pay period constitutes "proper notice." We will pay cash for unused vacation at the time of separation only if the employee gives proper notice.*

■ **A candidate may have to remain with his or her current employer through a certain date to receive a bonus or a commission.** If that date is relatively close, the person will want to remain until the payment has been received. However, the further away the date, the less likely he or she will ultimately join your firm.

A request for more money. With salary negotiations, you must be more careful. If you are offering an equitable salary, you have little reason to change it. If you do raise it, the compensation may no longer fit your company's compensation structure; furthermore, your action has suggested that the candidate can always force salary increases by exerting some pressure. That suggestion may haunt you in future salary dealings with that person and with your other employees (remember, they *will* find out).

> *The owner of a sporting goods store has a policy to never increase a salary offer. He says, "Every time I have, I have created a problem. That person spends his entire career with me trying to get additional increases. Also, I have discovered that many times all the person wants is a large offer, so he can use that to bargain additional money from his current employer."*

Some people, particularly salespeople, tend to ask for more—not because they expect to get it, but just because they need to be sure they have made the best deal they can.

At the same time, you may have to adjust your salary offer if the candidate is the only one to whom you would make an offer, if he or she possesses hard-to-find skills that your company requires, if you have to fill the position immediately, or if you must hire this person for some other reason. But do not raise your offer easily or quickly. Ask the candidate why he or she requires additional money. Sometimes the candidate will present legitimate considerations; if so, you can easily adjust the offer. If you are unwilling to increase the offer, tell the candidate. If you might increase the salary offer, accept what you have been told and take it under consideration. If you really want to give a highly desirable candidate more money but you don't want to disrupt your current salary schedule, you can offer a sign-on bonus without increasing the person's base pay.

Other issues. If your company requires a new hire to pass a drug test, polygraph test, or physical examination as a condition of employment, you need to inform the candidate. He or she may wish to take the test early to eliminate any complications before accepting the position. This is a reasonable request, and you should agree to make the necessary arrangements.

Depending on how the conversation has gone so far, you may or may not wish to provide:

- **A summary of all benefits**
- **Description of working relationships**
- **Outline of first-day schedule**
- **List of materials to bring**
- **Description of special conditions**

Depending on the call—for example, you and the candidate have disagreed on the compensation or the proposed start date—you may wish to hold back this information until you receive an initial acceptance of the offer. Some candidates, however, ask for all the facts before making a decision, and you should oblige them.

An offer in writing. It is good to follow up an offer with a letter reiterating the offer, and many candidates will request receipt of such a letter before giving a response. They want to be sure they have not misunderstood you, and they do not want to quit one job without a document confirming the new job offer. A typical letter might be as follows:

Dear Mr. Carlson,

I am writing to confirm the offer of employment I made to you on the telephone today. The position is service manager at our North Bendelton Service Center.

The working schedule is Monday through Friday, from 8:30 A.M. to 5:30 P.M., with an hour allowed each day for lunch.

Salary is $1,000 per week. Payday is every other Friday for the previous two weeks of work. We pay a 5% performance bonus quarterly, based on service sales.

I have enclosed a copy of our benefit plans.

We would like you to start on Monday, May 17.

If you have any questions, please call me. Otherwise, as we agreed in our conversation, you will call me with your answer by April 30. This offer is valid through that date.

Sincerely,

In some situations you may make the initial offer by letter; if so, you obviously have to adapt the wording. But, again, it is best to make the initial offer in person or on the telephone and then to follow up in writing.

An offer in person. An offer in person is similar to a telephone offer, but it also allows for the sharing of documents and for more questions and answers. The problem is that it often inconveniences the candidate, who may have to take additional time off from his or her current job. But if the request is logical, make it.

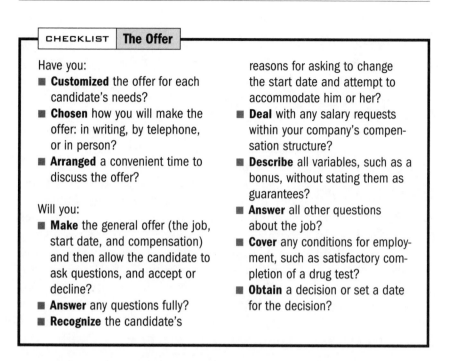

CHECKLIST | **The Offer**

Have you:
- **Customized** the offer for each candidate's needs?
- **Chosen** how you will make the offer: in writing, by telephone, or in person?
- **Arranged** a convenient time to discuss the offer?

Will you:
- **Make** the general offer (the job, start date, and compensation) and then allow the candidate to ask questions, and accept or decline?
- **Answer** any questions fully?
- **Recognize** the candidate's reasons for asking to change the start date and attempt to accommodate him or her?
- **Deal** with any salary requests within your company's compensation structure?
- **Describe** all variables, such as a bonus, without stating them as guarantees?
- **Answer** all other questions about the job?
- **Cover** any conditions for employment, such as satisfactory completion of a drug test?
- **Obtain** a decision or set a date for the decision?

Receiving the Response: Yeah or Nay?

It's hard to imagine, but you may not receive a response to an offer. That is why it is best to set a time limit on the offer. If you have not done that and have not received a timely response, it is best to formally withdraw the offer (see the discussion on page 159).

If the candidate declines your offer, do not become defensive. Remember, this is a customer or potential customer, so set forth the best-possible image for your company. Use this as an opportunity to gain information. Don't ask "Why?" which may put the person on the defensive. Instead, ask something similar to this:

"What factors led to your decision?"

or

"Can you give me some information that will help us in attracting other candidates?"

If you have no other candidates, you might ask the person

to recommend someone. If you keep things positive, the candidate may even contact you in the future for another job.

If the candidate accepts the offer, you can get into all the details you have not yet covered and send a letter confirming the acceptance. If the candidate will join you within a week, a letter probably is not necessary. You might also invite the candidate to meet with you and discuss details.

You do not want the hire to be a surprise, and you want to be the source of such information.

What do you do if the candidate accepts, but his or her current employer offers the candidate more money to stay? That does happen, and it often results in the candidate's not joining you, so treat this situation as you would any other declined offer. You do not want to get into a bidding war with the current employer. Moreover, the candidate may simply be attempting to obtain additional salary from you. If you think that's the case (but you generally cannot know for sure), review the earlier discussion on page 160.

If the candidate declines your offer, move on to the next candidate and begin again. A word of caution: It is amazing how many times a candidate will accept a job only to call the day before he or she is to start and decline it. Perhaps the candidate has had second thoughts. Many people find changing jobs—leaving the known for the unknown—traumatic. Or perhaps the current employer has made a counteroffer or a third party has made an offer. Most job seekers don't limit their efforts to one potential employer, but apply to many; so sometimes the candidate receives an offer after having accepted yours. Therefore, never dismiss other candidates until the new employee is actually on your payroll.

Notifying Others

After a candidate has accepted the offer, you need to inform your current employees and anyone else involved. You do not want the hire to be a surprise, and you want to be the source of such information. The first person to notify is the supervisor (if not you), who will notify anyone with whom the new employee will work. Finally, communicate with other employees and, if the new employee will deal with any of your suppliers and customers, let them know. Generally these notifications consist of the employee's name, start date, position, and reporting relationship. When the employee brings special skills or experience, you might make note of his or her former employment.

If the position is a key management one, if it will be of interest to the community or industry, or if it has public relations value for your company, you may also wish to notify the local or industry newspaper or magazine. Be cautious. You do not want to issue a general news release before notifying your employees and before the candidate has notified his or her current employer.

When you want to announce *before* the start date that someone will join your company, always ask for the person's permission.

A financial services firm extended an offer to someone for the position of credit manager. The candidate was currently working for a savings bank that provided an annual performance

---

| CHECKLIST | **Notifying Others** |

Will you:

- **Notify** the supervisor as soon as the candidate accepts the position?
- **Obtain** the candidate's permission to announce his or her decision to join your company?
- **Assign** the department supervisor to notify the department employees of the new hire?
- **Prepare** a communication to all other company employees?
- **Notify** customers and suppliers as appropriate?

- **Arrange** for a press release?
- **Prepare** letters to all other unsuccessful candidates for the position?
- **Hold** all letters to other candidates until you have confirmed the selection?
- **Keep** in mind that all other candidates are prospective customers or customers and treat them accordingly?
- **Notify** any outside agencies of the selection?

---

bonus. The company always paid the bonus—a significant amount of money (15% of base salary)—on the last payday of the calendar year.

The candidate accepted the position with the new company in late November, but requested a start date in early January so that he could receive his performance bonus.

The new company announced in mid-December that the person was joining the firm. His current employer heard the news and did not pay him the bonus.

It's also embarrassing to announce a new hire and later have to announce that the person will not join the firm after all.

Candidates best accept rejection when they perceive that you have treated them fairly and professionally.

As a rule, advise only the people who need to know—the supervisor and whoever makes the initial hiring arrangements, such as your human resources person—and hold off announcing to others until the person okays it or arrives on site.

Notify the candidates that who you are not hiring. Remember that they are prospective customers and may even be candidates for future opportunities with your company. Conclude the process professionally to protect your good image. You might consider personally phoning candidates whom you may want to consider in the near future or candidates recommended by employees, suppliers, or customers. However, do not promise future employment unless you mean it.

Or, you can use a letter similar to this:

Dear Mr. Johnson,

We have selected a candidate to fill the position of service manager, for which you also applied. It was a difficult decision because of the excellent qualifications of the candidates we interviewed.

We thank you for applying to our company, and we will maintain your résumé in our files for at least six months in case another opportunity develops for which we can consider you.

Again, thank you and best wishes for success in obtaining the position you desire.

Sincerely,

Keep in mind that no matter how well you convey the news, the candidate will see it as a rejection. Candidates best accept rejection when they perceive that you have treated them fairly and professionally. Do not get into the reasons—why the candidate selected is better than the one with whom you are communicating. That generally just adds to the feeling of rejection. What you want to do is retain a positive image with a future customer or candidate.

Be sure to notify all candidates as soon as the new employee has definitely accepted the job and reported to work.

If you used any employment agencies or search firms to help you fill the position, be sure to notify them, too. First, advise the agency or search firm from whom you obtained the successful candidate, and then notify the any other agencies, so that they can cease their efforts. If you use agencies or search firms, you want to maintain a good relationship with them. If they feel that you treated them less than professionally, you may have problems when you wish to use them in the future.

Summary

You have a candidate who has accepted the position. You have notified all other candidates of that decision and satisfactorily concluded the selection process. You have also notified all appropriate internal and external people of the new hire.

Next, you must prepare to bring your new employee on board. With proper planning, you can provide your new employee with an auspicious beginning to his or her new job.

Starting Employment

"To keep an organization young and fit, don't hire anyone until everybody's so overworked they'll be glad to see the newcomer no matter where he sits." —ROBERT TOWNSEND

O FAR WE HAVE DEALT WITH FINDING GOOD EMPLOYEES. The rest of the book emphasizes keeping them, and that begins with their first day of employment.

Usually, when people accept a job with a new company, the experience is a happy one. They have elected to change jobs—something that affects all aspects of their lives—and they generally do this only when they are positively motivated. They almost always approach their first day with a new employer with the highest and best expectations. Their optimism is an ideal base on which to build positive employee relations. Unfortunately, employers don't always take advantage of that opportunity.

A surprising number of companies carefully orchestrate hiring someone and then destroy a promising situation with a terrible first-day experience. It is not uncommon for a new employee to arrive at work and find that no one has prepared for his or her arrival. How would that make you feel?

Once again, your success in finding and keeping a new employee depends on proper planning and preparation. If you do your job correctly, a new employee's first day will confirm everyone's decision and establish a strong base on which to build a solid, employer-employee relationship.

First-day agendas differ by company, but let's deal with some typical aspects. The preceding chapter described the importance of communicating the selection to your current employees. You should never surprise them. The employee's supervisor, employees with whom the new employee will directly work, and any other company employees need to be told of the new employee's arrival and position.

Once a person has been hired, you may request information that was prohibited in the selection process. Some of this new information is required by law, such as evidence of U.S. citizenship. You may also need to know such things as age and the names of family members for purposes of insurance and retirement plan coverages. Once you have the information, you need to retain it in a separate file, and you are prohibited from using it to make internal employment decisions, such as promotions, transfers, or any other assignments. (See Chapter 9 for more on this.)

Employment Procedures

Who performs the various employment procedures depends on the size and type of company. It may be the owner, the owner's administrative assistant or secretary, a human resources professional, or the supervisor. Because that person must perform those procedures first, the new employee should report to that person or you should take the new employee to that person immediately after he or she arrives.

It's best to have a folder of materials ready for the new employee. What to cover will differ by state, locality, and company, but the following list should definitely be completed (unless some items were completed prior to the employee's first day):

Schedule. The first person to whom the new employee reports should describe the remainder of the first day: whom the new employee will see and what tasks are to be accomplished.

Federal proof of citizenship. This step is very important. Recall from the previous chapter the advice that you should instruct every new employee to bring along all appropriate documents you require. Any new employee who fails to comply should be sent home to retrieve the documents. By law you must have them before the employment begins. Some companies call the new employee on the day before the start date to remind him or her of what to bring. (See the list of acceptable proof on page 154.)

> **A surprising number of companies carefully orchestrate hiring someone and then destroy a promising situation with a terrible first-day experience.**

With the appropriate proof in hand you will need to complete a Form I-9, "Employment Eligibility Verification Form," which is available from the federal Immigration and Naturalization Service (check the blue pages of your phone book to find the closest regional office, or check online at: www.usdoj.gov/ins). Once completed, the form becomes part of the employee's personnel file.

Specifically required documents. Depending on your company and the job, you may require the new employee to furnish such job-related documents as a driver's license, a food handler's license, or a commercial driver's license.

Tests. If you require any tests as a condition of employment, such as a physical examination or drug tests, arrange for the employee to complete them before he or she reports to a supervisor for work or, as previously suggested, prior to the start date. But recall, you must require such tests of all employees or none (see previous chapter).

Security. You must assign to the new employee such security devices as photo identification, badge number, keys, and parking permits. You must also obtain any appropriate security documentation required by your company.

Compensation. Confirm base pay, overtime pay, pay dates, and any commissions and bonuses.

Direct deposit of pay. If you provide this option, review it and complete the necessary paperwork.

Tax forms. The employee must complete a Form W-4, "Employee's Withholding Allowance Certificate," the federal-tax withholding form. Your state and locality may also require their own tax forms. You can obtain the necessary forms from your accountant, employment attorney, or consultant. Federal forms can be obtained from the U.S. Internal Revenue Service (800-829-3676; www.irs.gov). For state or local forms, check with the secretary of state and local clerk's offices (again, see the blue pages in the telephone directory).

Benefits. You must explain any benefits that begin immediately and ask your new employee to complete any required documents. For example, the employee may wish to enroll dependents for medical insurance coverage, indicate beneficiaries for life insurance, or authorize payroll deductions for employee-benefit contributions. (You cannot make a deduction from a person's pay without proper authorization.) You should also provide written benefit information for the employee to take along for his or her reference.

If the employee isn't eligible for certain benefits immediately, tell the employee and provide written information anyway. Assure the employee that you will contact him or her and review the benefit(s) just before their effective date (more on this in Chapter 10).

Employee identification. If you issue employee identification, such as a badge or card, prepare it at this time. Instruct the employee in its use and required display.

Employee procedures. Cover any key procedures the employee immediately needs to know, such as where to park, which entrance to use, how to gain entrance, and what constitutes appropriate dress for the job, and supply the employee with a written description of such procedures. However, let the supervisor (if not you) review specific departmental and job procedures.

If you have an employee handbook, give a copy to the employee, and if required, have the employee sign a receipt as evidence that he or she received it.

Employment at will. If you hire under an employment-at-will policy and require that employees understand and agree to the policy, ask the employee to sign a statement to that effect. Some companies include the statement in their employee handbook. (See page 92 for more discussion. The Appendix contains a sample employment-at-will document.)

Code of business conduct and noncompete agreement. Some companies require employees to sign a code of business conduct— generally accepted business behavior as defined by the company—that the new employee agrees to abide by. It should include the company's rules and regulations and state who it covers and for how long. A noncompete agreement defines competitors and prohibited competitive actions, which the employee agrees to avoid. The agreement should state who it covers and for what length of time.

Generally, those agreements are limited to managers and certain professionals, but some companies require them of all employees. If specific elements apply to only certain classifications of employees, they should be identified.

Your employment attorney should determine whether you may require such documents and what they should contain. (The Appendix contains a sample.) If your company requires one or both of them, the employee should sign now.

CHECKLIST | **Employment Procedures**

Have you:
- **Prepared** for the new employee?
- **Gathered** all the required materials for the new employee?
- **Gathered** all necessary forms?
- **Arranged** to be available when the new employee arrives?
- **Made** all arrangements for placing the new employee on the rolls, including any external appointments for activities such as required tests or photographs?
- **Prepared** the employee's first-day schedule?

Special requirements. If your company has any special requirements, such as uniforms, use of personal automobiles, or lunch facilities, deal with them.

Conclusion. Conclude with questions and answers and be sure to welcome the employee on the most positive note before escorting him or her to the next activity.

You now you have a procedure for placing an employee on your payroll without surprises, because surprises begin employment on a negative note. If you properly informed the candidate when you made the offer (see Chapter 7) and if you follow this procedure, there should be no surprises.

The Supervisor

There are many clichés about first impressions, such as *Don't judge a book by its cover,* and they are all correct. However, the most important thing to remember about first impressions—whether positive or negative—is that they are difficult to overcome. So, make sure that the supervisor starts the employee off right.

The supervisor needs to have readied a work area and whatever materials the employee will require, such as a locker, computer, desk, sales book, or delivery van. One of the worst ways the supervisor can greet a new employee is like this:

> *"Oh, yes, you are starting today. You will be working in this area, but I haven't ordered a desk for you. I'll do that right now and it will be here in a couple of days. Till then, you can sit at the conference table."*

Wouldn't that make you feel really important and needed ? Contrast that with:

> *"Good morning and welcome. We are all so pleased that you have joined us. Let me show you where you will sit and introduce you to the others."*

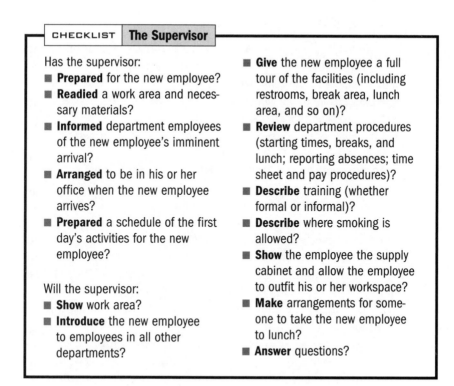

CHECKLIST | **The Supervisor**

Has the supervisor:
- **Prepared** for the new employee?
- **Readied** a work area and necessary materials?
- **Informed** department employees of the new employee's imminent arrival?
- **Arranged** to be in his or her office when the new employee arrives?
- **Prepared** a schedule of the first day's activities for the new employee?

Will the supervisor:
- **Show** work area?
- **Introduce** the new employee to employees in all other departments?

- **Give** the new employee a full tour of the facilities (including restrooms, break area, lunch area, and so on)?
- **Review** department procedures (starting times, breaks, and lunch; reporting absences; time sheet and pay procedures)?
- **Describe** training (whether formal or informal)?
- **Describe** where smoking is allowed?
- **Show** the employee the supply cabinet and allow the employee to outfit his or her workspace?
- **Make** arrangements for someone to take the new employee to lunch?
- **Answer** questions?

The supervisor also needs a checklist of what to cover during the employee's first day. Obviously, such a list will differ by company and job, but the checklist shows the kinds of things that the supervisor should be prepared to review. He or she will not only create a positive first-day experience, but will help the new employee be productive as soon as possible.

Training

Most new employees, even the most experienced ones, require some training that includes a general orientation to the new company and training in its specific procedures. In some cases such training is relatively brief. In others it requires considerable time.

Orientation

You should give all new employees a general orientation to the company as early as possible. It should cover:

- **The purpose of the company—its mission**
- **A brief history of the company**
- **A description of its organization structure**
- **The names of key personnel (and telephone numbers or other contact information)**
- **An introduction to the new employee's job and department**

To accomplish this orientation, some companies have very elaborate group programs using multimedia, such as videotapes, and presentations by senior executives. Others provide brief, one-on-one presentations. Still others have an individual video or pamphlet presentation for each employee. The choice of media and the degree of sophistication are far less important than providing the new employee with a broad picture of the company and where he or she fits in.

If you can accomplish the orientation in as little as 15 minutes (supplemented by a written document given to the employee), that will be 15 minutes well spent. You will have given the employee a context for the job—general knowledge about the company and his or her role in it. Some companies provide two orientations: a company orientation on the first day of employment and, if benefit programs begin later, a second orientation to benefits at that time.

Job Training

Training begins with a review of the job requirements and the new employee's qualifications. How much training does the person require to succeed? Is he or she new to the world of work and new to this type of job, or thoroughly experienced? One employee requires complete training and the other just an orientation to your procedures. If your company requires special skills, you may want to establish a standard training program for all new employees.

You or someone else has probably come up with a set of

procedures for every job in your company, that is, a best way to perform it. You have identified what the employee must accomplish and, often, how. That doesn't mean that individuality has no place, or that you should not be open to new ideas. You should allow for individual approaches and improvements, but even the most experienced professional needs to learn how you want things done.

A highly experienced waitperson has to know where things are kept, how and when to submit orders, and what the restaurant's specialties are. Even the most professional lab technician needs to know which procedures you use, how you report results, and how you handle materials. The most experienced shoe salesperson needs to know the styles and brands you carry, each line's strengths and weaknesses, and your inventory procedures.

With orientation, you will have given the employee a context for the job—general knowledge about the company and his or her role in it.

WHAT ARE THE OBJECTIVES OF YOUR TRAINING? Whatever the case, you need a list—an outline— of what you want the employee to know or do at the conclusion of training. Training professionals refer to the "behavioral outcomes" of the training— statements of desired behavior that represents what the individual has learned. For example, some of the behavioral outcomes for the training of a medical office receptionist might be the following:

- Answers all telephone calls in a friendly manner using the approved office greeting
- Transfers calls successfully as required
- Makes appointments as requested
- Registers appointments in journal and notifies doctor
- Greets visitors pleasantly
- Completes proper forms in preparation for patient's first visit

You can easily test those behaviors at the conclusion of training or observe them on the job. Whether you test or observe, you should always make an effort to evaluate the results of training.

A St. Louis marketing firm has order processors complete order forms for review at the conclusion of training.

A Wisconsin drugstore has employees locate items at the conclusion of training.

Some professionals require licensing or certification following standardized training or testing. For example, most states require real estate salespeople to obtain a license by passing a test. Some real estate offices hire people in nonsales positions while they attend school to prepare for the test. That can be an effective way to develop people skilled in your procedures even as they meet outside requirements.

WHO DOES THE TRAINING? Most training is done by current employees or by consultants.

Current employees. If your company is large enough, you may already have a human resources professional on staff who is skilled in training and would be an ideal choice. If you require a great deal of ongoing training, you may even want to hire a professional trainer to join your staff. Either way, you will have to ensure that the trainer possesses knowledge of the job content, as well as training ability.

If you don't have a professional trainer on staff, you can assign the training task to any employee who has expressed an interest in training or who naturally seems to help other employees learn new tasks. You may make a mistake, however, if you choose one of your current, best performers to train others. You may recall having had a teacher in school who knew the subject very well but was incapable of transferring that knowledge to students. Moreover, people tend to train others in how *they* do things, even if that will not or does not work for someone else.

Ultimately, you may simply have to assign someone to train a new employee and then evaluate how well the training is accomplished before assigning that person to train again. A side benefit of choosing someone who is already doing the job is that such a person is likely to improve his or her own job skills by training others.

Training consultants. You can also hire consultants to conduct the training for you. These practitioners have considerable training skills, but to be successful they also need to know your procedures or be skilled in the professions you hire. One source of such people is the membership directory of the American Society for Training and Development, which is also available online and can be searched (ASTD, 1640 King St., Box 1443, Alexandria, VA 22313-2043; 703-683-8100; www.astd.org).

Some outside services provide complete training programs. Some offer self-administering training programs. Others provide both programs and trainers. Depending on the subject matter and the skill of the trainer, you may discover numerous sources for all or part of your training:

A small amusement park in New Jersey uses a video training program in customer service for all its employees. It obtains the program from its trade association, the Outdoor Amusement Business Association in Minneapolis, Minnesota.

An Oregon computer-sales company sends all of its new employees to a "fundamentals of computers" course conducted by the local community college.

A small-engine repair center sends all of its new employees to a small-engine update seminar conducted by a major small-engine manufacturer.

A retail store has all new cosmetic salespeople spend a day at the store with a representative of the line they are handling.

A small manufacturer has all new supervisors participate in a "fundamentals of supervision" course conducted monthly by an employers' association.

A corporate legal department invites the developer of its matter-management (case-tracking) software to train its lawyers and paralegals in the use of the software.

The point is that you have many excellent sources to con-

┌───┐
│ CHECKLIST │ **Training** │
└───┘

Have you:

- **Prepared** an orientation program for all new employees?
- **Scheduled** orientation for all new employees on or shortly after their date of hire?
- **Identified** the training, if any, that each new employee requires and ensured that the supervisor agrees?
- **Given** the employee's supervisor responsibility for reinforcing the employee's training?
- **Selected** a person or organization to conduct training who has knowledge of the company's procedures and of the training being given?
- **Identified** a measure of training's effectiveness, either a test or observation on the job?
- **Considered** a mentor program?
- **Selected** prospective mentors and explained the mentor's role?

sider. Sometimes all it takes is a call to the local community college or your trade association or a review of trade magazines.

One final word about training goes back to hiring. Someone once said about the relationship between hiring and training: *If you want to make a silk purse out of a sow's ear, you better start with a silk sow.*

If you establish requirements for a job and hire someone adequately qualified to meet those requirements without further training, you obviously greatly reduce your training needs. Unfortunately, that is not always possible. In a tight labor market, you may have to hire less than fully qualified people and train them. In an especially tight labor market, some companies have even discovered that they have had to hire people who lack basic reading and writing skills and then provide that type of remedial training.

Mentoring

Companies often use a technique called mentoring to help new employees integrate themselves into the job and the company. The idea is to pair a new employee with a current employee who can answer questions and give general advice. Mentoring doesn't replace training, but complements it.

You should choose as a mentor someone who performs well

on the job and likes to work with other people, answer questions, and demonstrate skills. Do not choose the new employee's supervisor, because the reporting relationship can get in the way of the open give-and-take of mentoring. Ideally, the mentor is someone in a position similar to the new employee's.

The danger of mentoring is the same as when employees train other employees. Mentors tend to teach bad habits as well as correct ones. A mentor who complains a great deal can upset a person who has just joined your company. If you decide to use a mentor, select someone who can be a positive influence, and give the mentor literature or other information illustrating the mentor's role.

The U.S. Navy annually hires a number of recent college graduates for civilian positions, and it assigns to each a mentor who was a new employee within the past year. This practice helps the new employees adjust and perform up to standards more quickly and reduces new-employee resignations.

The Supervisor's Role in Training

The most effective developer of an employee is the employee's immediate supervisor—the person to whom the employee directly reports and who assigns work and appraises performance. The supervisor's opinions and suggestions carry significant weight with the new employee. When the supervisor supports training on the job, the results of training are usually quite effective. However, the opposite can also be true.

A small department store in Arizona has all new employees participate in two days of training. On completion they report to their department supervisors. Most supervisors support the training. They see it as preparing their employees for the actual job. However, one supervisor has established his own job procedures—procedures that differ from the ones covered in training. He generally greets his employees at the conclusion of their training with, "I hope you enjoyed your two days of relaxation. Now I'm going to tell you how to really do the job."

Not surprisingly, that supervisor's employees are the poor-

est performers and the most critical of training, and they enjoy the least personal development.

Because the supervisor must support training for it to be effective, supervisors need to know exactly what is being taught. Then, when the employee begins work, the supervisor can support and reinforce the training.

What If the New Employee Fails or Quits Soon After Hiring?

No matter how well you select people or how well you introduce them to the company, some new employees will quit shortly after joining you. Others may just not work out and you will have to let them go. These two problems require different approaches.

The Employee Quits

The most common reasons employees give for quitting soon after hiring are these:

- *"The job was not what I thought it would be."*
- *"I don't like the supervisor."*
- *"Another job I had applied for came through."*

The job was not what I thought would be may be your fault, especially if the selection process was not a two-way communication between you and the prospective employee. Other times, no matter how hard you try to correctly communicate the job, the employee may perceive things incorrectly. In their effort to obtain employment, people sometimes hear what they want to hear, and not what the employer actually said.

I don't like the supervisor may simply reflect a real personality conflict. Other times the employee's opinion may result from getting off to a bad start. If a supervisor tells a new employee things different from what was said in hiring or training, the person may leave.

Another job I had applied for came through is always a risk. People looking for jobs tend to apply at many companies, and sometimes they receive a second offer after accepting yours. However, they will usually stay with you once hired unless the other job is the one that they really want, they are disappointed in your job, or the other job offers a significant benefit, such as a much higher salary or a better location.

Whatever the case, you need to talk to the employee in an exit interview. You have invested in the individual, so you need to find out whether there is a problem that you can easily correct. Perhaps you can't save this employee, but you may learn something that you can correct, so that the same thing does not happen again.

Never make an exit interview confrontational and never become defensive, or you will learn little. Instead, make it an information-gathering meeting. You could approach it like this:

"Well, Allen, I understand you have decided to leave."

"That's correct. This job just is not what I wanted."

"Well, tell me, was it different from what we told you at time of hire?"

"Not really. But it was not something I want to do."

"It will help us in our future hiring if you can give me some specifics of things that bothered you."

"Well, I guess it was the way we had to work. I knew it was telephone work, but I thought it would be at a desk with some privacy. Instead, I was in this big open area in, like, a little cubbyhole. I couldn't stand it."

So should you redesign your offices? Not necessarily, but you should start giving candidates a tour of the work area so there are no surprises. And, as always, keep in mind that all departing employees are customers or prospective customers. At the least the employees will tell others why they left your company. You want their explanations to convey as much positive information as possible.

The Employee Fails to Perform as Required

No matter how well you and a candidate attempt to find out whether the job is right for him or her, mismatches will occur. A mismatch is the selection of an employee for a job that does not fit that person's skills or personal needs. Often an employee who quits has recognized such a mismatch. When an employee fails to perform, you may recognize a mismatch.

The key to confirming that you've placed an employee in the correct job is the evaluation of initial performance. As part of the job analysis, you established the standards of performance for the job—what an employee in that job must do to succeed—and you used those standards in hiring. But you need to reinforce the standards to each new employee as soon as he or she has joined your company, and you need to be absolutely sure that the new employee understands them. The job's standards of performance become the employee's guidelines, and each person needs to understand that you will use them to measure performance.

In some cases you will also need to communicate how long you expect a new employee will take before performing to standard. Establishing the breaking-in period gives you—and the employee—a way to measure the progress of the employee's performance and learning.

NO PROBATIONARY PERIOD REQUIRED. The hiring approach described in this book generally makes a probationary period unnecessary. Many companies still impose a probationary period, but it does not contribute to attracting good employees and becomes an excuse for the employer's failure to properly communicate what it requires and to train.

Consider the effect that a probationary period can have on the decision of prospective employee to join your company. In most cases, you are asking the person to give up a job. That is

---

> **CHECKLIST** | **An Employee Who Fails or Quits**
>
> Have you:
> - **Communicated** performance standards and measures to each employee when he or she begins a job?
> - **Measured** the performance of a new employee during the initial period of employment?
> - **Acted** positively to assist non- or underperforming employees to meet performance standards?
>
> - **Attempted** to transfer a good employee in the wrong job to one that better matches the employee's qualifications?
> - **Determined** the reasons why a newly hired employee has quit?
> - **Given** all departing employees an exit interview?
> - **Strived** to provide a constructive exit for an employee whom you must let go?

---

a permanent decision, yet you are not making an equally permanent decision. Instead, you are hedging your bet. You are saying that you will not make a final decision until after you see how the person performs. If you require a probationary period, do not be surprised if it reduces your offer acceptance rate.

In some situations a union contract may require a probationary period. Even so, stay with the approach described here. Employment should generally not be on a trial basis. It should be a serious commitment made by you and the candidate, one that you both work to make a success.

A POOR INITIAL EVALUATION. What do you do when the initial performance review indicates that the new employee is performing poorly?

First, you attempt to identify the problem. If it is something that you can correct, do so. Perhaps the employee is in the wrong job, but is otherwise a good employee—someone you wish to retain. If so, maybe a transfer to another job is in order. Try correcting the problem or transferring the employee before dismissal.

When there is no question that the wrong person was selected for the job, you must act. Delay will benefit no one. However, you need to also recognize that a person who left his or her job to join your company has a made a major investment, so consider that person's needs. Structure a separation that is the least damaging to the employee. Several weeks' notice, or pay in lieu of such notice, can ease the transition.

The way in which you let employees go communicates to your remaining employees how they might be treated. If they perceive your actions as fair and equitable, they will be more likely to give you the same consideration in all matters, and you will have contributed to good morale.

Learn from what happened. Determine why you both made the mistake, and then take measures to avoid making the same mistake in the future.

Summary

Always make the best possible selection of employees. Communicate exactly the desired performance and provide any necessary orientation and training. Review initial performance. If it is deficient, instead of letting someone go, attempt to discover what is wrong and correct it. That is good management and in the long run, that strategy will help you get and keep better employees.

So you've hired a new employee who is now trained and at work. Let's assume that nothing occurs during this initial period to cause the employee to leave, and you now have a permanent employee. How do you retain this employee and all other employees and keep them productive? That depends on how you treat them, a subject that is detailed in the next chapter.

Keeping Employees

"My advice: Don't worry about yourself. Take care of those who work for you and you'll float to greatness on their achievements." –H.S.M. BURNS

HY DO SOME EMPLOYERS NEVER SEEM TO HAVE problems retaining employees while others are constantly replacing employees who have left? The main reason is employment conditions.

A candidate who accepts a job offer generally wants the job and finds the described employment conditions acceptable. If the new employee discovers those factors live up to the employer's description of them in hiring, the employee tends to remain. Conversely, if employment conditions differ significantly from those described, employees tend to leave. (The exception occurs when the candidate accepts the job as a temporary one until a more desirable alternative turns up. In that situation, employment conditions are less significant.)

In the 1980s, a New England–based insurance firm decided it needed to recruit "bright, young, assertive, creative college graduates." Its theory was that as those people progressed through the organization, the company's culture would become more dynamic.

To fulfill this plan the company retained a consulting

firm. The firm structured a recruiting program that would appeal to the type of candidates the company wanted. The consultants sent campus recruiters who were similar to the desired type, and it carefully planned the interviews at the corporate office. Questions were developed and assigned. Interviewers were selected to project the "correct" image. Even the company's choice of hotel to house the candidates fit the desired image.

The company hired a total of 12 candidates after the consulting firm assured the company that they all had met its requirements. It assigned each new employee to a different department and created a development schedule for each one.

Two years later, all 12 had quit, and all for the same reason—they felt they did not fit the company's culture, its environment. The company had hired the type of employee it wanted, but its environment did not support "bright, young, assertive, creative" employees. When the bright, young employees discovered this, they asserted themselves and left for companies in which they believed their styles would better fit.

This example conveys a number of interesting messages for employers, but for the purposes of this chapter, the key one concerns the conditions under which the candidates accept their jobs. The company, through its consulting firm, projected an inaccurate image that appealed to the candidates but did not truly reflect the company's culture.

The first recommendation for keeping employees is for you to make sure that the realities of the job support what you told the candidates in hiring them. Employees, in their first few months, have little compunction about leaving. They haven't yet made a full commitment to your company and, in their job seeking, they may have interviewed with other companies that made them an offer even after they joined you.

You also need to create a working environment to retain *all* employees—not just those who you have recently hired. You must design that environment to meet your employees' needs and fulfill your company's mission simultaneously. This chapter and the next will examine methods that will contribute to your accomplishing that goal.

This chapter highlights the most significant factors that contribute to a positive employment atmosphere, while the next chapter deals with compensation and benefits.

Maintaining a Positive Work Environment

Most employees spend eight hours a day at their jobs, or about one-third of their normal day, in the work environment. Numerous studies have reported the following findings:

- **The employee's perception of the work environment** directly relates to job performance. A positively perceived environment produces positive performance, and a negatively perceived environment produces negative performance.
- **Employees think better of their jobs and their employer** when the environment is positive.
- **Improvement of the environment** generally improves employee performance.
- **A positively perceived working environment** contributes to employee retention, and a negatively perceived environment contributes to employee departure for other jobs.

You have everything to gain from creating and maintaining the most positive work environment possible for your employees.

Understanding the Hierarchy of Human Needs

Here's another way of thinking about how the working environment can contribute to or diminish employee performance and satisfaction: A number of years ago, the psychologist Abraham Maslow constructed what he called a *hierarchy of human needs,* which can be listed in inverse order of importance, as follows:

- ■ The need for "self-actualization"
- ■ Needs of the "ego"
- ■ The need for "socialization"
- ■ The need for "safety and security"
- ■ "Physiological" needs

Maslow theorized that these needs were common to all people and that people must satisfy their needs at one level before they begin to satisfy their needs at a higher level.

For example, meeting the most basic level of needs—physiological needs for oxygen, food, water, shelter, and health—is necessary to maintain life. Maslow's idea was that people attempting to fulfill their need for food and shelter won't concern themselves with issues of safety and security. Certainly, an employee who is deprived of oxygen won't be concerned with or even able to meet job standards.

In most cases, employers have already met their employees' basic needs, but perhaps not to the degree necessary for maximizing their performance and satisfaction. In other cases, there are jobs that attract employees who are seeking only to meet their most basic needs for food and shelter.

> *A chicken raising and processing company in the Southeast has a job called "chicken catcher." It is a terrible job. The employee must enter a large chicken coop (a dirty and unhealthy environment), scramble among hundreds of chickens, and grab the ones due for processing. The job has no redeeming features, so you might think it must have to pay a lot to find workers willing to do it.*
>
> *Wrong. The pay is very low. So how does the chicken company get employees?*
>
> *"These are people who are desperate for money," an operations supervisor confided. "They are generally rural people with little formal education who have somehow lost their small farms. They have no income and no skills. This job provides money for food, so they can continue to exist."*

Once an employee's physiological needs are met, the employer can consider the next level—safety and security.

Most companies make a major effort to provide a safe workplace. Studies have shown that numerous accidents in a workplace cause all the other employees to become concerned for their own safety, and their performance decreases.

Security can encompass not just physical safety but also the assurance of continued employment. The possibility of a layoff or reduction in employment tends to diminish productivity. Employees who feel unsafe or unsure in their employment won't make efforts to become a part of a work group (socialization).

A large company with a history of replacing older workers was rumored to be preparing to purchase a nonferrous metals fabricator in Texas. The rumor turned out to be untrue, but while it circulated at the nonferrous metals fabricator, production and attendance dropped and several employees quit. What was most significant, it was the better employees who quit.

The best employee performance is obtained when employees have had their lower-level needs met and are motivated by their higher ones:

- **Being an accepted part of a group working to meet common objectives (socialization)**
- **Being recognized for individual contributions (ego)**
- **Accomplishing one's own goals (self-actualization)**

Those needs contribute to superior employee performance and retention, but if employees begin to feel unsafe or insecure, they will concentrate on safety and security, performance will decrease, and employees will leave. For example:

When a postal worker shot several fellow employees, the national media reported it. During the next few days, other post offices around the country reported absenteeism and diminished performance. Postal employees no longer felt safe at work.

When an Atlanta day-trader shot fellow day-traders, a similar reaction occurred in small offices.

On-the-job harassment can also undercut an employee's sense of fulfillment at all levels, and in this case, the employee literally feared for his life.

> *An African-American state police officer resigned, citing continual harassment from white officers as the reason. He claimed not only that their actions affected his ability to perform his job, but also that he feared for his safety. He said he was unsure whether they would "back him up" in a dangerous situation.*

To maximize employee performance and motivate employees to stay, make sure that you are meeting their basic needs and providing both a safe environment and a sense of job security. Then you can concentrate on those factors that will produce high performance and employee satisfaction—socialization, ego, and self-fulfillment.

Let's take a closer look at the practical application of Maslow's hierarchy of needs to your company.

Meeting Your Employees' Physiological Needs

The most important employment condition that enables employees to meet their physiological needs is adequate compensation—enough to purchase food, shelter, and clothing. The required level of compensation to accomplish this varies with the region of the country and the employer, but whatever the amount, it must provide employees adequate income to support their perception of a minimum standard of living. (There are exceptions. Young employees and part-time employees often work for extra money rather than for money to support themselves. They may take a job between semesters or after school to obtain spending money or to add to savings. Some spouses may take a job mainly for outside-the-home socialization as well as extra money. Under these conditions, the employees generally aren't working to meet basic needs.)

When this book was published (and it may still be true), if you had visited the stores of a fast-food chain in different areas of the United States, you would have noticed that almost all had posted "Help Wanted" signs. Many of these signs stated the pay rate, and for the same jobs, it varied from the minimum wage (as of 2000, $5.15) to twice the minimum wage. Low unemployment was one reason for the differences. The stores may have had to increase pay to compete for employees, but even when unemployment was higher, differences existed. In some areas, the cost of living is simply greater.

A successful insurance agency representative in Iowa who wanted to move to California applied to several companies while he was on vacation there. A small agency offered him a job. In the interview he was asked what starting salary he wanted. The figure he gave was 10% higher than his current salary. The company agreed—with delight at having hired someone for so little.

After he had been on the new job for several months in California, he realized he had made an error. The income that had provided him a good living in Iowa plus 10% was barely allowing him to exist in California. Before the year was out, he had quit for a job paying more money.

The company should have known better than to take advantage of someone's ignorance of local costs.

Or consider this example:

The owner of a small department store in an affluent St. Louis suburb had difficulty attracting employees at the wage she was offering. She kept increasing the entry wage, but it still didn't produce results.

A consultant suggested that the owner was aiming at the wrong demographic group. Instead of seeking full-time employees, the consultant suggested that the owner create part-time positions for the many potential second-income wives in the area. Because those women would not be relying on their wages to meet their basic needs, the consultant reasoned, the rate of pay would not be an issue.

The department store owner created two half-day shifts

per week day and a full-day Saturday shift. She offered min-imum wage, a healthy store purchase discount, and flexibility with respect to time off. Within one year, she had full employ-ment and a waiting list of candidates.

Moreover, these women spent, on average, three-quarters of their pay at the store. A local competitor commented, "She's brilliant. Not only has she got a full workforce for the lowest possible wage, but the employees are also paying for themselves."

In this situation, the pool of prospective employees had already met their basic needs. By appealing to their desire for socialization and accomplishment, while simultaneously pro-viding flexible work hours, finding good help was no longer a problem.

Or this:

A small, garment-manufacturing company in the Northeast was sold. The new owner noticed that his stockroom man was paid only the minimum wage, but he had a family of five. The owner knew it was impossible for the man to support his fam-ily on such a wage, so he immediately doubled it.

To the new owner's surprise, the stockroom man was waiting to see him the next day. With tears in his eyes, he asked the owner to cancel the raise. He explained that the increased compensation made him ineligible for government assistance, and the assistance was of far greater value than the increase.

In this situation, more pay actually interfered with the employee's meeting his basic needs.

So far, I've discussed meeting physiological needs with a "livable wage." But compensation also contributes to an employee's ability to meet other needs further up the hierar-chy: security—extra income to protect against job loss and other emergencies; socialization—adequate compensation to participate with a desired group; ego—an income level that confirms your self-perceived worth; and self-fulfillment—attaining of individual compensation goals and objectives. (See Chapter 10 for more on this.)

The Importance of Benefits

Benefits are also relevant to meeting physiological needs, especially health insurance. Maintaining good health is a basic need, and doing so is increasingly expensive. Because health insurance meets such a basic need and is so expensive, it is almost always identified by employees as the benefit they most desire their employers to provide.

> *The owner of an automobile-collision repair shop in Atlanta had furnished health insurance for his employees for more than 20 years, and all of the employees had been with him at least 6 years. They had a good health and safety record, but the region and their industry didn't, and each year the cost of their health coverage increased.*
>
> *The owner finally decided he would have to cancel the coverage. He told the employees that he would increase their pay by the amount he had been paying for the premium, and they could purchase individual policies.*
>
> *Within 6 months, he had lost more than half of his employees. They had all gone to other shops that furnished health insurance.*

And another example:

A county in New Jersey decided to host a job fair for entry-level positions. It proved to be so successful that it became an annual event, well attended by employers and candidates alike.

At a meeting after one of the fairs, organizers asked the employers what questions candidates asked them most frequently. The top three were:
- *What is the starting pay?*
- *Do you provide health insurance?*
- *Do you have flexible hours? (The next chapter reviews that option.)*

Benefits, like other forms of compensation, are not limited to meeting just physiological needs. They also help employees meet other needs: Health benefits for dependents and life insurance for the wage earner enhance safety and security; vacations and employer-sponsored activities enhance social-

---

┌───┐

CHECKLIST | **Meeting Physiological Needs**

Have you:
- **Paid** your employees—particularly the lowest paid ones—enough to meet their basic needs (such as for food, shelter, clothing, and health?
- **Factored** into your pay decisions the cost of living in your geographic area?

- **Known** of any employee who is experiencing financial problems? Have you talked with the employee to see how you might assist, within appropriate limits?
- **Offered** health insurance for employees?

└───┘

ization; recognition of one's self-perceived worth feeds the ego; and attaining increased levels of benefits represents self-fulfillment. (Again, young people and part-time employees often work to fill time or earn additional money and have no intention of remaining with the employer. To them, benefits of any type have little meaning, and as one wag commented, "They think they're immortal anyway.") The next chapter covers benefits in detail.

Meeting Your Employees' Safety and Security Needs

Employees' need for safety and security applies not only to themselves but also to their dependents. Employees concerned for their safety and security will also have a difficult time producing the results you desire. Consider:

> *Al was employed as a research assistant to a Silicon Valley engineer. The work group had only four employees, but they were all confident that their work would produce major rewards within a year or two.*
>
> *Al had been married to his high school sweetheart for only three months when her doctors diagnosed her with a fatal form of cancer. They gave her only a year to live.*
>
> *Al and his wife were both orphans and lacked siblings or*

any other close relatives. They had only each other and literally no savings.

Al's work began to deteriorate as he took more and more time off to be with his wife. Eventually, he quit and enlisted in the U.S. Army. His reason? To obtain the free medical treatment he could not otherwise afford for his wife.

The engineering company Al left eventually went public. Its stock price soared, and today it is one of the largest employers in Silicon Valley. When I asked Al whether he ever regretted his decision, he said, "Absolutely not. I knew what the right priorities were."

A Redefinition of Job Security

The other type of security is job security. Employee opinion surveys consistently discover job security to be of major importance to employees. In the 1940s and 1950s, employees tended to accept jobs with the expectation of staying with a company until retirement, and companies desired and rewarded such loyalty. All that has changed in the past two decades. Today, employees accept jobs with little intention of remaining more than a few years (one consultant has suggested that the usual plan is for a three- to seven-year stay). Some companies even desire such turnover, and have replaced benefit programs that were designed to retain employees for many years with plans that are portable or can be converted to individual plans

Even so, job security can still be of major concern to employees.

A utility in Northern Virginia hired a consulting firm to "reengineer" its organization. The firm was noted for the results of its efforts, usually a reduction in workforce (or, as it is often called, "right sizing"). The employees knew all this, and rather than waiting for the inevitable results, many sought and accepted jobs with other companies. Those that found jobs quickest tended to be the better performers, so by the time the consulting firm had submitted its recommendations, many of the best performers had left.

Safety in the Workplace

Another important element of safety and security is the condition of workplace facilities. Most employers long ago learned that it is to their benefit, as well as to that of the employees, to ensure a safe and secure environment. In addition to the emotional and personal effects of accidents, the cost of injuries—both medical and time off—can be considerable.

WORKER'S COMPENSATION. All states require employers to provide some form of worker's compensation insurance. Although the specific requirements differ by state, they all basically cover medical costs and time lost because of injuries arising out of a person's employment. Worker's compensation is legally mandated, and the cost of purchasing such coverage is one of the normal costs of doing business. Of course, employers benefit because injured employees who receive benefits under worker's compensation usually may not also sue the employer. Because worker's compensation differs by state, you need to discover the specifics that apply to your employees. You can check your telephone book's blue pages for your state's labor department (or the equivalent) or ask your workers' compensation insurance carrier for such information.

OSHA. You also need to be aware of the Federal Occupation Safety and Health Act (OSHA), which applies to every private employer, with one or more employees, that is involved in interstate commerce. Very few companies don't fall within this classification.

OSHA requires the workplace to be free of hazardous conditions, and it covers a wide variety of issues, including smoking, restrooms, equipment, and sanitation. It includes provisions for inspections and enforced compliance. For a copy of the law and general information, you can contact OSHA directly at the U.S. Department of Labor—OSHA (Office of Public Affairs, Room N–3649, 200 Constitution Avenue, N.W., Washington, DC 20210; 202-693-1999) or visit its Web site (www.osha.gov).

If you are not familiar with the requirements of this act as they apply to your business, you need to obtain information

```
┌─────────────────────────────────────────────────────────────────────┐
│  ┌──────────────┐ ┌────────────────────────────┐                     │
│  │  CHECKLIST   │ │  Safety and Security Needs │                     │
│  └──────────────┘ └────────────────────────────┘                     │
```

Have you:
- **Ensured** that your company's work environment meets all federal and any state requirements?
- **Conducted** regular inspections of environment and safety conditions in your facilities?
- **Encouraged** employees to bring environmental and safety problems to the company's attention? Do you act on their suggestions?
- **Considered** the impact that company decisions may have on employee perceptions of safety and security, including job security?

and advice from an employment attorney or a safety consultant. Some worker's compensation insurance carriers provide assistance in complying with OSHA. They offer services such as employee training, workplace safety inspections, accident analysis, and industrial hygienists to test the air and noise in your workplace. Even when they do not provide such services, they can generally recommend someone who does.

Seeking Socialization, Ego, and Self-Fulfillment

Once employees have satisfied the first two levels of needs, they seek fulfillment at higher levels. These three levels—socialization, ego, and self-actualization—are referred to as psychological needs (although, to some extent, safety and security meet both physiological and psychological needs). In any event, you will most often deal with the psychological needs of your employees through these major activities: supervision, opportunity, equality, communication, and problem resolution.

Supervision

An employee's direct supervisor strongly influences whether the employee remains or succeeds with your company. The supervisor influences much of an employee's experiences through assignments, performance measurements, and attitude. In some companies the supervisor may be a department manager, a shift supervisor, or the owner of the business. The title isn't important. What is important is who directs the employee's activities. That person is the employee's supervisor.

The employee's supervisor is the employee's contact with the company's owner. The supervisor, by implementing the company's rules and procedures, creates the actual working conditions that the employee experiences.

A small-engine, sales-and-service shop in Minnesota was part of a large chain. The parent company had prepared an extensive set of employee procedures designed to retain and reward employees, and it gave each new employee a handbook outlining all those conditions.

The authoritarian manager of the shop continually ignored the corporation's employment conditions, and operated the shop and supervised its employees as he wished. The manager had the highest employee turnover of all shops in the chain. All the corporation's efforts to create a positive work environment were lost because of a poor supervisor.

Generally, people in nonsupervisory jobs gain little experience that prepares them to supervise others. Some people seem to be natural leaders—that is, natural supervisors—but most people require training in leadership skills. All companies need to train and educate all of their supervisors in their polices and procedures and ways to implement them.

Ideally, a prospective supervisor receives training just before moving into the position, or alternatively, just after moving into the position, say, for four hours a week during the first four weeks of work as a supervisor. Training provided too far in advance is forgotten by the time it is needed, and training provided too long after beginning the job must deal with habits—possibly some bad ones—already developed. The training should cover the factual matters of supervision—conditions of employment and their administration—as well as leadership skills: motivation, communication, performance measurement, discipline, and decision-making. Local community colleges, management or training consultants, and trade associations often provide courses to teach and develop leadership skills. Numerous consulting firms, as well as the the American Management Association, sell self-study packages. *Training and Development*, the monthly magazine of the American Society for Training and Development, contains many advertisements for such programs (look for it at your public library, or purchase a copy for $12 from ASTD, 1640 King St., Box 1443, Alexandria, VA 22313-2043, 703-683-8100, www.astd.org).

Never assume that a new supervisor naturally will know how to implement the job's requirements and represent your company's desires to the employees.

However, there are probably no standard or off-the-shelf courses that will cover your company's unique policies, procedures, and rules. Some small businesses hire a consultant (one experienced with their company, and its supervision and training techniques) to conduct training sessions or provide one-on-one coaching for new supervisors. Other companies supplement standard training courses with someone from the company who reviews their specific requirements with new supervisors. Others provide each new supervisor with a mentor—an experienced supervisor to coach and provide a source of on-the-job assistance.

The important point is never to assume that a new supervisor naturally will know how to implement the job's requirements and represent your company's desires to the employees. The supervisor is too important to maintaining a positive work environment to leave his or her actions to chance.

A consultant who assists companies in remaining nonunion reported that poor supervision is usually the main reason that nonunion employees form or join a union.

ASSIGNMENT. A supervisor makes many assignment decisions that affect an employee's work and work area, equipment, lunch, breaks, starting and quitting times, vacation, creation of work groups for specific projects, and overtime. Even with specific and detailed company rules, a supervisor can use assignments to reward or punish employees, and some organizations still traditionally haze new employees—a tradition that some supervisors not only allow but at times even participate in. Employee opinion surveys have revealed that when a company suffers from a severe morale problem, the source is usually poor supervisory performance.

At one time, employees put up with that sort of experience, but no longer. Today's employees believe that they should be treated fairly and with respect. You and your supervisors have to supply that kind of environment. You must properly train your supervisors in the company's rules and manage them to follow those rules.

The list that follows presents categories of rules that govern employee behavior on the job. Ideally, you should communicate these rules in writing to all employees and enforce them equally. The rules will vary for each company, but they generally should cover these topics:

- Punctuality
- Absenteeism
- Advance notification to the company of absence or lateness
- Emergency closings
- Dress code
- Use of alcoholic beverages and drugs on company property
- Use of company-owned equipment, including telephone, fax, copier, desktop computer
- Use of company-provided services, including e-mail, and Internet and intranet access
- Fighting and arguing on company property
- Possessing firearms on company property
- Time-reporting
- Breaks and meal periods
- Smoking
- Theft
- Confidentiality
- Abuse of company property
- Harassment, sexual or otherwise, of another employee

You must consider all these areas, plus any unique to your situation, and decide what sort of employee behavior is acceptable and unacceptable, contributes to the desired work environment and culture, meets your company's mission, and provides the type of customer service that most benefits you.

PERFORMANCE MEASUREMENTS. How you choose to measure an employee's performance will determine how well the employee performs, what training the employee requires, and how positive the employee will feel about the job and you as an employer. Performance measurement also provides individual and group recognition, and many times it determines an employee's compensation. Performance reviews are important to retaining good employees, and they generally accomplish their objective when employees perceive them as accurate and fair. That means they need to be based on measures and not opinion.

Supervisors and employees should share regular, informal, and continuing contact in the course of their normal work.

If you have defined the job well and developed, stated, and communicated performance standards or objectives as recommended in Chapter 3, objective and fair performance reviews will be relatively easy. Otherwise, you may have no basis for an objective review.

Generally, employers conduct performance reviews for a specific period of time—the most common seems to be annually—but a supervisor should never limit reviews to once a year. Supervisors and employees should share regular, informal, and continuing contact in the course of their normal work. If, at any point, a supervisor feels that an employee is having difficulty meeting standards or objectives or complying with rules, the supervisor should not wait for a regularly scheduled performance review. Such performance issues demand an immediate review with the employee.

When employees and their supervisors know the standards or objectives—that is, what constitutes doing a good job for the company—they both know how well the employee is performing and where he or she requires assistance. Thus, a performance review contains no surprises. Performance reviews are most effective when companies conduct them primarily for their employees' development—to improve performance where needed and to meet their employees' career objectives.

If performance reviews include salary adjustments, the employee's focus changes. Compensation becomes the paramount subject, and development discussions are less effective. For this reason, companies wisely separate the two types of reviews. They conduct a performance review first for development purposes. Then, a month or so later, they follow with the wage review. Obviously, the wage review will include information from the performance review, but compensation concerns don't affect the performance review. The supervisor can concentrate on helping the employee to improve performance and meet objectives.

CONDUCTING A PERFORMANCE REVIEW. In a performance review, the areas of needed improvement are identified and steps are developed to achieve that improvement. The steps should be as specific as other standards of performance and objectives, with completion dates and measures of performance. They then form part of the basis for the next performance review. A general outline of how to prepare for and conduct a successful performance review follows. The supervisor:

- **Documents** the employee's performance to standards
- **Identifies** the employee's three areas of best performance and the three areas of weakest performance
- **Notifies** the employee of a time and location for the performance review, which also gives the employee time to prepare
- **States** its objective at the beginning of the review and then reviews performance to standards or objectives
- **Allows** the employee to respond, thereby ensuring that the documented performance results are correct
- **Reviews** the employee's strengths and areas of needed improvement

The supervisor and employee discuss actions to provide for the necessary improvement or for the employee's further development.

The supervisor, with the employee's input, develops specific standards or objectives for the employee's next performance review.

THE SUPERVISOR'S ATTITUDE. Even when supervisors make assignments and conduct performance reviews by the book, they can become negative experiences if a supervisor has a poor general attitude toward the employee. You must concern yourself with how all your employees are being treated, reward the good supervisors, and correct or replace supervisors who are not performing as you desire. It's not enough that a supervisor gets the job done if the cost includes alienating valuable personnel, who end up leaving.

A study performed at a midwestern electric utility compared the results of supervisors who demonstrated a democratic style of supervision with those of authoritarian supervisors. It defined democratic supervisors as those who used good leadership skills (motivation and communication) and got their employees involved in decision-making, whereas authoritarian supervisors told their employees what to do and where, and were more concerned with results than with people. Over a 12-month period, the company gave both styles of supervisors a number of similar projects to accomplish.

The study found that, in the short run, the authoritarian supervisors achieved faster and better results, but at the price of the highest employee absenteeism, number of grievances, requests for transfers, and resignations. The other significant difference was that the authoritarian departments were less effective in dealing with any changes. For example, they did not easily accept new procedures.

The study concluded that employees will "take orders" for

CHECKLIST | **Supervision**

Have you:
- **Given** all employees regular performance reviews based on objective criteria?
- **Communicated** to your supervisors the type of management you wish practiced?
- **Provided** your supervisors with necessary training in management techniques?
- **Communicated** all company policies, procedures, and rules to your supervisors?
- **Included** employee relations as a part of supervisory performance reviews?

a short time and produce good results, but in the long run, employees who are involved in decision-making and are well managed perform better.

You can take three steps to ensure that your company has the correct style of supervisor.

1. You can hire or promote people to supervisory positions who see employees as a valuable asset of the company and want to work with them as well as through them. You can identify such supervisors by considering how they have dealt with people in their previous jobs and their interview answers. Some consultants offer tests that can provide insight (see the discussion of such tests beginning on page 115).

2. You must properly train your supervisors before they take on the role. Each should know what you expect, what the company's rules are, and how they can accomplish objectives through other people.

3. When you review the supervisor's performance, you should address how the supervisor is performing the portion of the job involving employees.

Opportunities

Benefits, compensation, supervision, and environment are all hygiene factors, as defined by Herzberg (see the discussion beginning on page 144). They don't motivate so long as they are present to the desired degree. When they are present to a greater degree, they encourage people to remain with you. When they are present to a lesser degree, they encourage people to leave. Herzberg identified some other working conditions as true motivators. A significant one is the opportunity for development and advancement.

Most employees work for more than just money; they work for accomplishment and recognition. Most employees are proud of what they do, and many people—not just those in professions—define themselves by their work. Also, our country's culture supports continually improving one's self. As a small-business owner or manager, you need to ask yourself these questions:

■ **How can my employees increase their job responsibilities?**

- **How can they learn more and develop new skills or greater excellence in their work?**
- **How can they become more satisfied with their accomplishments?**
- **How can I ensure that all employees receive proper recognition for their accomplishments?**

It's easy to assume that money is the primary motivator because employees usually want more of it, but Herzberg's hygiene analysis is accurate. Employees desire more money, but not just for what it can purchase. It is also how we keep score. More money means the employee is succeeding. It is recognition of accomplishment.

Even if your company provides very limited types of work, you need to consider the future for your employees—how they can push the limits of their present situations and grow in their work. Employees will remain if they see the opportunities for self-improvement like those in the paragraphs that follow.

CAREER PATHS. Career paths are outlines or descriptions of how an employee can progress with you. For example, a small advertising firm has an entry-level position of junior copywriter. The junior copywriter who achieves a certain level of experience and performance moves to copywriter, then to senior copywriter, and then to copywriting manager. In this example, all of the progressive positions are in the same area—copywriting—and form a job family.

It is possible to provide career paths that cross functional lines. For example, a career path at a financial-services company has an entry-level job of fulfillment clerk in the administra-

---

CHECKLIST | **Opportunities**

Have you:
- **Created** career paths and job families?
- **Encouraged** employees to obtain additional skills for promotion?
- **Offered** opportunities for advancement and growth through a promotion-from-within policy and by posting open positions?
- **Received** "lack of opportunity" as a reason that employees leave?

tion services department. From there the person normally moves to contract administration (contract-services department), sales administration (sales department), marketing representative (marketing department), and eventually a customer representative (client-services department). Here the career path is designed to provide experience in all functional areas before reaching the customer representative level.

PROMOTE FROM WITHIN. In Chapter 4 we discussed how to fill open positions from your current employees, and reviewed policies and procedures such as promotion from within and job posting. When those are your practices, your employees will recognize the opportunities they represent. However, if you have talented people with potential and you don't offer such opportunities, don't be surprised when employees leave for another company that does.

TRAINING. Sometimes an employee requires additional skills or knowledge to progress. You can provide what is needed through company training or some type of tuition reimbursement or assistance.

TRANSFER. You can also increase an employee's skills by transferring him or her—sometimes temporarily—to a job that has value and provides compensation equal to the employee's present one.

Equal Treatment

This book assumes and emphasizes the importance of treating all employees equally and fairly. Not only do employees who are not treated equally and fairly get upset, but other employees resent seeing their fellow workers treated unjustly.

Numerous federal laws cover discrimination in the workforce (see the discussion in Chapter 5). Most of them have different definitions of which employers the law covers, and many states have enacted similar laws that broaden those definitions. For example, the Civil Rights Act of 1964 prohibits discrimination due to race, color, religion, and national origin, and also prohibits sexual harassment. It applies to employers of 15 or more employees, but states have enacted similar laws that affect *all* employers. You need to know which requirements apply to your company. You can best accomplish this with the assistance of a human resources consultant or employment attorney.

Employees resent any sign of favoritism for any reason. Employees want everyone to be treated the same, whether required by law or not.

The same laws that regulate hiring practices also apply to employment decisions after you hire someone. Employment decisions include just about everything connected with work, from where someone sits to how much overtime one works. Making employment decisions on the basis of an employee's race, sex, sexual orientation, disability, religion, age, national origin, marital status, or veteran status is almost always unlawful unless there is a bona fide and justifiable reason for making a distinction. But, perhaps more to the point when discussing motivation, employees resent any sign of favoritism for any reason. Employees want everyone to be treated the same, whether required by law or not.

> *A fitness club hired a recent college graduate with a degree in physical education, and the club's owner quickly decided to train him to become the club's manager, in effect, predesignating him for promotion. The other employees felt that the new man was receiving special treatment and resented it. They were unfriendly toward him, and everyone else's morale and motivation suffered. However, the owner's strategy wasn't illegal. He may have displayed poor management, but there is no law against poor management.*

> *The director of a performing-arts organization in Tennessee fired her assistant. The rumor among the other employees was that the assistant had refused to date the director, and they felt that the assistant had been treated unfairly. Eventually, a delegation of employees complained to the director. Receiving no satisfaction, they took the matter public, opening up a can of worms that eventually got the director fired.*

CHECKLIST **Equal Treatment**

Have you:
- **Established** a nondiscrimination policy?
- **Communicated** your nondiscrimination policy to all employees by a handbook, bulletin-board notice, memo, or some other format?
- **Ensured** that all supervisors and managers follow your nondiscriminatory policy?
- **Described** a written grievance procedure for employees who believe that they have been treated unfairly or harassed, and have you communicated that procedure to all employees?

Discrimination means the act of distinguishing differences, say, in people. In many instances, that is a positive ability, but it is considered prejudicial and illegal if, when making an employment decision, you distinguish between people based on non-work-related differences (such as race, color, or national origin).

Your company should have a sound, nondiscriminatory policy that you communicate to all employees, and that your supervisors understand and implement. Such a policy should contain a specific procedure for notifying you of any discriminatory action. Here's a sample policy from a Connecticut-based company:

> *The company has a policy of nondiscrimination in all matters regarding the selection, hiring, termination, promotion, transfer, work assignment, scheduling, compensation, and any or all other conditions of employment. No decisions regarding employees will be influenced by race, sex, color, religion, national origin, age, disability, veteran status, marital status, or any other unlawful basis. No employee will be permitted to harass, intimidate, or subject any other employee to a hostile work environment because of that employee's race, sex, color, religion, national origin, age, disability, veteran status, marital status, or any other unlawful basis.*

SEXUAL HARASSMENT. Somewhat related to discrimination, sexual harassment is defined by most courts as unwelcome or unwanted conduct of a sexual nature (verbal or physical) when submission to or rejection of this conduct by an employee is used as a factor affecting hiring, evaluation, promotion, or other aspect of employment, or when this conduct substantially interferes with an individual's employment or creates an intimidating, hostile, or offensive work environment.

> *A small security firm hired its first female guard. The lunch-room walls were adorned with centerfolds from Playboy. The new guard complained, stating that she felt the environment was a hostile, sexual one.*
>
> *She talked to the owner, who told her that was "their way" and that she must adjust. Instead of adjusting, she quit and filed a complaint. The courts agreed with her. The Playboy pictures were removed, and the owner paid a fine and back pay.*

Management or supervisory staff are the people most often charged with discrimination in the workplace, whereas other employees are the people most often charged with sexual harassment. You can help prevent both charges by communicating to all of your employees the company's policy and the law, remaining vigilant, and being responsive to complaints of sexual harassment.

A GRIEVANCE PROCEDURE. To ensure that you correct any unfair or unequal actions, whether protected by the law or not, you need to have a published procedure for employees to bring such situations to your attention. You can distribute it to all employees as a separate document or as part of an employee handbook, or you can post it on a bulletin board.

Your procedure should include the following elements:

- **An assurance of confidentiality and no action against the employee who submits the grievance for having done so**
- **A statement of how and to whom the employee should submit the grievance**
- **A statement of when and how you will answer the grievance**
- **An appeal process for employees who disagree with the answer**

Those elements are also essential to your handling of any employee grievance.

FOR MORE INFORMATION. To learn more about federal equal-treatment and sexual-harassment requirements, you can contact the Equal Employment Opportunity Commission (1801 L St., N.W., Washington DC 20507; 202-663-4900; check your telephone directory's blue pages to find a regional office); visit its Web site (www.eeoc.gov), which publishes an abundance of material on pertinent laws, policies, and guidelines; or consult your employment attorney or consultant. You can also check with your state's department of labor, or the equivalent, to learn of any applicable state requirements.

Resolution of Employee Problems

No matter how well intentioned you and your company's management are, sooner or later problems will develop. Employees may disagree with their supervisors' actions, salary adjustments, or performance reviews, and employees may disagree with one another. All of this is normal human behavior. How your company deals with it will affect productivity and your ability to keep valued employees, so a procedure is needed to resolve such differences.

An informal procedure generally encourages employees to speak first with their supervisors. If that fails to resolve the problem or if the grievance concerns the supervisor, the employee should then speak with the supervisor's supervisor. Although a formal procedure almost always requires a written grievance, many formal procedures also recommend beginning with such an informal approach.

A formal procedure is generally more effective. Many grievances result from the interactions of employees with their supervisors, so unless employees have an excellent relationship with their supervisors, they tend not to use an informal approach and ultimately just quit. At its most basic and as outlined earlier, your procedure should describe the following points:

- How and to whom to submit the grievance
- When and how you will answer it
- How to appeal the answer

CHECKLIST | **Employee Problem Resolution**

Have you:
- **Established** a written procedure for resolving any employee grievances?

- **Communicated** the policy to all employees?
- **Investigated** and resolved all employee complaints?

AN OPEN-DOOR POLICY. Informal approaches are often part of an "open-door policy." At their simplest, such polices allow an employee to speak with any appropriate member of management concerning problems. Consider this example from a Florida-based real estate management company:

> *The company maintains an open-door policy—any employee may speak with any member of management. An employee who wishes to resolve a problem should do so by attempting to resolve it first with his or her supervisor and then with the senior manager of the division. If those discussions fail to resolve the problem, the employee may use the employee-grievance procedure or request a meeting with the human resources manager, vice president, or president. All parties will schedule and hold any such meeting at a mutually convenient time. If an employee disagrees with an action of his or her direct supervisor, another member of management, or another employee, the employee may use a grievance procedure.*

A FORMAL APPROACH. A typical, formal grievance procedure can be as follows:

1. Any employee who has a grievance should first discuss it with the person to whom he or she reports in an effort to obtain a satisfactory resolution.

2. If a discussion with the supervisor does not resolve the issue, the employee may then discuss the matter with the person to whom the supervisor reports. If the employee's grievance concerns some action by her or his supervisor, the employee may begin by speaking with the person to whom the supervisor reports.

3. If a discussion with the supervisor's manager fails to obtain a satisfactory resolution, the employee may make a request in writing for a review of the situation. The request must be signed by the employee, must state the specific problem, and must be received within 10 days of the incident causing the grievance. (Who should receive the request depends on your organization. If you have a human resources person, he or she may be the appropriate choice. If you don't and your company is small, perhaps it should go to you as owner. Some small companies deliver such requests to a consultant who provides human resources services as required; see Chapter 4).

4. Within 10 days of receiving of the employee's written request, the owner or designated person will meet with the employee to obtain information and with anyone else necessary to obtain additional information. The owner or designated person will notify the employee in this time period of the grievance's resolution.

5. If the employee is dissatisfied with the outcome, he or she may appeal the decision within five days. If the employee makes such an appeal, the owner or designated person (here again you must decide who will handle an appeal: a human resources person, an external consultant, or yourself) will meet with the appropriate people, including the protesting employee, and make a decision. The owner or the designated person will communicate that decision to the employee within 10 days and it shall be final.

Communication

The most common complaint in surveys of employee opinion is the lack of good communication. By good communication, employees mean accurate, timely, full, and direct communication from their employer. Employees want to hear official news from their management. Unfortunately, they often hear it from other sources, especially from other employees through the company grapevine. When this happens, they lose faith in their company's abilities to keep them informed.

A small wholesaler in Alabama wanted to move its warehouse from the north side to the south side of Decatur—not a significant distance. Before making a decision, they spoke with a number of commercial Realtors about available properties. One of the Realtors was related to an employee, and by the time the company announced its decision, all of the company's employees already had heard the story via rumor. The situation made the company look as if it had been holding back information.

Another example:

A motion-picture distributorship in Utah was notified that the building where it was located had been sold. The company decided to seek another location.

It began by meeting with all of its employees. The owners described the problem and asked for any suggestions. Eventually, the company leased space recommended by an employee. Even so, the employees suggested that management needed to communicate better.

GUIDELINES FOR GOOD COMMUNICATION. Accurate or not, employee perceptions determine whether communication is good or poor. You and your company will benefit by providing the best communication possible. Here are some guidelines that can help make your employee communications more effective:

You should be the source of information about the company—don't let the grapevine precede you. Be direct, complete, and truthful—even when the information may be unpopular. The longer you wait to communicate bad news, the worse that employees will perceive it.

Provide an open-door policy, a grievance procedure, or other ways to answer employee questions.

Listen to and interpret what employees say. Often they provide clues to bigger problems. For example, an employee will rarely say, "I'm insecure about my job." But an employee who asks questions about the future direction of the company may be expressing insecurity—and probably isn't alone in his or her concern.

Choose a regular format and schedule for whatever type of communication you choose. Employees should know how they will receive important information: at home by letter, in a department meeting, in a bulletin-board notice, or in a companywide meeting. What type to use depends on your company, its size, and the number of shifts and locations. Also, you may use different media for different messages.

For example, you might post open positions on the bulletin board. You could convey a change of business hours by individual memo to every employee, or a change in dress code at a department meeting with a handout of new pages for the employee handbook.

The point is to be consistent in the way you communicate and the media you use to deliver your messages, and select the medium that best supports your message.

Communicate as quickly as the message requires. If you see someone about to have an accident, you won't write a memo. You will intervene immediately.

> *Managers of a Washington, D.C., fuel-distribution company were considering relocation of its offices. They spent more than four months discussing the pros and cons of various sites. When they reached a decision, they called a meeting of all employees to announce it.*
>
> *The employees had had no indication that the company was considering a relocation, so the news was a surprise. The company also told the employees that they would be moving in two weeks, and encouraged no questions or discussion.*
>
> *The employees felt that they were being treated unfairly. Production dropped, several employees quit, and absenteeism increased.*
>
> *The owner of the company later said, "We really goofed! If we had communicated with our employees early on, they would probably have come to the same conclusion we did. Instead, we just told them what we were going to do. We did not give their*

needs any consideration. We lost a number of good people, and it took us almost a year to rebuild employee morale."

Head 'em off at the pass. An important fact of human behavior that business owners often overlook is that when people have information needs (and nothing creates such a need more than their employment) and the company fails to provide the correct information, they will create their own answers to their questions. When that happens, employers often find it difficult to persuade employees to believe and accept the truth because they must first dispel the faulty information.

A New York State nursery and landscaping company was considering closing one of its two locations. Before making the decision, the managers conducted a rather detailed study.

Ten employees learned about the study. Some asked the owner about it, but the owner refused to say anything until the study was complete.

Without real information, the employees decided that the real purpose of the study was to close both locations. By the time the owner announced the closing of one store, the employees had already convinced themselves that both were to close, so they ignored the owner's communication, and several employees quit in anticipation of a layoff.

When communication is two-way, you will also continually receive information you can use, and you will learn about your employees' needs. So listen. Be available. Accept what your employees tell you even if you know it is wrong. Remember, if someone believes something, it is their truth even if it's incorrect, and often what employees are saying is just a clue to some other message.

Two-way communication will also help you guard against malicious obedience.

A new supervisor decided to revise his department's internal work flow. His idea was good in principle, but he had based it on his experience at another company with different circumstances. His idea wouldn't work in his current situation.

One of his employees attempted to tell him so, but the supervisor defensively took the comment as mere disagreement with his idea. He said, "I am the supervisor, and that's the way I want it!"

The employees stopped commenting to him. As one said, "If that's the way he wants it, that's the way we'll do it!" And that's the way they did it, knowing full well that implementing the supervisor's idea would cause problems.

AN EMPLOYEE HANDBOOK. One of the most useful communication tools for employees is an employee handbook. It does not have to be large. Some handbooks are just a few photocopied pages. But whatever its length and format, the handbook provides each employee with a tangible summary of the rules and benefits of working for your company, and thus eliminates misconceptions.

The table of contents for a typical employee handbook follows. The good news is that you may already have written much of this as you have been following along in this book:

Introduction: A statement of the purpose of the handbook and how the employer will keep it current

---

CHECKLIST | **Communication**

Have you:

■ **Established** regular employee communication procedures, such as newsletters, bulletin-board notices, and meetings?

■ **Communicated** all company-related information as soon as possible to employees?

■ **Checked** all employee-related communications for completeness and accuracy?

■ **Established** a procedure for employees to ask questions?

■ **Furnished** all employees with written descriptions of employment conditions and benefits?

■ **Updated** all employee communications, such as handbooks, when you make changes to procedures or policies?

■ **Prepared** a manual for supervisors that covers company polices, procedures, rules, and the supervisor's role in their administration?

■ **Updated** all communications for supervisors, such as manuals, when you make changes?

Welcome letter: A letter from the company's owner or senior executive welcoming the new employee

Company mission: A statement of the firm's primary purpose

Key people: A list of them with relevant phone numbers and addresses. It could include pager and cell phone numbers, and e-mail addresses

Work schedules: The company's normal business hours and, if they differ, the employee's working hours

Employment-at-will: A statement of the company's employment-at-will policy, if it has one

Compensation: A description of pay periods and compensation policy and procedures

Benefits: A description of all benefits

Performance reviews: When the company conducts them, their purpose, and what records the company makes and maintains

Equal treatment: The company's equal-treatment policy and the grievance procedure for any alleged violations of that policy

Problem resolutions: A statement of how an employee can seek resolution of problems, including a description of any formal grievance procedure

Transfers, promotions, and training: Any policy on promotions and transfers, job posting, if available, and training programs provided

One caution: In a handbook you are making statements in writing, and aggrieved employees may be able to use them as the basis for breach-of-contract suits. For this reason, many handbook introductions contain a statement similar to the following:

This handbook is only a summary of conditions of employment. The details of all employment conditions covered in this handbook are governed by the master insurance policies and company policies and procedures maintained in the human resources office (if you have such an office or wherever you maintain them). Any differences between those documents and this handbook will be decided in favor of the formal documents. The company also has the right to revise all conditions of employment at any time, provided employees are given advance notice of any revisions. Any such notice will be provided as far in advance as possible. Times of advance notice will vary with government regulations and benefit carriers.

Some companies require employees to sign a statement that they have received the handbook, recognize that it is only a summary of employment conditions that the company can revise, and understand that they were hired under employment-at-will principles of the law, if it is applicable (see page 92).

A SUPERVISOR MANUAL. Just as an employee handbook is one of the most useful communication tools for employees, a supervisor manual can perform the same function for supervisors. It does not have to be large or specially written. It can be a collection of all company policies, procedures, rules, and forms. Whatever its length and format, it provides the supervisor with a ready set of instructions regarding the administration of company policies, procedures, and rules, and it can serve as a basis for training a new supervisor.

Here is a table of contents for a typical supervisor manual:

Introduction: A statement of what the manual's purpose is and how the employer will keep it current

Welcome letter: A letter from the company's owner or senior executive welcoming the new supervisor to his or her role

Company mission: A statement of the company's primary purpose

Supervisor's mission: A statement of the mission (objective or purpose) of a supervisor within the company

Key people: A list of them with relevant phone numbers and addresses. It could include pager and cell phone numbers, and e-mail addresses

Work schedules: The company's normal business hours and a description of any flexibility in working hours for employees

Employee rules: A definition of acceptable on-the-job behavior

Time sheets: An explanation of when they are required and how to complete them

Compensation: A description of pay periods, compensation policy, and procedures, and of the supervisor's role in wage adjustments

Benefits: A description of all benefits and ways in which a supervisor helps to administer them

Performance reviews: A statement of their purpose and a schedule for when the company conducts them

Equal treatment: The company's equal-treatment policy and the grievance procedure for any alleged violations of that policy

Problem resolutions: Methods an employee can use to seek resolution of problems, including a description of any formal grievance procedure and the supervisor's role

Transfers, promotions, and training: The company's policy on promotions and transfers, job posting, and training programs

Discipline: The company's policy and procedures regarding work-related infractions and the supervisor's role

In each area, the supervisor's manual includes any forms or records that he or she is required to complete or maintain.

Summary

Finding good employees can be time-consuming and cost-ly, just like obtaining good customers. Once you have a good employee, you should make every effort to retain that person. This chapter has dealt with some of the major considerations involved in retaining employees, by creating a positive work environment that meets their needs. The aim is to encourage you to develop specific goals for how you wish to treat and retain employees. Then create the policies and conditions of employment that will achieve your goals.

The Tangible Rewards of Work: Pay and Benefits

"The only way I can compete with large corporations is to treat my employees better, move them up faster, give them more money, and put mirrors in the bathrooms."

—JAMES R. UFFELMAN

 N THE PREVIOUS CHAPTER WE REVIEWED FACTORS THAT contribute to creating a positive work environment and meeting the needs of your employees. We examined Maslow's "hierarchy of needs" as it applies to conditions of employment. In this chapter we examine compensation and benefits, the relationship between them, and the contributions they can make to a positive work environment.

It is important to keep in mind that pay and benefits are both forms of compensation. Wages are cash compensation, while benefits are noncash compensation. Higher benefits generally accompany lower wages, and lower benefits accompany higher wages. Most employees perceive them as a package.

Establishing Compensation

In Chapter 7, we discussed compensation in the context of hiring. In considering a job offer, employees compare the compensation with what similar jobs in the industry and the community pay. Once hired, the new employee will compare his or her pay with the pay of other employees at the same company. As mentioned earlier, you can rest assured that employees know what other employees make.

To ensure that you pay all employees equitably, you must consider both the internal and the external worth of all positions. That will allow you to establish a compensation plan that reflects every job's relative value within the company and in the competitive marketplace.

There are dozens of systems to accomplish this. We review a basic one that deals with the key considerations.

Step One: Develop Your Company's Compensation Policy

Begin by stating your company's compensation policy. In creating your policy, consider what type of employees you wish to attract and retain, what you can afford and will agree to pay, and what your industry and community pay for similar jobs.

Here are some statements of compensation policies from three companies:

To pay wages competitive with similar jobs in the Central Alabama area as annually measured by a compensation survey.

To pay a base salary that is 80% of the competitive wage in the industry with a performance bonus that can increase total compensation to 140% of the competitive wage for employees who meet their goals.

To pay equal wages to all employees doing the same jobs and to provide individual incentives based on performance to standards.

No one compensation plan will serve all companies. Each of these three companies has established a policy that meets the individual company's needs and has developed a plan to meet the policy.

Once you have developed, written, and communicated the policy to candidates and employees, you must implement it as stated. Otherwise, it is a meaningless policy.

Step Two: Evaluating Job Worth

To determine internal equity, you must establish and define the relationships of jobs to one another and to the company. Begin by creating a list of all jobs in descending order of importance to the company. Then you can compare their relative worth to the company and assign each job a dollar value. Here are some ways to do this:

You can assign a specific number of points to similar key areas of each job such as required education, required experience, required skills, degree of independence (versus supervised actions), and degree of accountability (the job's value in terms of the company's budget or allocation of resources to meet the job's responsibilities). The total points that you assign to each job will establish its relative worth within the company.

A group of managers who know all the jobs in the company can rank the jobs (not the people in the jobs) in order of importance based on their experience with them.

Some companies use industry-published guidelines. If you are a member of an industry association, check with it.

The U.S. Department of Labor (DOL) provides several sources of assistance. The *Occupational Outlook Handbook* is available in print at bookstores and libraries, and is accessible online at http://stats.bls.gov/ocohome.htm. The DOL's staple *Dictionary of Occupational Titles* has been updated as the *O*Net Dictionary of Occupational Titles,* published by JIST Works, Inc. in cooperation with the DOL (8902 Otis Ave., Indianapolis, IN 46216-1033; 800-648-5478; also available in bookstores and libraries). These provide basic descriptions of most common job titles, and they will be helpful only if you have fairly standard positions.

The DOL's Bureau of Labor Statistics also publishes numerous "National Compensation Surveys" by city, which can also be downloaded from its Web site, which is located at: http://stats.bls.gov/opborder.htm.

Consultants provide this service (see Chapter 4 for more on how to locate them).

A small trucking company that completed this step compiled the following list of its jobs in descending order of importance (or value) to the company:

> Shift supervisor
> Route analyst
> Dispatcher
> Researcher
> Truck driver
> Hi-lo operator
> Data-entry clerk
> File clerk

Step Three: Job Compensation

The next step is to determine how much to pay for each job. One method is to research what your region or industry is paying for similar jobs. Wherever you are located and whatever your industry, an appropriate compensation survey will be available. Here are some possible sources of such surveys:

Some industries have trade associations that annually collect, compile, and publish compensation data from their members. If you are a member, check with it. If it doesn't conduct such surveys itself, it will know who does.

Chambers of commerce and employers' associations often perform similar services for the companies in their communities or know who does perform them.

Some management-and-accounting consulting firms conduct compensation surveys and sell them or provide them to their clients.

Check with your employment attorney or consultant if you have one.

For additional referrals, you can call:
- **The American Management Association** (1601 Broadway, New York, NY 10019-7420; 212-586-8100; www.amanet.org)
- **The Society for Human Resources Management** (1800 Duke St., Alexandria, VA 22314; 800-283-7476; www.shrm.org)

A survey may not cover all of your jobs, some of which may be unique to your industry or to your company, but some jobs are common to most. These common jobs and their corresponding industrywide or regional-average compensation can become *benchmark* jobs—that is, points of reference—for establishing your company's compensation structure.

For example, here is a list (in descending order of value to the company) of the positions from the small trucking company, mentioned earlier. The jobs in bold type are those for which the owner found similar positions in compensation surveys, so he highlighted them as benchmark jobs.

> **Shift supervisor**
> Route analyst
> **Dispatcher**
> Researcher
> **Truck driver**
> **Hi-lo operator**
> Data-entry clerk
> **File clerk**

Keep in mind that a job title alone doesn't identify the position. Its description or objective is what is important. A salesperson for an insurance agency has a job that is significantly different from the job of a tire salesperson. Job title may direct you to the correct grouping, but you must read the job's objective or description to discover if it applies. Surveys that do not supply such information have somewhat limited usefulness.

In the case of the small trucking company, the benchmark jobs had the following surveyed annual compensation:

Shift supervisor	**$40,000**
Route analyst	
Dispatcher	**$35,000**
Researcher	
Truck driver	**$32,000**
Hi-lo operator	**$30,000**
Data-entry clerk	
File clerk	**$22,000**

With this information (the external compensation for benchmark jobs and the relative worth of each job within the company), it was possible to assign a salary figure to each job:

Shift supervisor	**$40,000**
Route analyst	$37,500
Dispatcher	**$35,000**
Researcher	$33,000
Truck driver	**$32,000**
Hi-lo operator	**$30,000**
Data-entry clerk	$26,000
File clerk	**$22,000**

Once you have written a compensation policy, discovered competitive compensation information, and determined the relative internal worth of all jobs, you have a plan for paying a competitive wage that recognizes the proper relationships between jobs within the company.

Step 4: Individual Compensation

The last step is to consider the individual employees. Reconsider what you want to accomplish with compensation. Then create individual compensation to meet your objective and to recognize an employee's individual qualifications and performance.

One approach is to pay everyone in a similar job the same

wage, with increases based on productivity or changes in the cost-of-living index. For example, in one company all sales assistants received base pay of $8 an hour. The company adjusts that base once a year to reflect any increase in the cost-of-living index. However, individual employees receive a quarterly bonus on the basis of their performance as measured against standards.

Another approach is to create a range (or band) of pay for each job with the surveyed (competitive) rate as the range's midpoint. From the midpoint, a minimum and maximum are developed. With a maximum that is 150% of the minimum (not uncommon), a job with a surveyed rate of $40,000 would have a range as follows:

MINIMUM	MIDPOINT	MAXIMUM
$32,000	$40,000	$48,000

A salary range allows employers to pay employees according to their abilities and performance. They can hire new or inexperienced employees in the lower portion of the range, and increase their compensation as the employees learn the job and meet its performance standards. For employees who perform significantly above standard, the employer can increase compensation over the midpoint of the range.

In this system, the employer conducts an annual compensation survey, and as external competitive wages increase, the ranges move up. Likewise, any significant revisions to a job's responsibilities can result in a change to its internal and external worth and range.

Employers using this system typically create (often assisted by a consultant) and publish a matrix each year to provide a guideline for individual salary increases. The matrix reflects the amount the company can afford to pay, inflation, and competitive compensation. It relates increases in compensation to an employee's current position in the salary range and to his or her performance.

The following matrix was used by a firm in a region where a local survey projected average annual increases of 4% and where the previous year's cost-of-living index increased 3%. Because of the increased productivity of its employees and the resulting profit, the company felt it could give salary increases that were slightly higher than the cost-of-living and local increases.

Performance	Lowest Third	RANGE Middle Third	Highest Third
Above standard	7%–9%	5%–7%	3%–5%
Standard	5%–7%	3%–5%	1%–3%
Below standard	0%–3%	1%–3%	None

This company had assigned a salary range for every position. Employees in the middle third of a salary range earned approximately the competitive rate, while employees in the lowest third earned less than the competitive rate and employees in the top third earned more than that. The company also assigned standards of performance to every job, so that it could objectively measure each employee's performance during the previous year.

Surveyed compensation, benchmark jobs, salary ranges, and individual pay within a range are common elements of compensation plans, but as with benefits, there is no one correct approach for all companies:

A small Wisconsin confectionery manufacturer has compensation ranges, but only from the minimum to the midpoint. It hires new employees at a salary as low as possible in the range, but increases their pay to the midpoint as soon as the employees can perform to standard. Once an employee reaches the midpoint, he or she remains there with all other employees in similar positions until the company increases the midpoint in response to inflation. The company reviews its performance each quarter and pays employees a performance bonus in accordance with their department's or group's contribution to overall results.

An Iowa insurance company has salary ranges, but it pays above the midpoint only with an annual lump-sum check for performance above job requirements. This firm does not add increases to base pay.

An Illinois auto parts distributor pays a base wage within a salary range (minimum to midpoint) and then pays out a percentage of quarterly profits.

A Vermont specialty store pays all salespeople the same hourly wage plus 5% of the value of whatever they sell.

EQUAL PAY FOR EQUAL WORK. In 1963, the federal government passed the Equal Pay Act as an amendment to the Fair Labor Standards Act. It requires companies to pay both genders equally for similar work, except in the following cases:

1. If a valid seniority system governing pay exists. Often such systems are a part of union contracts, but some companies do give increases related to time on the job.

2. For some types of piecework. Piecework compensation pays the worker a specified amount for each piece of work accomplished (see the explanation in the next section). Small garment manufacturers and typing services commonly pay this way.

3. For merit-based pay plans. The level of compensation is based on performance.

Even these exceptions cannot result in a pattern of unequal pay for men and women.

If you do any of these, you need to consult an employment attorney to ensure that your system is valid.

OTHER COMPENSATION. There are many other forms of compensation. Chapter 7 reviewed bonuses and commissions. The same considerations mentioned there apply to retaining employees.

Some jobs are compensated in accordance with industry practices. Waitpeople typically receive a lower minimum wage (the law allows that) when they receive tips. Real estate and automobile salespeople receive commissions that are typical of their industries. But even where such industry standards exist, you can structure your company's compensation to retain good employees.

An automobile dealer in Michigan pays a standard commission to its salespeople, but it pays its exceptional salespeople (as measured by their sales) a higher commission—possibly the highest commission in the area. It's not surprising that the dealer has no trouble attracting and keeping good salespeople.

A small manufacturer in Georgia pays all of its employees 75% of the locally surveyed rate for manufacturing jobs, but it also pays a monthly bonus that is based on performance. The bonus allows high-performing employees to make as much as twice the locally surveyed rate. The owner commented, "It keeps the good employees and not the poor performing ones."

A Mississippi garment manufacturer pays on a piecework basis. New employees receive an hourly wage until they have acquired the skills necessary to meet performance standards. Then the manufacturer pays them on the basis of the number of pieces they produce in an hour. Again, the approach is designed to retain good employees—those who are good performers. (Most piecework plans must guarantee pay equal to at least the legal minimum wage.)

There may be as many compensation plans as there are companies. In this chapter we have reviewed one basic

---

CHECKLIST | **Compensation**

Have you:
- **Defined** the objective of your compensation program?
- **Written** a compensation policy statement?
- **Communicated** your compensation policy to all candidates and current employees?
- **Evaluated** the relative worth of all jobs in your company?
- **Researched** what competitive companies in your industry and region are paying?
- **Regularly updated** your information to ensure that your wages remain competitive?
- **Established** ranges of pay for each job, and put in place a system for determining what you will pay each employee within the range of pay for his or her job?
- **Paid** everyone equally for similar work or within legal exceptions?

---

approach, but there are others. The important considerations in determining your company's plan is to identify what you wish to accomplish, create the appropriate plan to meet that objective, and ensure that it meets all federal and state requirements. Whatever your plan, it can be a major factor in keeping good employees.

Now let's turn our attention to the other form of compensation—noncash compensation, or benefits.

Establishing Benefits

A company can choose to offer numerous benefits, most typically, paid vacation and holidays; medical and dental insurance; life and disability insurance; paid time off other than vacation and holidays, such as sick days, jury duty, and personal days; and retirement savings. Other benefits range from employee discounts on purchases of company products or services to on-site daycare facilities. As with compensation, a company should design its program of benefits to meet the company's goals, the needs of its employees, and its budget.

This book can't cover all possible benefits or even all of the usual benefits in great detail, but it will supply you with guidelines to make your benefits effective.

To begin, as with cash compensation, you need to recognize the type of employees you hire and their needs. For example, if you tend to hire young people, students, or spouses working for a second income, they probably won't see retirement savings as a significant benefit. If you tend to hire older people or married people with children, medical and dental insurance will probably have great appeal. If you tend to hire people who attend night school, tuition assistance will be well received. If your jobs attract people interested only in money, they may not care at all about benefits.

No one set of benefits will please all employees, but if you design your benefits to attract and keep the kind of people with whom you wish to work, you will also reinforce a positive environment for those employees. Keep in mind that, as an employer offering benefits, your choices will have tax consequences for your business and rules to follow. Therefore, before you proceed with any plan or offering, you should seek appropriate counsel from your accountant, lawyer, or benefits consultant.

Competitiveness

You should consider what benefits your competitors offer, and your competitors are other businesses who seek and hire similar people. If you have a small store and other small stores in your area offer their employees medical insurance, you'd better do the same to attract and retain your employees. If you are in an industry that normally provides free meals, you'd better do the same.

Your package of benefits must be competitive in the community as well as in your industry.

However, you do not compete for employees just within your industry. For example, a clerk will consider jobs with a variety of companies in any industry. This means you must be competitive in the community as well as in your industry.

When people look at jobs, benefits are not generally their first concern. They want to know what the job is and then what the compensation is. Benefits are usually the third consideration. Together, these three factors contribute to the candidate's decision, and their relative importance varies by individual. Once you've hired the person, benefits can be a major factor in retaining that employee by providing a degree of security.

You can design some benefits specifically to keep employees. For example, when you set up your company's retirement plans, you can choose a shorter or longer vesting period. Through the process of vesting, employees acquire a right to any contributions you made to their retirement plan. A longer vesting period encourages employees to stay with you. They want to remain until fully vested, and the longer employees stay with you, the less likely they will leave.

Or, as many employers do, you can plan to pay bonuses annually in January, so that employees probably will not leave from September through January. For this reason, it is not uncommon for job candidates to state that they are unavailable until the first of February.

Recall our earlier reference to Herzberg's theory (page 144) that compensation in the desired or assumed amount doesn't motivate people. The same is true of benefits. If employees feel that you haven't sufficiently provided the benefits that are important to them, they may leave or at least look for another job. On the other hand, if employees believe that another company can't match the benefits you offer, you have encouraged the employees to stay.

Identify the proportion of cash to noncash benefits that will appeal to your employees.

Although you might consider compensation and benefits separately, employees often consider them as a unit. Identifying the proportion of cash to noncash benefits that will appeal to your employees can produce benefits that support a positive work environment.

> *A firm in San Diego pays 20% above the going hourly rate for telemarketers. Its workforce is mostly second-income spouses and students who are primarily interested in the dollars they receive. The company recognizes that situation, gives money instead of benefits, and makes a point of communicating this policy to its employees—who are all happy with it.*

> *A small design and engineering group in Delaware employs engineers and designers, most of whom are in their 30s, are the primary wage earners in their families, and have several dependents. The firm pays wages that are slightly lower than those of its competitors, but it offers a fully paid insurance program that includes health, pharmacy, dental, and eyeglass coverage for employees and their dependents. By meeting its employees' benefit needs, the company enjoys very low employee turnover.*

Employees often overlook some employer-paid benefits that are legally mandated, yet are a significant cost to the employer. By law, employers pay for their employees' worker's compensation insurance, unemployment insurance, and one-half of their social security tax. You shouldn't hesitate to include those benefits in any illustration of the benefits package you provide to employees—its value to employees and its cost to you.

Cafeteria Benefits

One way to recognize and accommodate the varying needs of employees is to offer a "cafeteria benefit" plan. This approach assigns to each employee a total, annual-benefit "allowance," which he or she can allocate (spend) among a smorgasbord of benefits, each of which may "cost" a different amount. For example, a company could allow each employee $5,000 a year to purchase any combination of the following benefits:

Medical insurance	$2,000
Dental insurance	1,000
Life insurance	500
Disability insurance	500
Tuition assistance	1,000
Retirement savings	1,000
Vacation week	1,000
Personal day off	200
Total	**$7,200**

Obviously, $5,000 is not enough to purchase all the benefits, so employees must select those that are most important to them. Some cafeteria programs allow employees to purchase additional benefits with their own money, or to elect to receive money in lieu of benefits (subject to certain guidelines in the tax law).

Cafeteria plans not only provide the employees with options and control, but they provide the employer with a relatively easy way to control benefit costs, because the employer limits itself to paying a specific amount per employee. Still, a cafeteria approach to benefits may not be right for every employer. Such plans generally require additional administration time and record keeping. If you don't offer an adequate assortment of benefits, they are somewhat meaningless. If the majority of your employees desire the same benefits, they won't see the flexibility of choosing as an advantage, and if you have a workforce that, for whatever reason, is unconcerned with benefits, a cafeteria plan won't be worth your effort.

Time-Off Banks

Because benefits can play such an important role in finding and keeping good employees, companies continually look for new approaches. One such idea is time-off banks. The employer allots each employee a total number of days to be used as the employee wishes. Like a cafeteria-benefit plan, a time-off bank gives employees more control.

> **Decide what you want to accomplish— the reason you are providing benefits— and then design a benefit program to meet that objective.**

For example, if a company provides each employee with an average of two weeks (10 business days) of paid vacation per year and another five days for absences due to illness or personal reasons, the total comes to 15 days per employee per year. A time-off bank would allot each employee a total of 15 days per year to use for whatever purpose the employee wishes. This strategy gives employees greater flexibility and a greater sense of freedom in using their days off. It doesn't increase the number of paid days off, and it can assist in retaining employees.

Time-off banks are not good for every company. If you do not provide paid time off, you do not need one. If you have only limited time off, such as holidays and vacation, you do not need a time-off bank, and as with cafeteria benefit plans, the administration time and cost can be prohibitive for a small company.

Design of Your Program

You need to continually review your benefit program in terms of its objective and your employees' needs, and consider new approaches that may better meet both. First, decide what you want to accomplish—the reason you are providing benefits—and then design a benefit program to meet that objective. Your statement of objectives should answer questions such as these:

- **Do I want to use benefits to attract qualified candidates?**
- **Do I want to use benefits to help retain employees?**
- **What benefits are important to my employees?**

■ **What are the value and costs of each prospective benefit?**
■ **Do I want my benefits to be better than, equal to, or the same as my competitors' benefits?**

By answering such questions you can develop a goal for your benefit program—to meet the specific needs of your business. Then you can create a program to fulfill that goal. You can take the actions described in the section that follows to answer those questions and create your benefit program:

SURVEY YOUR EMPLOYEES. Identify the type of workforce you desire or have and the benefits that are important to them. If you believe you will be hiring young people for their first jobs, you can assume that a benefit such as retirement savings will probably be less important than vacation. If you expect to attract older people with dependents, you can assume that health insurance with dependent coverage will be important. (If you are just starting up and do not yet have any employees, you will have to make an educated guess.)

Do not ask your employees to vote for benefits. That strategy invariably results in a split decision, and the final outcome leaves many employees bitter. It also encourages them to act as a group rather than individuals. When that happens, the process becomes more of me-versus-them, and that, too, works against creating a positive work environment. (In some cases, allowing employees to vote has also been interpreted as recognizing employees as a defacto bargaining unit, that is, a union.)

As was suggested earlier, the best approach is to hire a consultant familiar with employee-opinion surveys to help you obtain the information without taking a vote.

CONSIDER YOUR COMPETITORS. Next, consider the benefits offered by other companies in your region and industry. Most communities have a local organization that annually conducts benefit surveys. Call your local chamber of commerce or employer's association and ask. If you are a member of an industry group, check with it. It may either conduct such surveys or know who does. If you have an employment attorney or consultant, check with him or her.

Also there are large organizations and professional associations that provide such services or know who does, such as the American Management Association (1601 Broadway, New York, NY 10019-7420; 212-586-8100; www.amanet.org) and the Society for Human Resources Management (1800 Duke St., Alexandria, VA 22314; 800-283-7476; www.shrm.org).

CONSIDER COST. Determine how much you can spend on benefits. Then compare what you can spend with what the benefits you are considering will cost. This comparison may lead you to make some adjustments.

Do not ask your employees to vote for benefits. The outcome often fails to promote a positive work environment.

If the benefits you are considering cost more than you can afford, you may have to decide which ones to offer—probably those that are of highest priority to your employees. Or, you may want to have the employees contribute to the cost. For example, you can pay for your employee's health insurance, but require the employee to pay for any dependent coverage (a common practice).

Most surveys report that the average cost of an employee's benefit package is between 25% and 35% of compensation. Of course, this figure depends on what benefits are included. Some companies include government-required benefits, such as social security and worker's compensation, and some do not. Some companies include the value of vacations, and some do not. Also, small companies may find that 25% to 35% of compensation will buy fewer benefits, because they often cannot purchase them as economically as larger organizations.

You need to determine just how much you can afford to spend on compensation and benefits—keeping in mind that there are tax consequences for your company. (Your accountant can assist you in determining what those will be.) Then rank the benefits you are considering by importance to your employees and calculate the cost of each. You can then determine which ones you can afford, and you can supplement them with some lower- or no-cost benefits.

In the process, consider such options as a cafeteria plan or a time-off bank, described earlier. Those relatively new approaches help employers simultaneously control benefit costs and give employees more control of their benefits.

Consider Maslow's hierarchy of needs and the options you might offer employees to help meet those needs.

LOOK AT LOWER-COST ALTERNATIVES. Here are but a few types of no-cost benefits to consider. They won't work for every business, but they demonstrate what some employers are doing. These are benefits that will probably be well received, but cost you relatively little. In each case, you must choose or develop options that suit the mission of your business. It gains little to make your employees happy if your work isn't getting done. On the other hand, don't just dismiss these ideas because you've never done it that way; take a look at how the following options, adapted to your business, might work for you and your employees.

Flexible hours. Employees generally see a lack of rigid starting and quitting times as positive. It gives them a degree of flexibility and control. A typical, flexible-hours program states that employees must be at work for eight hours per day (Monday through Friday) during normal business hours. The company's business hours are from 7 A.M. to 7 P.M.

Obviously, not all businesses can offer such flexibility. Retail stores and other businesses need to ensure that their employees are available when there are customers. They could still offer flexible hours, but require all employee to have their supervisor approve their choice to ensure that adequate staff are on hand when needed.

Some businesses believe that their employees must be available during the same hours for critical, face-to-face communication. Others have decided that such communication tools as voice mail, e-mail, and phone- and video-conferencing largely overcome that need. For example, it might be acceptable for someone to leave work early to meet family obligations and answer e-mail queries from other staff for a couple hours in the late evening, as long as other staff receives their answers by the next business morning.

Dress code. Many employees perceive a relaxed dress code as a positive benefit. They prefer the freedom to work in jeans and a sweatshirt versus more formal business attire. A casual dress code can save your employees the high cost of buying and dry-cleaning dress clothing.

But again, you have to be sure this decision supports the mission of your business. Customers do not always look favorably on dealing with employees in jeans or other casual attire, so you need to consider their perceptions, too. Some smaller companies get around this problem by announcing "clients on site" days, meaning that when customers are expected to visit the office, everyone must dress in standard business clothing. Other businesses, including some banks, have chosen a casual "uniform," such as khakis with a shirt bearing the corporate logo, for everyday wear, or have instituted "casual Fridays."

> **Part-time employees who prove valuable may be willing to move into full-time jobs when their obligations change.**

Whatever your strategy, make sure that all your employees understand what you mean by "casual" dress (for example, khakis but no jeans, and no shorts in summer). And, if you want to help your employees save money, make sure that your rules don't force them to go out and buy a new, "casual" wardrobe.

Part-time schedules. Many employers have discovered that in a tight labor market, it is easier to fill vacancies with part-time employees than with full-time ones. Often, the people interested in part-time work have other responsibilities, such as children in school or a dependent parent, or they are in school themselves. Or perhaps they don't need to work full-time, but want to work just part-time to get back into the workforce gradually, for fun, or to keep up their skills. They can work four or five hours a day, or two or three days a week, but not eight hours a day for five days a week. Part-time employees who prove valuable may be willing to move into full-time jobs when their obligations change.

Some full-time employees may wish to move to a part-time schedule, say from five days a week to four. If you can accommodate a valued employee who wants to work part time, you

CHECKLIST | A Wide Array of Benefit Possibilities

There are many types of benefits. Some, such as memberships for employees in a local health club, may be unique to a community, and some, such as retail-employee purchase discounts, may be unique to an industry. This list exemplifies the wide variety of employee benefits that exists:

Health
- Health care insurance
- Medical savings accounts
- Dental insurance
- Vision/eye glasses insurance
- Prescription insurance
- Reimbursement, flexible-spending or set-aside accounts

Time off
- Paid vacations
- Paid time off for illness
- Paid family leave
- Paid time off for personal reasons
- Unpaid leave of absence, such as for a sabbatical
- Combining of all time off into a single, employee-controlled bank of days

Retirement
- Employee-contributory investment program for retirement, such as a 401(k)

- Portable pension benefits
- Profit-sharing plans

Stock incentives
- Employee stock-ownership plans
- Stock options

Insurance
- Short-term disability insurance
- Long-term disability insurance
- Life insurance
- Long-term care benefits
- Accidental death and dismemberment insurance

Miscellaneous
- Organization day-care center or assistance
- Organization exercise facility or assistance
- Organization dependent day-care center or assistance
- A company-provided car
- Subsidized parking or transit pass
- Interest-free or bargain-rate loans
- Employee discounts
- Tuition and book assistance
- Financial counseling
- Preretirement counseling
- Legal assistance
- Dress-down days
- Rewards for accepted employee suggestions
- Identification of employee of the week, month, year

may well be further ahead than if you lose the employee altogether. However, make sure that you both clearly understand the arrangement: If you expect that a part-time employee will do five days' of work in three or four days for three or four days' pay, you and your employee are headed for frustration that could result in your losing the employee anyway.

Work at home. With the advent of desktop computers, networking systems, the Internet, and other types of home-office equipment and services, workers can perform many jobs as easily at home as they can in your facilities. If your work lends itself to such an approach, you should give it consideration. You may find that employees are even more productive at home, without wasting time in the daily commute or on office chit-chat.

For some employees, the distractions of home life, especially if they lack adequate child care, will prove counterproductive. You're not responsible for that. You must, however, make sure that your employees understand the standards of performance for their jobs—on site, at home, or elsewhere. If you expect to be able to reach an employee at home during regular business hours, say so. If the job has production requirements—say, 25 Internet queries processed per hour during an eight-hour shift—then by necessity, the employee won't be able to leave to pick up the kids or give the baby a bath.

Government Regulations

The government doesn't regulate the provisions of all benefits, but it has made laws and regulations that affect many of them. Generally, federal requirements do not apply to all small companies. For example, the federal Family and Medical Leave Act (time off for family needs) covers companies with 50 or more employees; the federal Consolidated Omnibus Budget Reconciliation Act (health insurance coverage for terminating employees) covers employers with 20 or more employees; and the federal Americans with Disabilities Act (protection of employees with disabilities) applies to employers of 15 or more. Each of these federal statutes affects benefits.

State regulations also will probably affect your provision of employee benefits. Different states focus on different benefit issues, and even when they focus on the same ones, their legal approaches to them may vary.

An employment attorney or consultant can help you meet the letter of the law, but you need to be aware of the following key, federal requirements.

ONE FOR ALL, AND ALL FOR ONE. While you must, by law, provide some benefits to all employees (for example, see ERISA, below), you will promote good employee relations by providing *all* the same benefits to *all* employees unless you have a justifiable reason for doing otherwise (for example, providing a car for salespeople who call on many companies in the area, uniforms for waitpeople in a theme restaurant, or a reserved parking space for mail-delivery people). Employees will accept such reasonable exceptions just as they do higher pay for higher positions, but they tend to resent differences in benefits without an apparent reason and often perceive such an approach as discriminatory.

BENEFITS FOR PART-TIME EMPLOYEES. Many companies hire part-time employees and pay them cash with no benefits, but there's a limit on that: When employees work more than 1,000 hours in a 12-month period, they are generally considered full-time and then are eligible for any full-time employee benefits, such as health insurance. Recognizing this situation, many companies base some benefits on the amount of time worked. For example, an employer may provide vacation as a percentage of total hours worked, so that an employee working half-time would receive 50% of a full-time vacation. At the least, you need to be aware of the number of hours part-time employees are working, so that if they exceed 1,000 hours, you can reclassify them as full-time.

ERISA (the federal Employment Retirement Income Security Act). Employers can choose whether to offer fringe benefits, such as health insurance or a retirement plan, to their employees. If they do choose to offer benefits, and they have six or more employees, then those benefit plans are governed by a federal law called ERISA. For instance, ERISA requires employers offering health insurance to make it available to all employees regardless of health status and, if participation is mandatory, prohibits employers from charging different premiums to different employees. (Employers must offer other types of benefits, for which they receive tax benefits, to all employees. For instance, employers often have special life insurance or retirement plans for top management.)

ERISA requires employers to file their benefit-plan descriptions with the U.S. Department of Labor. In many cases your benefit (insurance and retirement plan) providers will do this for you.

Some states require employers with six or more employees to offer health insurance. Check on this with your human resources consultant or with your employment attorney.

> **Employees who work more than 1,000 hours in a year are generally considered full-time and are eligible for any full-time benefits.**

THE OLDER EMPLOYEES PROTECTION ACT OF 1990. The federal Older Employees Protection Act of 1990 requires employers to provide benefits for employees over 40 years of age that are identical with those provided for younger employees and, in most instances, to pay the same amount in health premiums for all employees. This act also stipulates certain requirements regarding retirement and retirement benefits. It prohibits forced retirement before age 70 (except in the case of a company executive who is entitled to receive an annual company-paid pension with a legislated minimum amount after age 65). Also, it prohibits the firing of an older employee just before receiving retirement benefits.

COBRA (the Consolidated Omnibus Budget Reconciliation Act). COBRA is another federal law covering benefits. COBRA requires companies with 20 or more employees to offer employees and their immediate families an 18-month extension of health insurance when their employment with the company ceases. The employee must pay for the extended coverage, but COBRA ensures that he or she can retain similar coverage for that period.

If your company is covered by COBRA, you are required to notify employees of their rights at the time they separate from your firm and provide information about how they can obtain the extended coverage. However, COBRA does not require the employer to pay for the coverage.

THE FAMILY AND MEDICAL LEAVE ACT. The federal Family and Medical Leave Act requires a company to offer full-time employees who have worked at least 1,250 hours during the previous 12 months up to 12 weeks of unpaid leave per year to care for a newborn child or for a child or a parent who is seriously ill. Employees are guaranteed their job or one of equal status upon their return. State requirements may extend the period. For example, in the District of Columbia, employees may take up to four months of unpaid family leave.

MILITARY LEAVE. Companies must also allow employees in the National Guard and military reserve units to take time off to meet service requirements. (Some states require the employer to pay the employee regular wages for up to 14 days.) Their jobs (or ones of equal status) must be available upon their "timely return." Generally, timely return means 90 days after returning from duty, but if an employee is injured during service, the time can be extended as much as one year and 31 days.

THE JURORS' PROTECTION ACT. The law protects the jobs of employees who are called for federal jury service. Many states have passed their own such laws for courts under their jurisdiction, and you need to know what they are.

This section is not intended to make legal experts of its readers, but merely to acquaint you with a few of the federal and state requirements regarding benefits—the ones that most frequently involve small employers. (A 10-volume set of books, each volume containing some 1,000 pages, covers federal and state employment laws.) As a small-business owner or manager, you need to ensure that your company complies with all of them. The best approach is to obtain assistance from an employment-law attorney and a benefit consultant as you establish, administer, or redesign your benefit program.

Benefits are a key factor in attracting and keeping good employees. Whatever benefit program you offer should be based on that objective and be competitive with others in your industry and region. It must also be what you can afford and meet government requirements.

Benefit Administration

At this point you may be thinking, "How can I ever know and comply with all these regulations? Who is going to do all the necessary comparison shopping for benefits in the first place, not to mention the necessary record keeping, communicating, and other aspects of generally administering my employee-benefit plan?"

These are excellent questions for a small-business owner. Large companies generally have a human resources department staffed with professionals in these areas, but few small businesses can afford one. So, here are several suggestions:

Most of the required benefits (social security, worker's compensation, and unemployment insurance) can be handled by your accountant or whoever does your payroll; that person will make the necessary deductions and send payments to the appropriate state and federal agencies.

Employee insurance—such as life, disability, health, and dental—is usually purchased directly from an insurance carrier or through an insurance agent. Most types of insurance can be administered by the employer or by the carrier or agent on the employer's behalf. You can decide who will administer them, on the basis of the size and capabilities of your staff and the costs, when you purchase the insurance.

Time off for such reasons as vacation, holidays, jury duty, military service, sickness, and personal reasons is probably best administered by whoever prepares your payroll or your accountant. However, someone in house will have to let that person know when and how much to pay in accordance with the policy and procedures you establish. If you need assistance, you can obtain it from a benefits consultant or employment attorney or from a detailed benefits book.

Get a Lawyer

For help with deciding what benefits to offer, what legal regulations apply to your company, and what type of records to maintain, you need to hire someone with that knowledge or obtain such services as needed. This section contains some suggestions for finding a benefits consultant, employment attorney, and other source materials:

There are several sources for employment attorneys:

Call your local university's law school, if it has one. Often they can provide lists of attorneys, and some schools even have third-year students who will provide assistance for experience and a very small or no fee.

Call the attorney you probably used to help you set up or purchase your business. The attorney may have a colleague in the same office who specializes in employment law, or may be able to give a good recommendation to someone else.

Talk to other small-business owners and ask for their recommendations. Whom do they use and are they satisfied?

Look in the *Yellow Pages* under "Lawyers." Many lawyers state their areas of specialty. You want one that deals in benefits, labor law, or employment law.

Call the state bar association. It will not specifically recommend anyone, but it may give you a list of attorneys specializing in the appropriate areas. Your state's bar association may maintain a Web site with a referral feature. For example, the Minnesota State Bar Association features a search feature for the public in the area of labor and employment law.

Look for the *Martindale-Hubbell Lawyer Directory* in the reference section of your local library. It lists attorneys with their education and experiences. Even easier, use the Martindale-Hubbell

Lawyer Locator (http://web.lexis-nexis.com/marhub), which allows you to search online for a lawyer by a variety of criteria, including location, area of expertise, size of firm, and law school. You can read a detailed profile of each lawyer that the search produces.

Review the Westlaw and Lexis databases. For access to these services, available by subscription only, check with the reference librarian at your public library or at a law library, such as you might find at a university law school or a county courthouse or judicial center.

Find a Benefit Consultant

You can find benefit consultants through a similar search.

Check the *Yellow Pages* under both "Consultants" and "Management Consultants." Many advertise their specialties.

Ask your accountant. Many accounting firms have a consulting division or relationship with a benefits-consulting firm. Even if they do not, they may have worked with a consultant on another project.

Visit your public library and look for the *Directory of Management Consultants,* published by Kennedy Publications and Consultants News (One Kennedy Place, Rte. 12 South, Fitzwilliam, NH 03447). It is primarily a listing of search firms by type and region. A similar publication is the *Consultants and Consulting Organizations Directory,* published by Gale Group (Detroit).

Search the Internet. Start with the key words, "benefit consultant." You may discover the exact expertise for which you are looking.

Consider a Publication Service

Publication services will keep you abreast of what is occurring in employment and benefit law and regulation. Here are two such services that provide copies of federal and state laws and regulations, as well as regular update pages that describe new laws and court interpretations: *Guide to Employment Law and Regulation* and *The Employee Benefits Handbook* (both published by West Group). These are available by subscription, and cost at least a few hundred dollars per year; you can also look for them at your public library or at a law library at a local university or county courthouse.

How Do I Decide Among These Choices?

The publication service is excellent to have for continual reference, but you're probably better off not spending the money if you don't have someone who can and will use it and keep it up to date.

Employment-law attorneys will be able to advise you on the legality of your benefits. Some, but not all, are also excellent in developing benefit plans.

Benefit consultants are generally very good at developing benefit plans and setting up their administration, but sometimes they lack full knowledge of current legal requirements. As was mentioned in Chapter 4, some independent consultants furnish their time in increments as small as an hour. These people may be able to supply exactly the benefit services you require.

You might wish to take advantage, as needed, of the services of both a benefits consultant and an employment attorney. The consultant can help with designing your plan and the attorney with complying with all laws. If you contract solely for the services you require, the cost need not be prohibitive.

Let's assume you have several names. How do you determine whom to select? Here are some suggestions:

- **Obtain recommendations** from existing and former clients.
- **Check credentials,** including education, experience, and professional memberships and certifications.
- **Ask questions** to determine whether the person has experience and knowledge in your area of need.
- **Ascertain that the charges** will be within your budget.
- **Find out how detailed** the invoices will be.
- **Find out what type of expenses,** as well as standard fees, you will be responsible for.

- **Ask whether fees are charged** daily, hourly, or in some other way.
- **Check to see whether there is a minimum charge.** For example, one firm may have a minimum charge of one hour. If you have a 15-minute telephone conversation, it will bill you for one hour. Another firm may bill for actual time.
- **Find out whether you pay for services provided or pay a retainer** (usually a monthly amount guaranteed for a year or other contractual period), and if the latter, whether time is credited against the retainer or is charged in addition.
- **If you do not know the going rates,** interview at least three candidates for the service you need.
- **If you go to a consultant's office,** consider what the address and condition of the office says about the individual.
- **Be sure—most important of all—that the chemistry is right.** Does the consultant listen to you or tend to talk? Do you feel comfortable with the person? Is it someone who will correctly represent your company?

Summary

Compensation, whether in the form of wages or benefits, is a key element to both attracting and retaining employees. With careful thought, you can design a program that will significantly contribute to obtaining and retaining the type of employees who perform best for your company.

Throughout this book, we have emphasized the need to establish a clear objective or goal before undertaking any management activity. That's such a logical step that it's hard to imagine that anyone wouldn't automatically perform it, but in reality, managers, owners, and entrepreneurs often ignore it. Those people are all by their very nature active. They want to get on with things, so they tend to jump in without first deciding exactly what it is they wish to accomplish. If you take the time to establish a clear and specific objective, you will find that its implementation and your success will follow more easily.

Appendix

HIS SECTION OF THE BOOK CONTAINS COPIES OF the various forms mentioned in the text. They are presented in a format for photocopying, and permission to do so is hereby granted. However, you may find it more helpful to use these as a starting point for developing your own forms. Here are some hints for using some of the forms:

WORKFORCE PLANNING (PAGE 255). Use this form to adjust your calculation of employee needs for reality—for example, how many employees do you expect to be away from work during the year?—and let it guide your hiring for next year, too.

JOB DESCRIPTION (PAGE 256). Use this form to outline the key elements of any job you're trying to fill.

JOB POSTING NOTICE (PAGE 257). Use this form to announce job openings to internal candidates (current employees). Employers usually post it on a bulletin board designated for that purpose, along with application forms for the positions, or on a Web site.

APPLICATION FOR POSTED POSITION (PAGE 258). Employers usually supply this form adjacent to the job-posting bulletin board or present it as an electronic form on their Web sites. They may also make it available only on request.

EMPLOYEE RECOMMENDATION (PAGE 259). Provide it in the usual places (see above), or make it available on request. Employers often enclose it with an employment application in an envelope.

EMPLOYMENT APPLICATION (PAGES 260–63). This form is designed to be printed on two sides of an 11" x 17" sheet of paper and then folded in half to make a four page 11" x 8" booklet. Consider carefully the appearance of the completed application. Because candidates are also customers or prospective customers, give the application the same thought you would give any other public relations piece.

EMPLOYMENT REFERENCE CHECK RELEASE (PAGE 264). Whether you include it as part of your employment application or present it separately (as it is here) at the interview, you should obtain permission from every candidate to check the information and references that he or she provides.

EMPLOYMENT REFERENCE CHECK FORMS (PAGES 265–67). The forms presented here can be used to check employment, education, and personal references.

JOB OFFER (PAGE 268). You can use this form as a checklist for making a job offer by telephone or in person.

EMPLOYMENT-AT-WILL AGREEMENT (PAGE 269). If you require this type of agreement, have the new employee sign it on his or her first day of employment.

CODE OF BUSINESS CONDUCT/NONCOMPETE AGREEMENT (PAGE 270–75). Whether you should require your employees to sign such documents and, if so, what their content should be, are decisions you should make with the advice of your employment attorney. The sample, from a Florida-based company, is supplied solely as an example of what one company does and should not be used without first obtaining legal advice.

Workforce Planning

	JAN.	FEB.	MAR.	APR.	MAY	JUNE	JULY	AUG.	SEPT.	OCT.	NOV.	DEC.
Needed or required number of employees												
Minus adjustment for turnover												
Minus adjustment for absences												
Minus adjustment for vacations												
Minus adjustments for other factors												
Equals total needed or required number of employees												

Use of this form is described in Chapter 2, beginning on page 21.

Job Description

Title _____ Department _____

Reports to _____ Supervises _____

Objective: To _____

RESPONSIBILITIES

1. _____

2. _____

3. _____

4. _____

5. _____

6. _____

7. _____

8. _____

9. _____

10. _____

11. _____

REQUIREMENTS

Education _____

Experience _____

Special qualifications _____

Use of this form is described in Chapter 3, beginning on page 29.

Job Posting Notice

Title_____Department_____

Reports to_____Supervises_____

Compensation_____Date to be filled_____

MAIN RESPONSIBILITIES

1._____

2._____

3._____

4._____

5._____

REQUIRED QUALIFICATIONS

Education_____

_____

_____

Experience_____

_____

_____

Special qualifications_____

_____

_____

Application must be submitted by (date)_____

_____

_____

Use of this form is described in Chapter 4, beginning on page 52.

Application for Posted Position

Name_____ Department_____

Reports to_____ Date_____

Position applied for_____

QUALIFICATIONS

Education_____

_____

_____

_____

Experience_____

_____

_____

_____

Special qualifications_____

_____

_____

_____

Other_____

_____

_____

_____

Signature_____

Use of this form is described in Chapter 4, beginning on page 52.

Employee Recommendation

I recommend the following personl for employment consideration:

Name_____

Address_____

_____

_____

Phone number(s)_____

E-mail address(es)_____

Relationship_____

Position recommended for_____

A copy of the person's application or résumé is attached.

Recommending employee's signature_____

Date_____

Job title_____

Department_____

Phone number(s)_____

E-mail address(es)_____

Use of this form is described in Chapter 4, beginning on page 53.

Employment Application

Date_____

Name_____

Address_____

_____

Phone number(s)_____

Second (permanent) phone number_____

E-mail address(es)_____

Position, positions, or type of position desired _____

_____

_____

_____

EDUCATION

High school_____ Dates_____

Course of study_____ Degree_____

Grade-point average/class position _____

Community college_____ Dates_____

Course of study_____ Degree_____

Grade-point average/class position _____

College _____ Dates_____

Course of study_____ Degree_____

Grade-point average/class position _____

Graduate school_____ Dates_____

Course of study_____ Degree_____

Grade-point average/class position _____

Trade or professional school_____ Dates_____

Course of study_____ Degree_____

Certificates or licenses_____

WORK EXPERIENCE (List in order of most recent first)

Dates_____ Position_____

Employer_____

Address_____

_____

Phone number(s)_____

Reason for leaving_____

Starting compensation_____

Current or previous compensation_____

Department _____ Supervisor_____

Dates_____ Position_____

Employer_____

Address_____

_____

Phone number(s)_____

Reason for leaving_____

Starting compensation_____

Current or previous compensation_____

Department _____ Supervisor_____

Dates_____ Position_____

Employer_____

Address_____

_____

Phone number(s)_____

Reason for leaving_____

Starting compensation_____

Current or previous compensation_____

Department _____ Supervisor_____

Continued on page 262. Use of this form is described in Chapter 5, beginning on page 90.

Employment Application (continued)

Dates_____ Position_____

Employer_____

Address_____

_____

Phone number(s)_____

Reason for leaving_____

Starting compensation_____

Current or previous compensation _____

Department _____ Supervisor_____

Other training related to desired job (dates, schools, and description)

_____

_____

_____

_____

Experiences related to desired job (dates and description)

_____

_____

_____

_____

Skills related to desired job (description and amount)

_____

_____

_____

_____

Any limitations related to successfully performing desired job

_____

_____

_____

_____

REFERENCES

Two personal references (names, addresses, phone numbers, and relationships)

_____

_____

_____

Two professional references (names, addresses, phone numbers, and relationships)

_____

_____

_____

The candidate certifies that all information provided in this application is true and complete, and recognizes that in submitting this application, authorization for the investigation of all information is given. Furthermore, the candidate understands and agrees that any misrepresentations or omissions will be sufficient cause for cancellation of the application or termination of employment if already employed.

The candidate grants the company the right to contact any or all places and people mentioned on this application (with the exception of the current employer) and any institution, school, or agency for information about the applicant with respect to the applicant's qualifications, and hereby discharges and exonerates the company, its agents and representatives, and any person supplying information.

Your signature to this document indicates your understanding of this policy and agreement with it.

Signature_____ Date_____

Use of this form is described in Chapter 5, beginning on page 90.

Employment Reference Check Release

As an candidate for a position with (company name), I grant (company name) the right to contact any or all places and people mentioned on my application and résumé or in an interview (with the exception of my current employer) and any institution, school, or agency for information about me with respect to my qualifications, and I hereby discharge and exonerate (company name), its agents and representatives, and any person supplying information.

Signature_____ Date_____

Use of this form is described in Chapter 5, beginning on page 105.

Employment Reference Check

Candidate_____ Date_____

Company called_____ Phone number(s)_____

Name of contact_____ Title_____

Dates of employment_____ to_____

First job_____ Department_____

Last job_____ Department_____

Starting compensation_____

Ending compensation_____

Reason for leaving_____

Performance_____

Problems_____

Attendance_____

Personal relationships_____

Accomplishments_____

Recommendations_____

Other_____

Reference check conducted by_____

Use of this form is described in Chapter 6, beginning on page 129.

Education Reference Check

Candidate_____

Date_____

School called_____

Phone number(s)_____

Name of contact _____

Title_____

Dates of attendance _____to_____

Curriculum_____

Major_____

Year graduated_____

Degrees_____

Class standing_____

Grade-point average_____

Rewards and achievements_____

Problems_____

Record of attendance_____

Relationship to candidate_____

Recommendations_____

Other_____

Reference check conducted by_____

Use of this form is described in Chapter 6, beginning on page 131.

Personal Reference Check

Candidate_____

Date_____

Person called_____

Phone number(s)_____

Relationship to candidate_____

Dates of relationship: from_____to _____

Applicant's qualifications_____

Areas of needed improvement _____

Problems_____

Relationship to candidate_____

Recommendations_____

Other_____

_____

_____

_____

_____

_____

_____

_____

Reference check conducted by_____

Use of this form is described in Chapter 6, beginning on page 132.

Job Offer

Candidate _____

Date _____

Time called _____

Phone number(s) _____

Position _____

Start date _____

Starting compensation _____

Additional compensation _____

Supervisor _____

Department _____

Report to (whom) _____ Where to report _____

Items to bring (e.g., proof of citizenship) _____

Benefits to describe _____

_____

_____

_____

_____

Use of this form is described in Chapter 7, beginning on page 157.

Employment-at-Will Agreement

(Company name) hires all employees under an employment-at-will policy. The terms of this policy allow the Company at any time to terminate any employee (unless otherwise covered by the terms and conditions of a specific employment agreement with the employee), and any employee to terminate employment at any time by providing proper notice (one full pay period). Any statements regarding discharge, promotion, or other aspect of employment shall be interpreted consistent with an employment-at-will relationship between the Company and its employees, regardless of whether such statements are in written form or transmitted orally to employees. The policy of at-will employment shall be applied consistently for all employees without regard to their position, length of service, and standards of performance. The policy may be varied in the case of an individual only by a written agreement with the employee that is signed by an officer of the Company.

Your signature to this document indicates your understanding of this policy and agreement with it.

Signature_____ Date_____

Use of this form is described in Chapter 8, beginning on page 173.

Code of Business Conduct/Noncompete Agreement

1. POLICY

The Company holds its employees to the highest standards of business conduct. To provide employees with guidance in identifying business situations that create, or have the potential to create, legal and ethical problems, or the appearance of such, and to provide direction in handling actual and potential situations, the Company has developed a Code of Business Conduct.

2. SCOPE

The conditions of employment contained in this policy and procedure apply to all departments and employees of the Company.

3. ACCOUNTABILITY

3.1 Human Resources is accountable for obtaining at the time of hire, and updating each calendar year, a Code of Business Conduct statement signed by the employee indicating the employee's understanding of and agreement with the Company's Code of Business Conduct.

3.2 Every employee is accountable for performance that fulfills the specific terms and conditions of the Company's Code of Conduct as well as its intent.

3.3 All managers are accountable for ensuring that their employees operate within the specific terms and conditions of the Company's Code of Conduct as well as its intent.

4. FORMS

A Code of Business Conduct statement for employee signature.

5. LAWS

The Company intends to operate in full compliance with all laws, so that each employee is to conform his or her business conduct to the requirements of local, state, and federal laws. The Company's Code of Conduct requires faithful compliance with all laws by all employees, even if an employee believes that noncompliance does not present ethical implications.

6. ETHICS

Compliance with local, state, and federal laws does not eliminate the necessity for employees to consider the business ethics of their activities. All employees must be aware of the fact that a legal business practice can still present an ethical problem.

7. APPEARANCE

It is critical to avoid even the appearance of any illegal or unethical behavior. Employees must behave in a fashion that retains the trust of our clients, other employees, stockholders, and the public.

8. CODE OF BUSINESS CONDUCT QUESTIONS

Any question regarding whether or not a specific behavior is covered by the Code of Business Conduct should be presented to the Human Resources Manager. The Human Resources Manager will have the question reviewed by the appropriate parties (generally the Senior Vice President of Operations and the General Counsel) and return an answer to the employee.

9. ASSOCIATE

For purposes of the Code of Business Conduct, an associate is a member of an employee's immediate family, a trust of which an employee is a trustee, or a trust in which a member of the employee's immediate family has a beneficial interest.

10. CODE OF BUSINESS CONDUCT

10.1 Outside Employment

As a condition of employment, every employee is expected to devote his or her full professional efforts to the Company's business. Therefore, outside employment should not be accepted if it in any way interferes with job requirements or performance. It is recommended that an employee notify his or her manager prior to accepting any such outside employment, and the manager will advise the employee of any possible conflict with Company employment.

10.2 Personal Financial Interest

Employees are expected to exercise their judgment and discretion in the best interests of the Company. To avoid any conflict of interest or appearance of conflict of interest:

10.2.1 All employees and their associates should not have a direct or indirect interest or investment, other than minor ownership of publicly traded stock, in any business enterprise that is doing or seeking to do business with the Company.

10.2.2 Employees (and their associates) in positions to influence, make, or carry out investment or purchasing decisions should avoid investment in any business enterprise in which the Company has an investment, from whom the Company may make, has made, or is making a pur-

Continued on page 272. Use of this form is described in Chapter 8, beginning on page 173.

Code of Business Conduct/Noncompete Agreement (continued)

chase, and from whom the Company is receiving products or services.

10.3 Confidential and Proprietary Information

During the course of employment, employees may obtain access to information with respect to the Company's business or the business or personal affairs of its customers or other employees. All such information must be kept confidential, and employees must adhere to all local, state, and federal privacy laws. This responsibility continues after an employee is no longer employed by the Company, and the Company will pursue all available legal remedies to prevent current and former employees from benefiting or misusing such confidential Company information.

10.4 Corporate Opportunities

No employee may appropriate, for his or her own or any associate's personal profit or advantage, any business venture, opportunity, or potential opportunity discovered or developed in the course of employment that is in any way related to any business in which the Company is or may become engaged. No employee may, directly or indirectly, compete with the Company in the purchase or sale of any property, right, interest, or information; nor may any employee or associate knowingly acquire, directly or indirectly, anything of probable interest to the Company without the prior written consent of the Company.

10.5 Dealings in Securities

Federal law prohibits security transactions based on nonpublic information. Generally, such laws apply to a person when purchasing, selling, or otherwise trading the securities of, or any other proprietary interest in, any business or enterprise in which the person participating in the transaction is in possession of material information concerning the transaction which:

10.5.1 Relates in any way to the business or financial condition, present or prospective, of such business or enterprise; to its products, services, or facilities, whether already available or in the process of development; to the market for its securities; or to the Company's investment intentions with respect to such business or enterprise, and

10.5.2 Has not been made generally known to the public, and

10.5.3 In the case of any such action taken by an employee or any associate of an employee on the employee's or associate's behalf, has been obtained in the course of such employee's employment with the Company.

10.6 Gifts, Entertainment, Loans, and Other Favors

All transactions between the Company and customers, suppliers, and vendors must be based solely on the merits of each decision. Employees and associates may not accept or give gifts, entertainment, loans, or other favors from or to any business, enterprise organization, or person that is doing business or seeking to do business with the Company, which is a competitor of the company, or with which the company is considering investing.

10.6.1 The prohibition against loans does not apply to loans made in the ordinary course of business from established banking or financial institutions.

10.6.2 The prohibition against the giving and receiving of gifts and other favors does not apply if the gift, entertainment or other favor is of such nominal value that it could not be reasonably regarded as placing the recipient under any obligation to the donor.

10.6.3 The prohibition against the giving and receiving of entertainment does not apply if the gift or receipt of a gift is approved in advance by the company, reflects normal business practices, is of nominal value, is legal under applicable law, meets generally accepted ethical standards, and would not embarrass the Company if disclosed.

10.7 Political Contributions

Federal and state laws regulate the conditions under which a corporation may make political contributions or may ask employees to make such contributions. Except as allowed by law, the Company forbids the use of Company funds or resources for contributions to any political party or committee or candidate or office holder of any government – federal, state and local.

10.7.1 Employee will not be reimbursed by the Company for any individual political contributions.

10.7.2 The Company may authorize resources to defray administrative expenses of a Company affiliated political action committee to the extent clearly permitted under law.

10.8 Protection of Company Assets

All employees share the responsibility to protect Company property – both property specifically assigned to an employee as well as common property and property assigned to other employees.

10.8.1 No employee shall take, sell, lend, or give away any Company property, regardless of its condition or value, without prior written authorization.

10.8.2 No employee has the right to receive or give away Company services, information, use of information, use of facilities or use of equip-

Continued on page 274. Use of this form is described in Chapter 8, beginning on page 173.

Code of Business Conduct/Noncompete Agreement (continued)

ment without prior written authorization.

10.9 Relationship With Competitors

Because an employee's knowledge of the Company's business and information is one of the Company's most valuable assets, employees may not render advice or give service, gratuitously or otherwise, to any organization or individual engaged in the same business as the Company without prior written authorization.

10.9.1 No employee shall at any time enter into a written or oral under-standing or agreement, expressed or implied, or participate in any plan or scheme, formal or informal, with any competitor concerning prices, offers, information, terms, conditions, contracts, contacts, sources, or any other information.

10.9.2 No employee shall engage in any other conduct that, in the opinion of the Company's legal counsel, violates any antitrust law.

10.10 Standards of Conduct

The Company maintains internal standards of conduct that seek to pro-tect employees from harassment and from discrimination (see Conditions of Employment policy and procedure). Similarly, employees who represent the Company in activities or in business transactions involving nonemployees should conduct themselves in strict compliance with the same standards of conduct.

11. DISCLOSURE

The following procedures have been established to allow disclosure of any material interest, affiliation, or activity on the part of any employee that conflicts with, is likely to conflict with, or may appear to conflict with the duties of any employee, the Company, or the Company's Code of Business Conduct.

11.1 On an annual basis the Human Resources Manager will distribute to all managers a questionnaire to elicit disclosures of conflicts or possible conflicts.

11.2 Human Resources will distribute to each newly hired management employee at time of employment a questionnaire to elicit disclosures of conflicts or possible conflicts.

11.3 Any employee who at any time becomes aware of a potential conflict should immediately contact the Human Resources Manager to obtain and complete a questionnaire.

11.4 All completed questionnaires are returned to Human Resources Manager, who forwards to the Senior Vice President of Operations any that indicate a possible conflict.

11.5 All information reported by questionnaire is treated as confidential except to the extent necessary for the protection of the Company's interests or as required by law.

11.6 Employees who are not subject to the disclosure procedure as represented by completion of a questionnaire are not excused from the Code of Business Conduct.

11.7 Each year Human Resources will distribute to every employee a Code of Business Conduct and a memo stating the Code of Business Conduct was previously signed by the employee and is still in full force and effect.

11.8 Human Resources will obtain a signed Code of Business Conduct from each newly hired employee at time of employment.

12. SANCTIONS

Any infraction of the Company's Code of Business Conduct or requirements of this policy and procedure may subject the employee to disciplinary action, including termination of employment.

Index

About the Author

J OHN H. MCCONNELL, DRAWS ON MORE THAN TWO decades of experience working with companies, large and small, to help them find and keep the best people. McConnell has undergraduate and graduate degrees in educational psychology. He has held executive human resources positions with Wolverine Tube, Garan, Inc., M&M Mars, and National Liberty Insurance.

McConnell is president of McConnell, Simmons & Co., Inc., a New Jersey firm that specializes in consulting services and products for human resources professionals. The firm, founded in 1974, has furnished services and products to a wide range of organizations, from those employing only two people to those employing a cast of thousands. His clients have included Philip Morris, the U.S. Navy, Colonial Penn Group, Ford Motor Company, British Air, Management Centre Europe, Caterpillar, East Ohio Gas, the U.S. Department of Labor, and the American Management Association. McConnell has authored numerous articles and business books, including *An Introduction to Human Resources, Meeting Management,* and *Using the Computer as a Management Tool.*

McConnell has produced and toured several theatrical musicals, and once owned a circus. He is currently developing a book that combines his management-consulting and circus-operating experiences: *This Company Is Nothing But a Three-Ring Circus.*

He can be contacted as follows:

John H. McConnell
1 Skyline Dr.
Morristown, NJ 07960
973-539-6481